Writing for Magazines

A Beginner's Guide

Cheryl Sloan Wray

NTC Publishing Group
a division of NTC/Contemporary Publishing Group
Lincolnwood, Illinois USA

Library of Congress Cataloging-in-Publication Data

Wray, Cheryl Sloan.
Writing for magazines: a beginner's guide / Cheryl Sloan Wray.
p. cm.
Includes bibliographical references (p.) and index.
ISBN 0-8442-5961-6
1. Authorship. I. Title.
PN147.W664 1996
808'.02—dc20 96-24828
CIP

Acknowledgments
p. 21: Reprinted with permission by The Des Moines Register, 1983.
p. 26: From *Martha Stewart Living.* © 1994. Reprinted by permission.
p. 28: © 1995 by Janice Williams. Reprinted by permission.
p. 31: Reprinted with permission from the March 1995 issue of *Texas Monthly*.
p. 34: © 1990. Reprinted by permission of *Alabama West.*
p. 38: Reprinted with permission from *Family Fun*, 1996.

Published by NTC Publishing Group
A division of NTC/Contemporary Publishing Group, Inc.
4255 West Touhy Avenue, Lincolnwood (Chicago), Illinois 60712-1975 U.S.A.

Printed in the United States of America
International Standard Book Number: 0-8442-5961-6
5 6 7 8 9 VRS/VRS 0 5 4 3 2

CONTENTS

PREFACE

So you want to be a magazine writer?

For some reason, at some point, you decided that writing for magazines is something you would like to do—or at least *try* to do. You have read articles in magazines and thought, "I could do as good as that." Or you have read articles in magazines and thought, "I could do *better* than that."

Based on my experiences, I can tell you that there are a lot of people out there who think thoughts similar to those. There are many people who will say, "I really should write that down" or "That would make a great story." I hope this book takes you from being one of those people and transforms you into someone who will act on his or her words and big dreams.

I see and talk to people all the time who want to start writing for magazines. I have talked to them at writers' conferences where I have spoken on this same topic (the genesis of my idea for this book, by the way). They say they have dreamed of being a writer for years (or they have just discovered that they want to write and might have the talent for it), but they just don't know where to start. They want to know how to get from "I want to . . ." to "I can do it, and I know how."

WHAT THIS BOOK DOES

This book is quite basic. It does not go immediately into a description of how to write that blockbuster article (although it does start to take you through the steps in Chapter Seven). Instead, it starts you where you need to start—at the beginning.

This book will tell you about what a magazine writer does, the magazines out there to write for, how to think as a writer, how to get ideas, how to find the time to write, how to set goals, how to acquire the tools of a writer, and how to defeat writer's block. Then, and only then, does it try to show you where to go from there: from the first draft and revision, to the basics of grammar and the development of your style, to the mailing of your first article.

Along the way, I will give you examples of magazine articles that are effective and enjoyable to read. I will give you advice from editors on how to get published. I will provide information about resources that can aid you as a new writer. At the end of every chapter, I will give you "Jumpstart" exercises to get you started writing. I hope that you become an active participant while reading this book—that you will do the exercises and, in the process, be actively putting into practice the information and advice you are receiving.

ACKNOWLEDGMENTS

In preparing for this book—in getting everything here that I needed to get in here—I had help from many different sources. Because of that, I must thank a number of people for their help.

Thank you, first of all, to my closest writing friends. Ella Robinson, your constant encouragement has always been wonderful, and your assistance in reading and analyzing the manuscript at all stages was a great help! Sammie Barstow, your words of support and love meant everything to me. All the members of my writing group in Tuscaloosa, your questions and comments helped tremendously.

Thank you, also, to those friends who don't share my love of writing. Malia Hughes, you have always made me feel like I could do anything; your joy at my successes fills me with thanks. Angela Nelson, you're my dearest and oldest friend and, as always, thank you.

Thank you to Jim Stovall and George Frangoulis at the University of Alabama, who helped me get this project going in the first place. Your suggestions on writing and marketing this book were invaluable.

Thank you to David and Joanne Sloan, my parents and fellow writers. Your love of writing is in good hands!

Of course, thank you to my wonderful daughter and husband. McKenna, you are the light of my life (I could write volumes about being your Mom!). Gary, you are the rock of my life. Your unconditional love, encouragement, and support are sometimes hard to believe. I thank you for always believing in me. And, although we haven't met yet, I must acknowledge the child who will arrive not long after this book is put to press. Whoever you are—Delaney or Dylan—you were there with me the entire time I sat at the computer and revised these words.

Thank you, finally, to all the aspiring writers I have met out there. Your honest questions and passionate dreams inspired this book. I hope I give you some inspiration in return.

So now, let's get to the fun part. Let's learn how you can become a magazine writer.

CHAPTER ONE

SO YOU WANT TO BE A MAGAZINE WRITER?

When posed with the question, "Why do you want to write?" aspiring magazine writers will give a variety of responses:

- "I've always loved to write."
- "I feel like I have something to say."
- "Uncle Ed says I should do it."
- "I don't really want to do anything else."
- "I can get rich."
- "I think I have some talent."
- "I dream of seeing my name in print."
- "Writing can't be *that* hard."

And on and on and on. If you listen to the responses you get from asking that question to aspiring writers (or if you honestly ask it of yourself), you will find that most of the answers revolve around the image people have of magazine writers and the writing lifestyle. To get this point across, let me introduce you to a few magazine writers.

Connor is a full-time freelance magazine writer. He even has business cards that proudly proclaim his profession: "Connor Covington. Writer." Connor has always known he would be a writer. He says he's known it since the third grade, when his teacher, Mrs. Thompson, told him his talking dog story was brilliant. He skipped college, ignored most of the advice he was given (even by writing professionals), and jumped right in. Today, he writes one to two hours a day and has five hundred published credits to show for it. He's a regular contributor to four major magazines and is now considered an expert on several issues—his favorite ones right now are environmental justice and political reform. Several times a week he goes to lunch with his agent or writer friends. When he does sit down to write, the words seem to flow from his brain to his computer screen. He loves writing; the lifestyle has become so relaxing and lucrative, he can't imagine doing anything else.

Does anyone smell a rat? Although the half-truths and flat-out impossibilities in this story seem quite obvious to me, many aspiring writers actually believe that this is the type of life they could lead. Big checks, hob-knobbing with agents and fellow bestselling authors, days of endless inspiration—the images of easy days and easy money ahead fill their minds.

Why do people seem to think that writing is an easy life? Why do people dreamily ask of freelance writers, "Well, what do you actually do all day?" It comes as a shock to find out that magazine writers actually get rejected, they actually struggle to find the right words, they actually work. To set the record straight, let's meet a few *real* writers.

> *Sandra just recently learned to respond, "I work at home as a writer," to the question, "What do you do for a living?" For years, she would say she was a mother or mumble something about not really doing much of anything. She dreamed of being a writer for years, but she never did anything about it. "I don't have the time," "I don't know what exactly to write about," and "My kids are more important than my crazy ideas," were her excuses. After ten years of dreaming, she now knows that she likes to write personal experience articles and how-to articles on parenting. She's had one story published in her local newspaper and a filler printed in a regional parenting magazine. She's proud of her progress, and now, with the support of her husband and three children behind her (they proudly state "My mom's a writer"), she knows she will only improve.*

> *Jack works all day as a welder at a large factory. He gets little satisfaction from his job, but as a single father he has to do it. He dreams of turning his part-time writing work into a full-time job, but he knows he can't support himself and his young daughter on the irregular and infrequent paychecks. In the meantime, he gets up at 4:30 in the morning—two hours early—to work on his magazine articles. He reads about writing as much as he can, attends writer's conferences when he can get off of work, and has a regular goal of sending out ten query letters and one magazine article a month. For all his hard work, he has had about twenty-five rejections in the last year and a half—and three articles published.*

Sandra and Jack are real writers (actually, they're composites of many writers I know), and they have learned the realities of the writing life the old-fashioned way—they have had it stand up and knock them in the face. Although they both know about disappointment, lack of confidence, and rejection, they also know about those qualities that make an aspiring writer really feel like a writer. They know that determination, education, confidence, goal-setting, perseverance, and pure enjoyment will go a long way in getting started and continuing writing.

> *"It is not without reason that writers in our country are called engineers of the human soul."*
>
> NIKITA KHRUSHCHEV

If you picked up this book, you probably think you can be a writer like Sandra and Jack. Perhaps now, though, you realize that being a writer is a lot tougher than you ever thought. You may have stopped yourself in midsentence a few moments ago and said, "He's only sold three articles in almost two years? I want to get something published soon!" You *can* succeed at your writing dreams—you simply need to have a solid understanding of the struggles you may encounter and the concrete tools needed to write and market your work.

> *"All life is an experiment. The more experiments you make, the better."*
> RALPH WALDO EMERSON

DO YOU HAVE WHAT IT TAKES?

To gauge your opinion of the magazine writing life and to see whether you have "what it takes," answer the following questions. (I promise that this will be the first and last "test" in this book.)

1. I want to be a magazine writer so
   (a) I can go on "Oprah."
   (b) I can be rich and famous.
   (c) I can have people say, "I read your article in *ABC Magazine.*"
   (d) I can get some sense of personal satisfaction and accomplishment from my efforts.

2. I knew I wanted to be a writer when
   (a) I saw a story on John Grisham and his millions of bucks on "60 Minutes."
   (b) I ruled out being a doctor because I can't stand the sight of blood.
   (c) I realized that everyone else thought I could write well.
   (d) my kindergarten teacher put "Not Bad" on my first short story and I excitedly raced home to tell Mom about it.

3. My first sale will probably net me
   (a) $500 and assignments galore.
   (b) $250 and a photo byline.
   (c) $50.
   (d) two issues of the magazine.

4. My first sale will probably be to
   (a) *Esquire.*
   (b) *Cosmopolitan.*
   (c) *The National Enquirer.*
   (d) *Trout Fisherman's Monthly.*

5. The last thing I read was
   (a) *Huckleberry Finn*—back in the ninth grade.
   (b) my automobile manual.
   (c) last week's Sunday paper.
   (d) it is hard to pick—I'm currently reading two novels, one nonfiction book, and the five magazines to which I subscribe.
6. I'll find the time to write when
   (a) there's nothing better to do.
   (b) I'm truly inspired.
   (c) I need to get the job done.
   (d) I have it on my appointment book. (I dedicate myself to work certain times and give myself deadlines to back it up.)
7. To me, organization means
   (a) shoving all my notes and ideas under the bed.
   (b) shoving all my notes and ideas in a big box.
   (c) knowing I have everything I need, just not knowing exactly where they are.
   (d) keeping information labeled and categorized in some fashion, such as in file cabinets or spiral notebooks.
8. Grammar, spelling, and punctuation are
   (a) things I last thought about in tenth grade.
   (b) as terrifying as tarantulas.
   (c) important, but not everything.
   (d) extremely important.
9. Research is
   (a) boring.
   (b) "I have to do research?"
   (c) something I'll do only if I have to.
   (d) exciting.
10. My own response to "If at once you don't succeed" is
   (a) "Give up."
   (b) "Chalk it up as one of life's experiences and then give up."
   (c) "Give it one more college try."
   (d) "Try, try again."
11. My network of support consists of
   (a) my dog Spot.
   (b) family and friends who get a sick look on their face whenever I broach the topic of writing.
   (c) me.
   (d) family and friends who, although they may not have the same passion as I do, still encourage me in all my endeavors.

12. If I couldn't write, I would
    (a) not lose a lot of sleep over it.
    (b) become passionate about coin collecting.
    (c) get a lot more sleep than I do now.
    (d) die.

If you answered mostly "a"s and "b"s, you have no reasonable understanding of what a magazine writer's life is like. You think that writing magazine articles will gain you instant success and wealth. You think that magazine writing takes little time and effort. (Sorry, but you can't sit around in your bathrobe all day and then crank out that $1,000 essay in one afternoon.) You also have little understanding of why you want to be a magazine writer. The fact that writing can be a personally satisfying venture isn't high on your reasons for wanting to write.

If you answered mostly "c"s, you are well on your way to understanding what being a magazine writer is all about. Yet, you still aren't completely sold on the idea that you need to be dedicated to your writing aspirations in a practical way—the same way you would be about a "real" job or passion.

If you answered mostly "d"s, then congratulations are in order. You would truly die (or at least feel very ill) if you couldn't write. Writing brings meaning to your life and enriches it. You understand that magazine writing takes a lot of hard work—yet you still want to do it.

FROM THE EDITOR'S DESK

"Effective organization of ideas is important. The successful writer must be willing to cut, polish, check, rewrite, and condense."

BETTY GAREE, *ACCENT ON LIVING*

HERE'S WHAT IT TAKES

I believe there are seven essential ingredients to being a successful magazine writer. In no particular order, they are:

1. *Understanding of the field and markets.* You need to know what you are getting into. Going into any venture blindfolded will make the work difficult, if not impossible. Talk to writers whenever you can, read about writing, and orient yourself to the marketing skills you will need to succeed.
2. *Perseverance.* James Joyce's *Ulysses* was rejected by twenty-five publishing houses before it was accepted. Today, it is recognized as one of the classics of modern literature. Robert Pirsig's *Zen and the Art of Motorcycle Maintenance* is even more of a success story. It was rejected 122 times before it went on to be accepted and sell millions of copies. A writing friend of mine wanted to write for magazines for years but never had the courage to send out her articles. After she

got over her fear, she also learned to accept rejection. It took her two years, but she got her first personal experience story accepted. Today, she writes and gets published on a regular basis. Perseverance is especially important to new magazine writers. You must learn to stick your neck out—again and again and again. Don't get discouraged in the face of rejection. You *will* be published if you persevere.

3. *Organization.* Although you don't have to be a neat freak, you do need to set up some sort of organized system for your writing projects. I like to set up file folders for different projects; I also keep a special file folder just for ideas. I keep track of the status of my projects on a desk calendar and in a submission log (for those projects I'm sending out for publication). Whatever works for you is fine, provided you understand your system.
4. *Belief in your work.* In my first draft, this ingredient was actually called, "Disregard for what others think or say." I realized, however, that this might encourage you to never listen to professionals' advice and words of wisdom. You do need to listen to advice, but don't take all advice as knowledge set in stone. When others ask what you have written lately, proudly state that you just completed an article (even if you haven't sold it yet). When others question why you are spending so much time on writing efforts that don't seem to be paying off, tell them that you love writing and have confidence that your hard work will pay off soon. Belief in your work and in yourself will get you a long way in this business!
5. *Willingness to improve.* While you must believe in your work, you must never believe that it is perfect. Even the best writers can get better. Always be on the watch for areas in which you are consistently struggling. Then, dedicate yourself to learning more about and improving in those areas. For example, if you have problems with grammar and punctuation, invest in several good grammar handbooks and memorize the rules. Never be afraid to ask questions, as this is perhaps the best step to improving your writing. By letting more experienced writers answer questions for you and tell you about their own failures and successes, you can vastly improve your own writing. If you get to the point where you are working with editors, take their advice on a regular basis. They are the editors for a good reason—they know the type of material and the style of writing that will be published in their magazine!

> *"I do not want to be a doctor to live by men's diseases, nor a lawyer and live by their quarrels. So, I don't see that there is anything left for me but to be an author.*
>
> NATHANIEL HAWTHORNE (TO HIS MOTHER)

6. *Open eyes, ears, and mind.* You can probably spot writers amongst the crowd of Saturday afternoon mall shoppers. They are the ones sitting on the bench in the middle of the busy halls just looking at people! Learn to be observant in all ways. Watch people, listen to the sounds around you, and observe trends in society. Most importantly, never write anything off as inappropriate to your magazine writing.
7. *Passion for writing.* Real magazine writers don't just love the *idea* of writing, they love to write! They love to come up with ideas, to research (although some writers love this step a little less than others), and to write the finished piece. And they love, of course, to see the finished piece in print. What would you rather do than write? Chances are, if you truly yearn to be a writer, you can't think of another single thing you would rather do. You might, on those cold nights when no words are getting from your head to the computer, yearn to love gardening or coin collecting with the same fervor. But, when those words finally come to you, you breathe a sigh of relief and realize that there is nothing in this world you want to do more than sit at your computer and implore those words to come.

FROM THE EDITOR'S DESK

"Freelancers can best break in by offering us stories of national interest that we won't find through other channels. Well-written self-help articles also are always welcome."

LISA RAPPA, *YOUR HEALTH*

Jumpstart Exercises

1. Buy a notebook for use as your personal writing notebook or journal. If you prefer to write on a computer, start a journal file or folder that you can add to as you go along. Do the "Jumpstart" exercises throughout this book in your journal.
2. Write three or four paragraphs in response to the question, "Why do you want to write?"
3. Look critically at your personality. In light of the characteristics necessary to be successful as a magazine writer, what personality traits will help you in your dreams? What traits will hinder you?
4. Imagine that it is twenty-five years from now. You have succeeded at all you want to do as a writer. Write a sketch in which you describe your lifestyle, your greatest triumphs, and your struggles along the way. Do you have dreams yet to fulfill?

CHAPTER TWO

THE WONDERFUL WORLD OF MAGAZINES

Have you ever gone to a bookstore and just stared at the number of magazines on the racks? There are approximately eleven thousand magazines in print today. Approximately three hundred magazines start up each year (although less than 10 percent of those make it past the first year). There are magazines on every topic imaginable—from lumber (*Southern Lumberman*) to chile peppers (*Chile Pepper Magazine*) to teddy bears (*Teddy Bear Review*).

If you have never gone to your favorite bookstore and studied the magazine rack, do it sometime soon. Look at the wide variety of magazines out there; look at the topics covered and the audiences being reached. Then, take a look between the covers of the various magazines. See the wide array of articles published. Notice the different topics and the different forms the articles take. Read through the first paragraphs of a few articles and see the different tones and styles the writers use.

To get ready to write for today's magazines, you must understand several elements of the business. In particular, you need to understand the types of articles published in magazines and the wide fields of magazines predominant today. Then, you need to determine where you fit in this picture. What types of articles do you want to write? What do you want to write about? Which magazines do you want to write for?

TYPES OF MAGAZINE ARTICLES

A quick look at magazines today will show you that there is a wide variety of articles being published. There are practical articles that teach readers how to do something and there are poignant, personal stories that touch readers' hearts, to name but a few types.

To get ready to write, you need to have a thorough understanding of the different types of articles being published today.

How-to Articles

One primary reason people read magazines—or newspapers, or nonfiction books, or many other resources for that matter—is to learn how to do something. Most magazines strive to provide information for their readers that will make their lives easier, more productive, less stressful, or more enriching. How-to articles fill this need by providing step-by-step, usually simple, information for readers.

Look in any magazine and you will find plenty of how-to articles. Readers are told how to do almost anything, from how to lose weight, to how to improve job productivity, to how to encourage their child's creativity. Most beginning freelance writers should consider writing this type of magazine article. How-to articles are some of the easiest types to write, simply because they are usually straightforward and not too complex. Anyone can tell someone else how to do something; everyone has an expertise. Therefore, the how-to article can often be written from personal experience. If a writer does not have personal knowledge of a subject, it is usually quite easy to find an expert on a topic who can be interviewed.

> *"Why do writers write? Because it isn't there."*
> THOMAS BERGER

Although I say how-to articles are quite easy to write, this does not mean that they should not be written well. Even with a simple idea, you should be challenged to write it in a way that a reader will find entertaining. Therefore, write your how-to article with an interesting lead, entertaining anecdotes, and relevant examples. A story on something you might consider a bland topic ("How to Get Straight Answers from your Automechanic") can still be written in a creative manner. For a shining example of how-to writing, read Robert James Waller's "Romance" at the end of this chapter.

Looking through a stack of magazines in my living room, I saw dozens of how-to articles. Among them were:

- "I Finally Feel Good About Myself: Six Ways to Boost Self-Confidence" (*American Woman,* January–February 1995)
- "It's a Wrap: Finding the Perfect Coat" (*Redbook,* October 1994)
- "Twelve Ways to Win Readers (and Editors)" (*Writer's Digest,* December 1991)
- "Helping Domestic Violence Victims" (*Mothering,* Spring 1994)
- "How to Negotiate a Raise" (*Cosmopolitan,* December 1994)

Descriptive Articles

Closely related to how-to articles, descriptive articles also provide readers with useful information. Instead of primarily providing information on how a person can *do* something, however, the descriptive article simply provides a person with a storehouse of knowledge about a subject.

Few beginning writers consider writing descriptive articles, primarily because they have a reputation for being bland. An inspired writer, however, can make a descriptive article informative and enjoyable to readers—

especially if it's centered around a topic about which the writer feels passionate.

Descriptive articles do take a fair amount of research. You should have the goal of providing your readers with as much information about the topic as possible. Provide good quotes, up-to-date statistics, resource information, and true-to-life stories. Read Katherine Whiteside's "Violets" at the end of this chapter to see how descriptive articles can be informational, yet also entertaining and well-written.

Descriptive articles may not be the most exotic of articles, but magazines eat them up! My perusal of househould magazines turned up tons of descriptive articles. Among them:

- "Reelin' in the Ozarks" (*TravelSouth,* Summer 1992) (*Note:* Travel articles often fit into the descriptive article category because they contain so much information—descriptions of the area, listings of restaurants and hotels, resources for more information, etc.)
- "Invasion of the Privacy Snatchers" (*Cosmopolitan,* February 1994)
- "Talk about Your Muscles" (*Chickadee,* March 1994)
- "Wild about Blackberries" (*Cooking Light,* July/August 1994)
- "Birth over Forty" (*Mothering,* Spring 1994)

Personal Experience Articles

The old adage, "Write what you know," certainly applies to new magazine writers. And many magazines pay for what you know and what you have experienced in the form of your personal experience article.

The key to a successful personal experience article is in finding the element of your experience that applies to readers. A reader (and an editor) does not simply want to hear about "My Summer Vacation" or "My Son's Chicken Pox." With what aspect of your experience can readers identify? Was it an especially harrowing event, a side-splitting happening, a truly enlightening experience, or a bizarre (even unbelievable) occurrence? Can they identify with your feelings, find some comfort in them, or learn how to improve their lives from hearing about them? Find what is common ground and highlight that element of your article.

> **FROM THE EDITOR'S DESK**
>
> "Editors want to know they are getting something from a writer they cannot get from anyone else. Good writing should be a given, a starting point. After that, it's what you know."
>
> KAREN BISCHOFF, *DOLLS*

Janice Williams "The Image in the Mirror," reprinted at the end of this chapter, shows you how a personal experience article can be informational, enlightening, and emotional.

Personal experience articles crop up in almost all magazines. Some of the ones I found included:

- "Suffer the Little Children," about a woman's experience with Christian Science (*Redbook,* October 1994)
- "My Life in Tabloid TV" (*Cosmopolitan,* February 1994)
- "We Talked and We Built," a story of a child's first friend (*Mothering,* Spring 1994)
- "A Mother's Story: As Beautiful as Kate" (*McCalls,* November 1994)
- "My Husband Controlled My Money" (*Good Housekeeping,* February 1994)

Personality Profiles

People like to read about people, and they especially like to read about people who are either famous or extraordinary. Therefore, the most popular types of personality profiles in magazines today are those that focus on celebrities or on ordinary people who have become in some way "extraordinary," such as people who have been through a crisis and come out stronger, have an unusual hobby, have achieved financial (or other) success, have a special expertise, or who make a difference in other people's lives. They are people who, in some way or another, will make an impression on your reader.

Writing a personality profile involves two major ingredients: (1) someone interesting to interview and (2) the time to devote to the interview and development of the story. In writing an article for a college alumni magazine about a civil rights activist and graduate, I found myself doing extensive research. I read old newspapers, learned about her career track, and talked to friends and family—all before I called her and arranged an interview.

"Lee Harvey's Legacy," presented at the end of this chapter, is an excellent example of a personality profile. Personality profiles like these make it into magazines everyday:

- "The Grisham Brief" (*Writer's Digest,* June 1993)
- "Profile: Home Missions Pioneer" (*Dimension,* January/February/March 1995)
- "The Call of the Wild," a profile of three adventure-seeking women (*Woman's Own,* February 1995)
- "Glenn Close: Very Up Close and Personal" (*Cosmospolitan,* February 1994)
- "Vivian Malone Jones, Activist" (*Alabama Alumni,* September 1994)

Historical Articles

People are fascinated with the past. It's filled with colorful figures and important (and often surprising and unusual) events. And while people like to read about history—especially when it is told in an entertaining way—

there are few magazine writers who write these articles. This, then, might be a niche you can fill.

In writing historical articles, remember that your goal is to impart information in an entertaining way. Make the past relevant to your reader's life; make the events and characters of the past as interesting as possible.

Thomas Hardy worked full-time as an architect until his fourth novel was published.

You can sell historical articles if you tie a historical happening in with a magazine's theme and if you keep up with anniversaries. Buy a reference book that charts historical events and look for events that will be celebrating fiftieth, seventy-fifth, one-hundredth, or even two-hundredth anniversaries. Then, pitch the idea to an appropriate magazine.

Catherine Corbett wrote about the one-hundred-seventy-fifth anniversary of a Civil War happening. Her article, "The Phoenix of the South," is at the end of the chapter. These other historical articles were pitched and sold to magazines:

- "The Beginning of a Beautiful Friendship," a story about *Casablanca*'s fiftieth birthday (*Entertainment Weekly*, March 1994)
- "Blue Plate Specials," an article about classic diners (*Family Fun,* April 1995)
- "Lest We Forget," a twentieth anniversary article about the end of the Vietnam War (*Alabama Alumni,* April/May 1995)
- "No Limits," a retrospective look at "Austin City Limits" (*Texas Monthly,* February 1995)
- "Phillips Brooks: Author of 'O Little Town of Bethlehem' Remembered" (*Mature Living,* December 1994)

Humor Articles

If you can make your reader laugh, you have done them a great service—and you have done something that a lot of magazine writers can't do. Humorous articles are very popular in today's magazines, and editors are always looking for good ones—ones that truly make you laugh and that are written in a casual, not stilted or forced, manner. ("Don't send me a humor article that isn't funny!" said one of the editors I talked to.)

The best humor articles are those that spotlight an experience most people have had. They tell about the hazards of potty training or the frustration of living with a remote control hog. They don't try to inform or explain, they simply entertain.

Humorous articles can run the gamut of styles. They can be written as essays, quizzes, or how-to pieces. "Daddyspeak Happens," presented at the end of the chapter, takes an ordinary slice-of-life and makes it relevant and funny to all readers. I found myself laughing out loud at these other humorous articles:

- "The Ten Commandments of Roadside Dining" (*TravelSouth,* Summer 1992)
- "Proud to Be a Big Mouth" (*Redbook,* September 1994)
- "Weddings I Have Performed," humorous stories of unique wedding ceremonies (*Modern Bride,* January 1995)
- "Martha Stewart Hell" (*New Woman,* October 1994)
- "Ten Things I Thought Would Happen After Graduation . . . But Guess What?" (*The Student,* May 1993)

Short Pieces

More and more magazines are purchasing short pieces of writing. Short pieces include everything from jokes to book reviews to quizzes to funny quotes to departmental articles to restaurant reviews to lists. They are usually quite easy to write (and much of the research can usually be accomplished over the phone). The pay, even if it's just $50, isn't bad for a 150-word article.

In my early days of writing, I discovered that writing book reviews could put a few extra dollars (and a free book) in my pocket each month. Don't forget to consider this and other short article outlets as possibilities for you as you get started. See Exhibit 2.1 on page 14 for a list of the types of short articles you can write for magazines today.

ANATOMY OF A MAGAZINE

To truly understand how magazines are contructed today, what types of material they publish, and what freelance writers need to know about them, it is good to learn how to analyze a magazine from cover to cover. In completing this analysis, you will come to understand what I like to call the anatomy of a magazine. By the time you are ready to market your articles to magazines (see Chapter 12), you will already understand the magazine for which you want to write, and you will know how your writing fits into it.

Casual readers of magazines—most of the American population—understand magazines only in a superficial way. They notice the covers, sometimes pay attention to the ads, and read the articles that interest them. There is, however, much more to magazines.

As an aspiring magazine writer, you should be much more than a casual reader. You should be a student of the magazine field. You should be able to read through a magazine and understand what the editors and writers are trying to accomplish.

Think of a magazine you like and, ideally, for which you would like to write. Obtain a copy and analyze it according to the following items:

- *The cover.* What type of picture is on the front page? Is it a cozy, personal illustration or photograph? Is it an informational graphic or

EXHIBIT 2.1 TYPES OF SHORT ARTICLES

Types of short articles you might be able to write include:

Book reviews
Children's pages
Departments
Devotionals
How-to tips
Humorous anecdotes
Inspirational thoughts
Mini-profiles
Play reviews
Product reviews
Puzzles, games, and brain teasers
Quizzes
Recipes
Reminiscences
Restaurant reviews
Travel shorts
Video or music reviews

For more information on writing short pieces, I recommend Connie Emerson's *The 30-Minute Writer: How to Write and Sell Short Pieces,* published by Writer's Digest Books. It gives you detailed information about all of these possible markets.

illustration? Look at the cover blurbs. These are the words that tell you what articles are in the issue of the magazine. Both the cover illustration and the cover blurbs will let you know to what type of material the editors give high priority.

- *The table of contents.* This is one of the most important elements in your analysis of a magazine's anatomy. It will tell you what types of feature stories and department material the magazine accepts. You can also get the tone of the writing from looking at article titles and the information provided about the story.
- *Editorial page.* Some magazines have a page where the editor makes comments. Take a look at it to see what type of writing the editor uses him or herself and to see what types of articles he discusses.
- *The stories themselves.* Analyze every page of editorial content individually. When looking at articles, analyze the leads, article structure, special features (sidebars, photographs, charts, etc.), and conclusion.

This analysis will show you what the magazine's writing is like. When you begin to select magazines to write for, you will try to write in a style similar to your chosen magazines.

- *Advertisements.* Ads will give you another glimpse into the magazine's reader. From ads, you can learn about a reader's age, salary, family life, and hobbies. When you begin to write articles for publication, you want to know as much as possible about your potential reader—ads can help you learn a little bit more.

Use Exhibit 2.2 to help you analyze magazines.

THE MAGAZINE FIELDS

The annual *Writer's Market* (an irreplaceable resource for magazine writers that is more extensively discussed in Chapter 12) lists forty-nine categories of consumer magazines. They are:

animal
art and architecture
associations
astrology, metaphysical, and New Age
automotive and motorcycle
aviation
business and finance
career, college, and alumni
child care and parental guidance
comic books
consumer service and business opportunity
contemporary culture
detective and crime
disabilities
entertainment
ethnic/minority
food and drink
games and puzzles
gay and lesbian interest
general interest
health and fitness
history
hobby and craft
home and garden
humor
inflight
juvenile

EXHIBIT 2.2 HOW TO ANALYZE A MAGAZINE

In analyzing an individual magazine, look at the elements of its anatomy and ask yourself the following questions about each element.

Cover

- Does the cover picture or illustration tell me anything about the magazine?
- What do the cover blurbs tell me?

Table of contents

- What are the feature articles about?
- What are the departments or columns about?
- What types of articles does this magazine seem to use a lot of?
- Can I learn anything about the tone of the articles from their titles?

Editorial page

- What does the editor comment about this month?
- Can the editor's comments tell me anything about the magazine's content?
- Does the editor have a particular writing style?

Articles

- Are the articles similar in style and content or are they varied?
- What types of leads do the articles have?
- How are the articles structured?
- Do the articles include sidebars, photographs, graphic elements, etc.?
- What types of conclusions do the articles have?
- Do the articles have writer identifications at the end of them? If so, are most of the authors freelance writers?

Advertisements

- Is there a lot of advertising in the magazine or is it mostly editorial copy?
- What products are advertised in the magazine?
- Can these products tell me anything about the magazine's typical reader (salary, education, interests, hobbies, etc.)?

literary and "little"
men's
military
music
mystery
nature, conservation, and ecology
personal computers
photography
politics and world affairs
psychology and self-improvement
regional
relationships
religious
retirement
romance and confession
rural
science
science fiction, fantasy, and horror
sports
teen and young adult
travel, camping, and trailer
women's

FROM THE EDITOR'S DESK

"We are open to working with new writers who present a good article idea and demonstrate that they've done their homework concerning the article subject itself."

NICHOLAS DRAKE,
CIRCLE K MAGAZINE

There are an additional sixty-three trade magazines listed in the book. These trade magazines also take material from freelance magazine writers and are a market that shouldn't be overlooked.

With so many magazines in existence on such varied topics, it's easy to see why many magazine writers choose to specialize. As you get started writing, you should consider whether you want to be a generalist (a writer who writes on a variety of topics) or a speciaist (a writer who writes on one topic, or a select few, related topics).

One writer friend of mine writes exclusively on religious topics and, almost exclusively, for religious magazines. Her writing is very diversified (she's written everything from personality profiles to travel pieces), yet it is all designed for a religious audience. She feels comfortable in this area and feels, in fact, that her writing is a ministry. She has found her place in today's huge magazine field.

Another friend writes primarily about entertainment topics. He is very knowledgeable about television, movies, and technology, and focuses his writing energies on those areas. He, also, has found his place in today's huge magazine field.

FINDING YOUR NICHE

It is best to go into any venture with your eyes open. Before you start writing, you should have some idea of where you want to focus your energies. You should ask yourself, "What types of articles do I like to write?" and "What topics do I want to write about?"

To determine what types of articles you like to write, take a critical look at your personality. Take a look at the way you live your life, the ideas you consider valuable, and your personality traits. All of these should give you hints as to the types of articles for which you are best suited.

- Do you like to do research? Do you feel some sort of obligation to teach others? If you do, you would do well writing how-to or descriptive articles.
- Do you enjoy meeting new people? Do you have a gregarious personality? Do you fit well in other people's environments? If so, you might consider writing personality profiles.
- Do you have strong opinions about issues? Do you like sharing your opinion with others? Do you like telling others about things that have influenced your life? If so, perhaps personal experience articles, humor articles, or opinion pieces are in your future.

Of course, there is no better way to learn than to actually write. Write a personal experience article and see how it feels. Write a historical article; was it an experience you would rather not try again soon? Try several article types on for size. You will find your niche.

In addition to determining what style of writing you like to follow, you need to decide what topics you enjoy and to identify those about which you can realistically manage to write. I have found that the easiest way to find topics of interest and expertise is to fill in the "Interests/Expertise Worksheet" (Exhibit 2.3 on page 19). It is amazing how many students and conference attendees of mine have filled out this worksheet and determined that they were skilled in something they had never before considered or realized that their life roles were more than wife and mother or businessman and husband.

After completing the worksheet, look at your twenty words or phrases and ask yourself how your hobbies, talents and gifts, professional skills, and roles can help you determine on what topics you would like to write. In completing the worksheet myself, I discovered that my love of cooking and entertaining (listed as hobbies) and the fact that I'm a mother (one of my roles) were the areas of interest and expertise that fascinated me the most. Today, I try to focus most of my writing energies on the topics of parenting and entertaining.

> *John Grisham wrote his first book,* A Time to Kill, *on yellow legal pads during court while he was a lawyer in Mississippi.*

EXHIBIT 2.3 INTEREST/EXPERTISE WORKSHEET

Hobbies:

1.
2.
3.
4.
5.

Talents/gifts:

1.
2.
3.
4.
5.

Professional Skills:

1.
2.
3.
4.
5.

Roles:

1.
2.
3.
4.
5.

Jumpstart Exercises

1. Complete the "Interests/Expertise Worksheet," if you haven't already. Were you surprised by any of your responses?
2. Using your worksheet responses, and by looking at the list of types of magazines from *Writer's Market,* select three or four topics in which you are interested and/or have a special expertise.

3. Select one of your favorite magazines and analyze the types of writing prevalent in the magazine. Are there a lot of how-to articles? personality profiles? Are the articles effective? Were the writers successful in getting a point across to you, the reader?
4. If you haven't already, select a magazine to analyze. Write down any impressions you have about the magazine's cover, table of contents, editorial page, articles, and advertisements.
5. Read the sample articles on pages 21–40. After reading each one, write a short paragraph identifying the elements or attributes that made the article effective.

HOW-TO ARTICLE

The following article by Robert Waller was written two years before the phenomenal success of his novel *The Bridges of Madison County.* It was published first in the *Des Moines Register* in 1983 and then in *Ladies Home Journal.*

This is an article on how to acquire and keep romance in your life. I will bet, however, that it's unlike any other how-to article you have ever read. It's far from the cliches we often think of in respect to how-to writing—boring, dry, and very unexciting. Waller's article does tell us, step-by-step, how to do something. It also happens to be poignant, stylish, and poetic.

"Romance"

by Robert James Waller

Romance dances just beyond the firelight, in the corner of your eye. She does not like you to look at her directly; she flees from the cold light of logic and data collection when it is turned toward her. If you persist in trying to study her, however, she first disintegrates, then dissolves into nothing at all.

E. B. White once said a similar thing about humor, which "can be dissected, as a frog, but the thing dies in the process and the innards are discouraging to any but the pure scientific mind." You can't get at romance, then, by good old Western reductionism.

Understand, I am not just talking about romance in the sense of love between two people. You can't really have a romance with someone else unless you are, first of all, a romantic yourself. Most people I know are not very romantic. They were once, or had the chance to be, but romance got lost along the way, drowned in the roar of our times, beat out by overly analystic teachers, drummed out by those who scoff at romantics as foolish and weak. In those people, romance looked around and said, "I'm not living here; too cold."

What do romantics look like? You can't really generalize. Besides, to make a list of characteristics would be to commit the sin of breaking romance down into small pieces, which I cautioned about before. The best way to tell a romantic is to just be around one. You will know. There is a sense of passion about them, a sense of living just a bit too far out at the edge emotionally sometimes; a caring for what seems to be dumb things—an old chair you sat in during your graduate student days and in the early times of your career, a knife that lies on the desk year after year, a simple wooden box. You can tell a romantic by the voice—it dances because the mind is dancing.

And I can tell you this for sure. All romantics like dogs and cats, and maybe some other creatures, preferably animals that come in off the road for a little sustenance and decide to stay around and participate in the craziness they sense in this place of food and laughter. Animals like romantics, for they know they will never be let down by them.

It's important to note here that you do not have to be a poet or a painter or a musician to be a romantic. In fact, I know quite a few folks in these areas of endeavor who are downright unromantic. On the other hand, Andrew Carnegie was a romantic. So was Joseph Smith when he led the Mormons westward. And I have seen more than one insurance salesman, in the bars where I have played, grin outwardly and inwardly when I launched into a song about the wind and the flowers and the highways that run forever.

Robert Pirsig puts it well, in his book Zen and the Art of Motorcycle Maintenance, *when he says, "The Buddha resides quite as comfortably in the circuits of a digital computer or the gears of a cycle transmission as he does at the top of a mountain or in the petals of a flower. To think otherwise is to demean the Buddha—which is to demean oneself."*

In a sense, romance is practical. It fuels your life and propels your work with a sense of vision, hope, and caring. Because you are working for others, not just for yourself, your work takes on a certain quality that it will not otherwise have. I suppose you can say romance puts meat on the table, though, as I say that, I feel more than just a slight drain on my system as romance prepares me to leave.

Let me turn now to the matter of getting and keeping romance. Romance is hard to get, hard to keep, and fairly easy to drive away. If you are really intent on getting rid of romance, though, here are a few brief suggestions:

Become obsessive about neatness, particularly in the way your desk looks.

Install excessive shag carpet in your house, so that when the dog throws up or one of your friends spills a beer, all hell breaks loose.

Don't listen to any good music. Ignore Bach, Mozart, Pete Seeger, and the Paul Winter Consort. Instead, listen only to top-40 radio. This is a first-rate approach to giving romance a shove out of your life, for she likes subtlety and low decibel counts.

Excessive focus on detail and procedure at the expense of vision, of dreams, of reflection, is another good way to get rid of romance.

Buy birthday cards, anniversary cards, and the like instead of making up your own. All of us are poets, some have just lost their voices for a while. As Ray Bradbury once said, about people in general, "And they were all, when their souls grew warm, poets."

Finally, the surest way to lose romance forever is to do things just for money, even though your cells tell you this is not what you should be doing.

Now, in no particular order, here are some suggestions for keeping romance around you (or getting her back if she has flown):

Read some poetry every day. For starters, try a little Yeats, then some Kipling (along with some of his stories). I know Kipling must be terribly out of fashion nowadays, but romantics never concern themselves with fashion anyhow.

Set a new schedule for yourself and do your reading then. Try this: Instead of flopping around in bed, get up early—maybe 4 a.m.—on a Sunday, in the winter, when a classic Iowa howler is blowing in from the Dakotas. This works pretty well. Besides, you have the secret pleasure of being reasonably sure you are the only one in the Western Hemisphere reading Kipling at that very moment.

Here's another idea. Sometime in your life, build your own house or at least the most intimate parts of it. Design it, too, with lots of thought. You will get endless pleasure and romance from walking through doorways and knowing you put the door there with your mind and your hands.

Collect little things, like the old knife on your desk or the small box you had for keepsakes when you were a child. At a time in my life when I was just overcome with administrative burdens, and my face showed it, one of my faculty gave me a small wooden flute along with a note that said, "Don't let your muse slip away." I keep the flute where I can see it.

Play a musical instrument. Something you can get out on those early mornings when reading is not the thing. Don't tell me you are not musical and, for heaven's sake, don't tell me you are tone deaf. I simply, if you will pardon the expression, won't hear of it. If all else fails, or even if it doesn't, buy an Appalachian dulcimer. You can get warm, exotic sounds out of it right away without knowing anything formal about music at all. Try reading some ancient Chinese poetry while you strum the dulcimer. It works wonders.

Travel is good for romance. But don't just travel, travel. *Here's what you need: notebooks, a small compass, a pocket atlas of the world, and a spyglass for looking out of airplane windows or across the rooftops of Paris or far down the country lanes in England. A word of warning is needed here: If you are traveling with your boss and he or she is not a romantic, be careful. You may not want to be seen with your compass and a spyglass on an airplane. If you are a true romantic, however, it won't matter much, because you will be good at what you do and your boss will just shake his or her head and mutter about what one has to put up with to get qualified work these days.*

Keep good journals of your life and travels. This is vitally important. I delight in reading and re-reading my adventures in the old markets of Saudia Arabia, where I bargained for gold and silver to bring home, and my wild ride through the streets of Riyadh late at night with a Bedouin cab driver who played Arabic music on a tape deck and tried to give me a short course in his language, while the best I could do was teach him to say "Kleenex" by pointing to a box of it on his dashboard.

I like knowing that I was in Richmond, Virginia, at 7:55 a.m. on June 8, 1981, or that I was in Paris in the snow in January 1982, or that I was once in Montego Bay, Jamaica, in the spring.

One of the most haunting entries in my journal reads, "12:24 p.m. Back in Iowa. Georgia and Rachel are sleeping (3:24 a.m.), and I'm over Egypt." When I wrote that, I remember feeling very far away, in more ways that just miles, somehow.

My secretary leaves me alone when I fall behind in an especially unappealing piece of work, and a cold, gray, November rain is splattering against the third-floor windows of Seerley Hall. She knows I'm traveling. I stand, put my hands in my pockets, stare out those windows, and I'm comforted by the knowledge that somewhere the big planes are turning for Bombay or Bangkok, for Brisbane or Barcelona, and romance is skipping along their wings.

But romance is not just outward bound. She also rides your shoulder when you turn for home, with your notebooks full, your suitcase packed with dirty clothes, when it's only a few days before Christmas and London's Heathrow Airport is pandemonium, with all flights overbooked. But then you're on, in your seat, London falls behind, Ireland is below; you get out the notebook again, and you write, "God, all I want now is to see Georgia, Rachel, the pups, Roadcat, and eat a giant plate of Georgia's world-famous spaghetti."

Finally, you have got to work at remembering that romance is all around you. It's not somewhere else. Here are two examples.

I had to go to the Hawaiian island of Oahu a while back. Everyone told me, before I went, how crass and junky Oahu and, particularly, Honolulu have become. It certainly looks that way, at first glance. "But," I said to myself, "romance must still be here somewhere." At first I couldn't see her. My vision was blocked by Don Ho standing around drinking a pina colada. But something caught my eye—and there was romance, right behind him, jumping up and down and waving to me. So, I got up before dawn, went down to the beach, rolled up my jeans, waded in, and stood there in the pre-dawn grayness, playing my flute with the water washing around me and thinking about what this must have looked like when Captain Cook first came around Diamond Head, his sails flapping in the trade winds. There were a few other people on the beach, but they paid me no mind; they were there for the same reasons. When I finished, I heard the sound of applause from a long way off. I turned; it was romance. I caught a glimpse of her, just as the first ray of morning sunlight struck the barrier reef while she danced along it. And, my notebook says, "Soft winds blow easy, here in the night time, as Oahu lies bathing in the sweet scent of orchids. This skyplane will ride the west wind to morning and land in L.A. just after dawn."

The second example has to do with Iowa. Iowa is a very romantic, mystical place. I can't explain it, but it's here. Anybody can see the Rocky Mountains—they're obvious. It takes a little more perspective to see the beauty of Iowa or the romance in the long sweep of North Dakota prairie west of Larimre. Once when I was working in the woods south of Wadena, in northeast Iowa, it started to snow late in the day. I worked on. As I did, I began to feel a presence. What was it? The woods were filling up with snow. What was there? It took me a moment, but then I knew: It was Iowa. Iowa, like romance, doesn't come up and pirouette before you, saying, "Hey, look, I'm beautiful." She just lies there, on hot June days, like a woman in the sun, while romance splashes around where the Winnebago runs to kiss the Shell Rock, just two miles below the place of my growing.

Well, that's enough. You get the idea. All I have left for is a test of sorts (you knew there would be a test, didn't you?). How are you going to know if you have lived the romantic life? Here's how. On your dying bed, after all the living and doing, you must run this poem by turn-of-the-century poet R. M. Rilke through your mind:

> *I live my life in growing orbits,*
> *which move out over the things of this world.*
> *Perhaps I can never achieve the last,*
> *but that will be my attempt.*
> *I am circling around God,*
> *around the ancient tower,*
> *and I have been circling for a thousand years.*
> *And I still do not know,*
> *if I am a Falcon,*
> *or a storm,*
> *or a great song.*

When you have done that, on your dying bed, if you can smile and nod quietly to yourself, you will have succeeded, and romance will ride your shoulder as you turn for home.

Go well. Remember the flowers. Remember the wind.

DESCRIPTIVE ARTICLE

Descriptive articles also often get a bad rap. They chief goal of descriptive articles is to inform readers, so they can't be that interesting, right? Wrong.

Here's an article by Katherine Whiteside that appeared in the April/May 1994 issue of *Martha Stewart's Living*. It gives a lot of information about violets (gardening tips, historical tidbits, and pollination information), but readers don't feel like they're getting overwhelmed, as this information is presented in an attractive, enjoyable way.

Especially note the strong lead and conclusion. The lead paragraph does an excellent job of grabbing the reader's attention, making him want to continue reading. The lead also lets the reader know that he or she is going to get a little more than a straightforward article about violets—he or she is going to learn about something a little deeper than that.

"Violets"

by Katherine Whiteside

Whoever first called the violet "shrinking" or "shy" wasn't really paying attention. That little flag of a flower may seem to be waving in surrender, but don't let a peep of purple fool you. Violets are strong, sly survivors, reminding the truly observant that sometimes the simplest things have the greatest staying power.

In the wild, violets are great adapters. Diversity in habitat is one of nature's first lines of defense, and there are more than five hundred Viola *species, which show up everywhere from alpine scree to coastal plains, in bogs and prairies, alongside streams, and in dry forests.*

As for the flower's downcast appearance, what seems to be a timid, retiring look is actually an artful dodge. Each stalk curves downward at the blossom end to prevent spring's copious rains from washing away the violet's storehouse of nectar. This nectar is attractive to bees (who use the wide, flat lower petal as a landing pad), and in case there is any bumbling over where the goodes are stored, tiny black lines draw an insect's attention irresistibly toward the source.

Yet the violet's real survival secret is that it doesn't need pollinators at all. The relatively showy spring blossoms are followed by a summer crop of tiny green cleistogamous (closed) flowers, which self-pollinate and produce the bulk of violet seeds. The seeds grow in tough little capsules that split open with such force that the next generation is tossed well away from the parents. These tricks and traits of the genus Viola *should dispel any illusions about the violet's delicate disposition. The wild violet has been around for thousands of years, and nature doesn't long tolerate a wimpy plant.*

Because violets are largely self-pollinated, their appearance has hardly changed since the days when the ancient Greeks grew them. A scented violet, most likely Viola odorata, *was the symbol of classical Athens and a desirable flower for ornamental and medicinal purposes. The same violet of Athens became the sweet violet of the cut-flower and perfume industry. Huge amounts of the flowers were cultivated in Rhinebeck, New York, to supply demand for nosegays at the turn of the century, while in Devon, England, they were grown for the essential oil ionone. (It is still possible to buy little round bottles of violet water in drugstores in Devon.)*

The violet's famous scent offers another hint of wiliness. If sniffed for more than the briefest moment, the perfume anesthetizes the olfactory system so that the sweet smell seems to disappear. Place distance between blossom and nose and the soporofic effect wears off, so that the perfume may be experienced once again.

Although some violets are celebrated for their perfumes, the ubiquitous Marsh Blue Violet (V. cucullata), *native to moist, shade areas all over the East, has no scent at all. Another species,* V. labradorica, *grows as far north as Alaska and is desirable more for its mauve flowers and purple-tinged leaves than for any trace of perfume. The genus also has white violets, such as* V. blanda; *yellow violets, such as* V. rotundifolia; *and the charming* V. tricolor, *a purple, yellow, and white wildflower that served as one of the parents of the hugely hybridized clan of pansies.*

Wild violets are just about perfect when it comes to self-preservation, but like any other plant, they could disappear forever if indiscriminately collected. A far better idea is to grow violets yourself. Plant them in the spring under hedges, in the shade of rock walls, or in a small early border with grape hyacinths. Give them a bit of leaf mold, but avoid the temptation to fertilize. Just leave them alone and they will quickly grow into the sturdy clump of leaves that signals a good batch of flowers next year.

With all the other work to be done in the garden this season, it's comforting to learn that one of the simplest pleasures of spring is also one of the most stalwart of flowers. Even when totally ignored, violets will reseed and return, establishing entire colonies that defy banishment. Just relax and remember Napolean's boast as he set sail for Elba: "I will return with the violets in spring!"

PERSONAL EXPERIENCE ARTICLE

Writing from your personal experience can be difficult to do. You, in effect, are baring your life for hundreds (probably thousands, perhaps millions) to see and analyze. The following article is a good example of this. It tells of a young woman's experience with eating disorders—and the heartache involved is very obvious.

This article is a good example of a personal experience article because it does have this honest quality to it. It is also effective because it makes it personal to readers; it gives advice to others who may have had a similar experience.

This article appeared in the December 12, 1995, issue of *Woman's World.*

"The Image in the Mirror"

by Janice Williams, as told to Eva Unga

Not long ago, my two daughters watched in amazement as I ordered a burger and fries. "Mom's really eating," Robynne, 10, exclaimed, while Brandie, 13, stared in awe.

To most people, that meal would be no big deal, but for me, after battling an eating disorder, it was a triumph.

At 5'7" and 130 pounds, I'd always been slim. Then, during my first pregnancy, I gained 30 pounds. Although I lost some of the weight after Brandie was born, I didn't lose all of it.

Sure, it bothered me a little, But I had a precious new baby to feed, change, cuddle and just marvel at. I figured I'd take off the extra pounds once I adjusted to life as a mommy.

Then a few relatives teased me about my weight. "Hey, Janice," one said. "You're looking a little wide in the rear end."

I should've shrugged it off. Instead, my mind flashed back to my childhood. My brother had been overweight, and other kids had tormented him about it. As his big sister, I had defended him. But secretly, I'd been glad that I wasn't like him.

So I panicked. You have to get thin now! a shrill voice inside my head screamed. For the next few weeks, I ate nothing but fruit and salad. The pounds melted off until I was slimmer than I'd been before I got pregnant. Now everyone told me how wonderful I looked, and I was ecstatic.

But once I started eating normally again, the weight returned. And now, even back at 130 pounds—where I'd been happy before—I felt bloated.

I can remember how my battle with anorexia began. Although I loved being a mom, I was just 18 when I had Brandie, and I was scared I wouldn't be a good parent. My whole life had changed—and my body and my metabolism, too. Anorexia was my way of taking control.

But back then, all I knew is that the woman in the mirror didn't look like the woman I wanted to be.

"You're not fat," my husband, Doug, would soothe. "You're beautiful just the way you are." But I didn't believe him. Instead, I kept dieting.

I stopped when I got pregnant. But after Robynne was born, I started all over again. I thought about food all the time. But, although I cooked huge meals and baked tons of goodies for my family, I hardly tasted a bite. Instead, I'd urge them to eat while I ate a salad.

Then one day while I was shopping at the mall, a scout from a modeling agency gave me his card. I was flattered, so I went for an interview. The agent's words devastated me. "You would have to lose ten to fifteen pounds," he said.

Now even the 118 pounds that I weighed wasn't slim enough for me. Models who are taller than you weigh less! I berated myself. So I began taking diet pills—up to 50 a day! They made me dizzy and gave me headaches, so I swallowed handfuls of aspirin too.

Somehow, love gave me the energy I needed to look after my children. But from the moment I kissed them good morning to when I tucked them in at night, I thought about food.

Taking so many diet pills made my hands shake, and I began to have heart palpitations. But no matter how much I lost, I still saw myself as fat. It was like looking in a fun-house mirror—my self-image had become distorted.

My husband watched with worried eyes. One day, after I'd insisted on having only salad again, Doug finally exploded. "Look at you!" he yelled at me. "Your clothes are hanging off you!"

That's because they're such a huge size, I told myself. But they were only a size five! My heart twists now when I remember how my daughters would ask, "Mommy, why don't you eat anything but salads?" What kind of message was I sending them?

In bed at night, my heart would race so fast I'd be afraid to sleep, fearing I'd never wake up again. I'd tiptoe into my daughters' room and stroke their hair as they slept and pray for relief.

But part of me must have known that I needed help. Because one night, I had a dream that woke me up. In it, I opened a newspaper to a headline that read, "Mother of Two Dies From Diet Pill Overdose." Beneath the headline was a picture of me.

I woke shaking with fear. I have to stop this now! I thought. I'm slowly killing myself, I realized. And I can't do that to my family.

The next morning, I called my doctor, who referred me to a support group for people with eating disorders. It was weeks before I had the courage to stand up and say, "I have anorexia," but their nods of understanding filled me with relief. I wasn't alone.

Through therapy, I learned my obsession with food was a way to avoid dealing with my feelings of low self-esteem. I realized that people loved me for me. I started to eat normally again, and one day my daughters and I smashed my scale! It was one of the proudest moments of my life.

This past fall marked the second anniversary of my recovery. Now I eat what I want—in moderation, of course. I'm a size 12, and when I look at myself in the mirror, I like what I see. No, I'm not a teenager anymore, and I'll never be model-slim. But I'm happy to be alive and be a wife and a mother, and I feel beautiful.

PERSONALITY PROFILE

How do you capture an individual's true personality in words? How do you convey to your audience an honest, vivid representation of someone's actions and attitudes and beliefs and lifestyle? Those who write personality profiles know that it's always difficult to do so. Good writers of personality profiles know that one of the secrets is in the old adage, "Show, don't tell." You don't say someone is "nice" or "greedy," you show it—through descriptions, through retellings of a person's actions, and through the person's own words.

The following excerpt is the first half of the article "Lee Harvey's Legacy," from the March 1995 issue of *Texas Monthly.*

"Lee Harvey's Legacy"

by Keith Kachtick

The Texas Chili Parlor is a neighborhood bar without the neighborhood. Stuck in the no-man's-land between the state capitol and the University of Texas campus, the Chili Parlor is so steeped in Austin tradition that its decision several years ago to begin offering chili with beans got coverage on the local TV news. The bar's decor consists chiefly of scuffed wooden tables and junkyard scraps nailed to the walls—rusted license plates, cow skulls, yellowed newspaper clippings, and a hand-scrawled sign above the cash register noting that "Tippis is not a city in China." Old Life *magazine photographs used to hang on the walls, including one of Jack Ruby shooting Lee Harvey Oswald. "I don't even think anybody I worked with ever thought twice about it," Rachel Oswald said. "You see that image everywhere; it's easy to take it for granted. But it was still depressing, seeing my father shot every time I came to work."*

For seven years Rachel was a waitress at the Chili Parlor while she put herself through nursing school. One night at the end of her shift, she and I shared a bowl of queso, chips, and $2 Bloody Marys. I asked Rachel how many people in the bar knew who she was.

"Who I am?" she asked. "Or who my father was?"

I nodded that I appreciated the distinction.

"The people I have worked with the longest know. A few of the regulars."

The late-night air had become a distinctive Texas medley of cigarette smoke and day-old chili fumes. Stevie Ray Vaughan was turned up loud on the radio. In a bar filled with pretty women, Rachel was striking enough to turn heads. She wore a purple dress from a vintage clothing store, platform shoes, and a black string choker. Even at 29, she had a tomboyish quality, and when she laughed, she seemed to be all elbows and collarbones. In conversation, Rachel could be both reserved and outgoing, and though she speaks with a slow drawl, her dark eyes, high cheeks, and thick, heavy eyebrows make it clear she is of Slavic descent. She looks a bit like Helena Bonham Carter, who, coincidentally, played her mother, Marina, in a 1993 TV movie about the Oswald family.

It is difficult to imagine what life must be like for the child of a celebrity—having a recognizable name, a childhood in the spotlight. But imagine the life of a child fathered by a villain, a child cursed with a name like Booth or Oswald. Especially Oswald. Even now, three decades after President Kennedy's death, the name still stirs up strong emotions—particularly in Texas. To much of the world, Texas is still Dallas, the place where JFK was shot. Most Texans resent this with a passion, and many of them blame Rachel's father.

"You know, it's interesting if you think about it," Rachel said, lighting a cigarette. "Probably the only other people in America who have to routinely see their father being killed are the children of President Kennedy." She blew a long stream of smoke toward the ceiling. "Kinda strange, huh?"

Audrey Marina Rachel Oswald was 33 days old when President Kennedy was killed, 35 days old when Jack Ruby killed her father. She was born in Dallas' Parkland Memorial Hospital, the same hospital where both Kennedy and her father were transported after being shot.

Rachel's mother, Marina, then barely in her twenties, had arrived from Minsk, Russia, only a year earlier and spoke very little English. According to Rachel, in the months immediately after Lee's murder, Marina, Rachel, and her two-year-old sister survived chiefly on the charity of the churches in the Dallas suburb of Richardson.

I asked what it was like being named Oswald and growing up so close to Dallas.

Rachel thought for a minute. "I didn't know my family was any different until I was about seven. One day, my mother sat my sister and me down on our big green couch and told us that the man who had raised us as our father—our stepfather, Kenneth—was not, you know, our real father, that our real father's name was Lee Oswald and that he had, well, that he had been accused of killing the president of the United States." Rachel smiled. "This helped explain why our school bus was sometimes followed by news teams, why our mailbox got shot at, why kids at school would ask, 'Did your daddy shoot the president?' At home we rarely discussed Lee. We were just trying to be a normal family. Every once in a while my mother would say that I looked like him, that I ate like him, that my legs looked like his legs, but for the most part we just didn't talk about it."

I asked her what else she remembered about growing up.

"I remember that my mother was very beautiful, that she had been writ-

ten up in Life *magazine. When we moved to Rockwall, which was much smaller than Richardson—people lived there for farming and football—everyone in town knew my mother. She was this delicate Russian beauty, widowed by a man who shot the president. We were of interest to people. For the most part, folks were nice, but they were always whispering things. I remember that a helicopter flew over my mother's wedding to my stepfather, that it was sort of a big deal in the news."*

In 1982 a national tabloid newspaper ran an unauthorized cover story on Rachel and her sister claiming, OSWALD KIDS DON'T HAVE DOGS OR DATES. *The word "Oswald" was stamped in red ink over photographs of the two girls. According to the story, Rachel was a miserable, lonely child—her dogs had been poisoned, she had never been asked out on a date, she had no friends, her family couldn't even afford to buy albums for her record player. In truth, Rachel was a healthy, active teenager. She studied gymnastics and ballet, made good grades, was a varsity cheerleader, and was even voted most popular student by her classmates.*

"Don't get me wrong," Rachel said, blushing a little. "I was shy—and I chose not to date much—but enough of the article was false that we filed a lawsuit and they settled out of court. I mean, things weren't completely normal. Sometimes when the cheerleading squad went to football games in different towns, people in the stands would shout stuff at me—'Your daddy shot Kennedy' or 'Good thing your daddy's dead and buried.' But mostly things were pretty normal. The kids didn't care much one way or the other. It was usually the parents who did the weird stuff."

HISTORICAL ARTICLE

The following article appeared in a regional magazine in Alabama. It is an effective historical article for several reasons. First, it makes the story (something that happened almost two centuries ago) seem relevant to modern readers. It does this by showing the setting as it appears today, so that readers feel comfortable. The article also does a good job of making the events and characters seem alive through the use of accurate facts and descriptions.

"The Phoenix of the South"

by Cathy Corbett

The University of Alabama—the very mention of the name brings to mind the sprawling campus bordered by the Black Warrior River, shaded by ancient oaks, watched over by Denny Chimes, dedicated to its purpose of higher education, and filled with students from all over the United States and countries beyond.

There is little about the University today that would suggest to the casual onlooker that the campus was at one time a target of the Union's campaign to bring the South under submission. It was, however, and April 4 marks the 125th anniversary of the day that brought Union and Confederate forces into conflict in Tuscaloosa, and ultimately, the University campus to its knees.

The burning of the University of Alabama campus, while tragic, adds to the overall stirrings of history about the institution and gives students and faculty alike an almost unexplainable feeling of protective loyalty toward their University.

At the University's inception in 1831, however, this student loyalty wasn't so great. The expectations of the administration were high as the University opened its doors, but the students, regrettably, did not live up to these expectations. As Alabama was a frontier society, few students could meet the academic admission requirements, and the University was forced to admit unprepared young men. Conflict between high faculty expectations and poor student preparation and behavior created tensions.

As discipline problems worsened in the late 1850s, the president of the University, Landon Garland, sought to remedy these problems by converting the University to a military academy. He succeeded in convincing the legislature in 1860 of the benefits a military institution would provide should the growing tensions between the North and South develop into war.

Consequently, in the Fall of 1860 when the young men returned to campus, they returned, not just as students, but as the first members of the Alabama Corps of Cadets. Within nine months after the introduction of the military system, the students' unruly image had been wiped away.

In 1861, with the predictions of war having come true, the cadets petitioned President Garland to "suspend college duties" so they could go to war. President Garland firmly denied their request saying that they would be better prepared for war if they stayed on and trained to be officers. He also did not want the war to come to a close and leave Alabama "destitute of cultivated intellect."

Many students, however, obtained their parents' permission to leave, and by September 1862, the senior class had no members, and the junior class consisted of only three. To make up for this loss, the University lowered its admission age. Between the years of 1862–1865, the majority of students on campus were 15 and 16 years old. Many of these young men entered and stayed only long enough to learn the basics of military life, then joined the war without graduating. The University's reputation as an efficient military training school continued to grow.

By 1865, a major problem facing the University was the lack of sufficient food and supplies. The Corps had reached its limit of 200, but President Garland admitted 100 more candidates. He did require that each pay a portion of his tuition with 200 pounds of bacon. Garland used the bacon to barter for other supplies. Despite his efforts to get better equipment, the cadets' weapons were often substandard.

As the sounds of the Civil War edged closer to Tuscaloosa, President Garland did all he could to prepare his men to fortify the campus. He knew that the city of Tuscaloosa was on two of the most likely routes to railroads and furnaces of Selma. He also feared that the University, because it was a valuable training ground for the Confederacy, was a likely candidate for destruction.

President Garland was right.

The night of April 4, 1865, was rainy. The Corps was fast asleep—tired from having been on patrol for several days before because of a false rumor about a Yankee invasion. One young cadet stayed up late in he sentinel box trying to prepare for the next day's classes. Shortly after midnight, he heard President Garland run across campus and break the quiet drizzle of the rain with shouts of "Beat the long roll! The Yankees are in town!"

Federal troops, under the leadership of General John T. Croxton, had been making their way toward Tuscaloosa for several days. On the morning of April 3, they began the forty-mile journey along Watermelon Road to Northport. They reached the outer limits of Northport by night, and General Croxton and 150 men moved to the bridge over the Black Warrior River. Croxton discovered that the home guard had learned of his presence and were trying to tear up the bridge. Knowing he could wait no longer, he invaded Tuscaloosa.

Union soldiers roamed the town, burned factories, and interrupted a wedding party at Dr. S.J. Leach's home. All the while, the Alabama Corps of Cadets slept on unaware of the soldiers' presence. Finally, Dr. Bryce, supervisor of the Insane Hospital, ran to the University and alerted President Garland of the raid. The corps sprang into action immediately upon hearing President Garland's shouts.

Colonel James T. Murfee took charge of the 300 cadets. He ordered one squad to go retrieve the University's two cannons that were stored in a stable, and instructed them to move them to the top of River Hill. He then ordered his brother, State Captain John Murfee, to take a group of cadets, form them into a line and march them into the city. The main body of the Corps and some professors would follow.

As the Corps turned onto Greensboro Street (which led to the river), they were challenged with "Who comes here?" When the Corps identified themselves, shots rang out. The Corps dropped down and returned the fire. However, they were at a distinct disadvantage because they were armed with old-fashioned Springfield rifles that would only fire once before needing to be reloaded. Meanwhile, the Federals were armed with Winchesters that could fire 16 times before needing to be reloaded. A few moments later the firing stopped, and Dr. Garland, Colonel Murfee, and a Confederate officer could be seen in a serious conversation.

The Confederate officer was Captain Carpenter who had just married Emily Leach when the Federals surprised the wedding party and took Captain Carpenter prisoner. He had obtained permission from General Croxton to return to his bride and tell her that he was all right. On his return, he stopped to meet with Dr. Garland and give him grim news. The Union troops, which were 1400 strong, had captured the University's cannons, they held the bridge, and were fortified behind cotton bales.

President Garland realized that under the circumstances it would be a useless sacrifice of the lives of his young men to fight on. He ordered the Corps to retreat to the University.

Once there, they filled their haversacks, and by 2 a.m., were on the march to King's Bridge, eight miles east of Tuscaloosa. They crossed the bridge, tore up the floor, and fortified themselves against a hill in a position to ward off an attack should they be pursued.

Early in the day, the boys heard the explosion of the magazines and saw the smoke ascending from the burning buildings of "the University they would have given their lives to protect."

As soon as the destruction of the University was completed, General Croxton left without making any attempt to pursue the Corps of Cadets. Total casualties of the skirmish: 23 Union soldiers killed or wounded; one retired Confederate officer killed; several members of the home guard wounded; and four members of the Corps, including Captain Murfee, wounded.

Following a council of war that morning, Dr. Garland and several other officers decided to march to Selma and attempt to join General Forrest's forces. Upon their arrival in Marion, they learned that Selma had fallen on April 2, and General Forrest had passed through Marion two days before. With no way to locate General Forrest, the University lying in ashes, and rations becoming very short, Dr. Garland finally decided to disband the Corps with orders to reassemble at Auburn in thirty days. Before this time, however, Lee surrendered on the 9th and Johnson on the 26th. With that the Civil War was brought to its end. "Thus also ended the career of the first Alabama Corps of Cadets."

The words of John Massey, a professor at the University at the time of the invasion, about his beloved Corps, is a fitting epitaph to their days of glory. "It fell (my) lot . . . to witness great enthusiasm over (the Corps) origin in 1860, to watch with absorbing interest its checkered and stormy life of five years, and to experience genuine sorrow at its untimely end amid the gloom of April 1865.

Reluctantly leaving its Alma Mater in ashes and its native land bathed in tears, it vanished, like the spirits of the heroic dead, with no stain on its honor. Its good name will live as long as the University of Alabama endures."

HUMOR ARTICLE

The number one rule regarding humor articles is a simple one: be funny. One of the best ways to write a humor article is to take an experience that a large number of people experience—something people can identify with—and put a humorous spin on it. You will have a lot of people shaking their heads, laughing, and saying, "Yeah, that is what it's like."

The biggest way to score a zero with your humor article is to have your humor sound forced. Try not to think of how many one-liners you have come up with or how many clever phrases you have invented. Write in as natural a way as possible.

The following article, published in the March 6, 1996, issue of *Family Fun,* is effective because it is one of those topics of mass appeal and because the humor is natural.

"Daddyspeak Happens"

by Andrew Marlatt

Not long ago, my friend Dave and I were in a grocery checkout line having just scavenged the aisles for baseball game provisions—a six-pack, pretzels, hot dogs, the usual. As the impassive young lady at the register rang up our purchases, Dave rooted in his pockets and then turned to me, frowning.

"Um, can you cover this?" he asked. "I left my wallet at home. What a silly bunny."

I froze. The woman behind us, who had been unloading her groceries, paused. The clerk raised an eyebrow.

"New father," I explained, hastily pulling out my own wallet and paying the bill.

The clerk nodded in sympathy as I dragged Dave toward the exit, gripping his elbow hard.

"What?" he whined, as the electric doors hushed close behind us.

Safely in the car, I turned on the ignition key and stared through the heat-baked windshield. Sitting next to me was a mature, articulate, self-aware man, a respected medical research scientist who daily bandied about terms such as tubulointerstitial nephritis *and* coccidioidomycosis. *A man who had just uttered in public, without any prompting . . .*

"Silly bunny," I said quietly.

"What?"

"You said . . . 'silly bunny.'"

"When?"

"Just now. In the store."

"I did?"

If Dave was surprised, I shouldn't have been. Within months—no days—of his son's birth, he seemed unable to pronounce even the simplest of words. Milk bottle *became "moo-moo ba-ba."* Bath *became "splishy-splash." And his son, whom he himself had named Daniel, became, inexplicably, "Wiggleworm."*

At first, I convinced myself this was an isolated case, but then the rising tide of fatherhood engulfed my circle of friends. One by one, it swamped them all in what I began to call Daddyspeak. I stood by helplessly as Larry, a brusque, burly man who looks as if he extinguishes oil well fires by yelling at them, described his fidgety daughter as "such a flappy birdie." I shook my head as John, a public relations executive who makes his living choosing his words carefully, began calling his son "William the Wub du Wompas." And in silent awe, I watched a home video of my friend Tony as he gave his eight-month-old daughter, Jessica, a bath. I had known Tony for years. As a fellow reporter, I had seen him deal with Mafia dons and predawn rubouts. As a friend, I had bonded with him at countless New York Mets games. And yet there he was, naked in the tub, bathing his daughter and squealing, "Soapy! Jessie's all soapy!" Moments later, the camera cut to Jessica asleep in her crib. Tony, sitting next to me on the couch, stared at the vision on screen and sighed, "She's such a snugglebug."

It unnerved me, especially after my wife, Susan, and I began to discuss parenthood. Would I speak differently, too? Surely not, I thought. But when I mentioned my resolve to my friend Leonard, a therapist and new father, he set me straight. "The bottom line," he said, "is that while you may think of yourself as a dignified, professional human being, you become a father and that all goes down the poopy drain."

"Ha," I retorted brazenly, but the joke was on me. Even then I suspected what I know now: the descent into Daddyspeak is inevitable. It is subtle and irrevesible, like balding or bad credit. Adjectives mutate into gibberish. Pronunciation dies a slow death. Singular concepts such as sleep become multihypenated, rhyming sillyisms such as "nappy-nap-nap." In Daddyspeak, there are no grammatical violations, and there are no humiliation police. Men who once had a hard time with sensitive concepts, like love and kiss, turn into softhearted, limp-lipped beings who babble phrases such as "Does my Wiggleworm want his Nook-Nook?"

Fatherhood was thrust into my arms on November 21, 1994, at 4:53 p.m. I did not immediately respond in Daddyspeak because my son, Walker, at ten pounds nine ounces, appeared to be the size of an eight-year-old. Within a few days, however, as he began to whine for a feeding, I uttered my first Daddyphrase: "Hold on, yum-yum's coming."

Yum-yum? *Where did that come from? Could this be a cathartic release from machismo? A turning point in my life that signified I was becoming a softer, more sensitive soul? After careful reflections, I concluded it was more like a sneeze. "Yum-yum" was in me somewhere and needed to get out. In fact, I now believe that the need to say "yum-yum" or "wiggleworm" is deeply embedded in the male psyche. Like the instinct to hunt or procreate or wear dark socks while mowing the lawn, the urge to speak nonsensically with one's child has been with us since the beginning of time. Primitive Dad doubtless had his own version of yum-yum, though it might have boiled down to a difference in the inflection of the word* Gak.

With the advantage of hindsight, I now believe there's a reason we speak gibberish with our babies: Daddyspeak strengthens the tentative bond between father and child. For one, it helps level the playing field. My son can't talk yet and so, to be fair, I act as if I can't either. When I say, "How's my wooka-boo?" and he answers "Nanana," we are both staring into each other's eyes and think, "I have no idea what you're saying, but I'm happy." Also, while the adult male voice is often demanding and even scary, Daddyspeak is soft and inviting. This is how I want Walker to perceive me. I don't want him to think of me as demanding and scary until he's a teenager.

Finally, how else are you going to entertain an infant?

CHAPTER THREE

WHAT'S THE BIG IDEA?

David, a magazine writer, settled comfortably into his airplane seat for the flight to his parents' home. He had thought he would never make it—he had waited till the last minute to book his flight, something you can't exactly do during the busy holiday season. He took out his notebook to work on some article outlines when the man sitting next to him struck up a conversation. He was an insurance sales representative on his way back from a stress-reduction seminar. They had a nice conversation—the sales rep did seem quite rested—then David turned his attention back to his notebooks.

He suddenly had an idea.

Six months later, David had an article entitled "Stress-Free Sales" published in both an executive training magazine and an insurance association's magazine. A spin-off, "Letting Go of Stress," was published in a men's magazine. In all the articles, David quoted the sales rep he met on the airplane.

From his airplane flight, he had several other ideas evolve into published articles. He wrote "Survival Tips for Holiday Travel" for a women's magazine and "You Can't Go Home Again" (a humorous article about visiting family for the holidays) for a general interest magazine. He also came up with a list of ten possible article ideas just from reading the in-flight magazines on the airplane.

David has learned the valuable art of idea-gathering. He is always on the lookout for article ideas—even when he's on an airplane flight (and probably when he's in the grocery store checkout line, at a party, or simply daydreaming). Then David *does something* with his ideas. He writes the ideas down, approaches magazines with his ideas, and transforms his ideas into actual magazine articles.

Idea-gathering is one of the most important skills for new magazine writers to develop. Yet, for some reason, it's a skill that many of them think is impossible to acquire. I am constantly amazed at the number of aspiring writers who tell me, "I want to write, but I don't know what to write about."

Ideas are everywhere. Once you know how to find them, you won't know what to do with all of your ideas! In fact, I would bet that if you consciously looked for article ideas all day long, you could have at least a hundred by the end of the day. See Exhibit 3.1 on page 42 for more evidence that ideas are everywhere.

EXHIBIT 3.1 IDEAS ARE EVERYWHERE

Here are some ideas for magazine articles I developed from looking back on a normal day of doing errands, working on articles, reading, and doing other random activities. It took me about fifteen minutes to come up with this list.

1. "Making Creative Easter Baskets" (yesterday was Easter Sunday)
2. "Making Healthy Easter Baskets" (my daughter, McKenna, ate way too much chocolate as part of Easter)
3. Essay on how spring makes me think of new beginnings, such as how to do spring cleaning, get organized for spring, make spring resolutions, etc.
4. "The Ten Best Videos for Children" or something else on the video-watching tendencies of children (from watching McKenna watch "The Lion King" before school this morning)
5. "Dealing with Spring colds" (from giving my daughter congestion medicine this morning)
6. "Tax Tips for Tax Dummies" (from mailing my taxes in today)
7. "Tax Tips for Freelance Writers"
8. "Dealing with a Child's Independence" (from hearing McKenna repeatedly say, "I can do it, Momma" all day today)
9. "How to Write a Winning Term Paper" (from teaching a writing class at the local college today)
10. "Symptoms You Should Never Ignore" (from checking in on my mother, who has recently suffered a burst blood vessel in her brain)
11. "Creative Ways to Cut Wedding Costs" (from planning my own wedding, just five weeks away)
12. "Get Your Fiancé Involved in Wedding Planning" (ditto)
13. "Second Weddings Can Be Just as Special" (ditto)
14. "Can Getting a Tan Be Healthy?" (from getting ready for a honeymoon in Aruba)
15. "Country's Hottest Young Stars" (from listening to a country radio station while writing this chapter)
16. "Celebrating Earth Day in Your Own Home" (from watching a report on the local news)

Although many of your ideas may not be very good (I don't think I would actually want to write about tax tips), you can usually find one or two ideas that you like.

(EVERY)WHERE TO FIND IDEAS

To become an expert idea-gatherer, look at the following simple sources.

Reading

As a writer, you should also be an avid reader. You should be reading a wide variety of materials, including novels, nonfiction books, biographies, poetry, magazines, newspapers, and reference materials. In fact, you should be reading anything and everything you can get your hands on.

As a new writer, you must teach yourself to be in a constant state of reading. If your mind is not expanding, if you are not opening yourself up to new information, be aware of it and make a change. Do things that will encourage you to read. Have a corner in your house designated for reading. As a break from writing, go to the bookstore. Treat yourself to a new book as a reward for finishing an article. Subscribe to writer's magazines; they will motivate you and give you ideas.

Reading is important, because it teaches several things. First of all, it teaches you to become a critic of writing. You get to the point where you can decide what is both good and bad writing. Reading also opens you up to a wealth of information that you cannot acquire any other way. And, for our purpose in this chapter, reading can provide you with innumerable ideas for your own writing.

Ideas can come from a variety of reading sources.

Magazines • Look to magazines to see what type of material is being published. If you are interested in writing for a specific magazine, read it and see what slants its writers take on topics. Read articles and let your mind wander to similar topics about which you have some knowledge or interest.

You can also recycle ideas from magazines. Magazines often publish the same types of articles every two or three years. (Have you ever noticed, for example, that you see something like "Getting Your Child Ready for School" in August issues every year?) Someone has to write these "old" articles. Why couldn't that writer be you?

Magazines can also provide you with writing techniques to use in your own writing. If you like the way an article lead is written, tear it out to refer to later. If you like the way a writer groups her information together, clip it and keep it in your files. You never want to plagiarize another writer, but you can get a good deal of inspiration from another writer's good idea.

Newspapers • Daily papers are great reading material for a number of reasons. First of all, they tell us what is important in the world today. Look at articles to see what issues people are concerned about and to see what trends are hot. Look especially at articles that talk about national findings or new studies about a subject or trend. These topics could also be very appropriate for magazines.

Newspapers also tell us about interesting people and events. I have found that the best place to find article ideas in the newspaper is in the feature section, as it is here that you read about unique festivals, fascinating individuals, and so forth. Look at these local stories and see which ones could be written for a national audience. You already have the basic information from the newspaper article, so much of the research is already done for you. Ask yourself what information needs to be added for a national audience, then interview the individual or talk to someone who can fill in the details.

> *"I think why my mother wanted so badly for me to be a writer was simply because of this: She wanted me to be the voice of her family, especially her voice. And families like Mom's and mine are voiceless for centuries. And suddenly we go to college, and we read the great books of the world. And we look around and we realize our family has stories also."*
>
> PAT CONROY

In reading newspapers, don't forget to look at those places that many people might overlook. The letters to the editor, for example, are invaluable in letting you know what issues are of greatest interest and concern to people. If you write a magazine article about an issue you read about in a letter, you could even use the letter-writer as a "real-world" source. Advertisements and classified ads also tell you about what is popular and important to the general public. Who knows? Your perusal through the classifieds could give you the idea for an article entitled "Couples Who Found Love Through the Personals" (or a different take, "How to Write a Personal Ad"). An ad you see in the travel section might lead to "Ten Tips for Cruise Travel" or "Crime-Proofing Your Home While You Are Away."

Other Sources • Also look at unusual reading materials, such as the Yellow Pages, technical manuals, brochures, menus, and atlases. The message here is that you can get ideas—you guessed it—everywhere. You never know where an idea will present itself.

The Yellow Pages, for example, are great for those times when you can think of absolutely *nothing.* Go through the pages and look at all of the businesses. You might ask yourself why someone would want to hire a massage therapist, giving you the idea for an article entitled, "Do-it-Yourself Massage." You might wonder about the historical home advertised in your town, leading to an article entitled, "Rivertown's Confederate Heritage."

Never discard any type of reading material. Your first published credit may come from reading your dishwasher manual!

Books • Read books both for ideas and as a break from idea-gathering. Fiction and nonfiction books, especially if they are popular ones, let you know what types of stories attract and interest people today. Classic books tell us about eternal themes and show us what good writing is all about. Books can give you the idea for a topic or provide an idea for an episode or anecdote to use in your article (in my experience, this second type of inspiration is usually more prevalent).

Books on writing can also give you lots of ideas. They might give you tangible ideas through writing exercises, or they might simply provide you with inspiration ("If this writer wrote about all of those things, certainly I can come up with some ideas of my own").

Books are also a good way to give yourself a break from writing. Reading for pure enjoyment is very important on its own, and it can provide a much-needed change of pace from the work you are doing. If you write a lot of informational articles, a suspenseful whodunit can give you a nice break. If you write how-tos, a juicy biography might be just the antidote for a tired mind. Just take this warning to heart: Once you learn to look for ideas, reading for enjoyment will be interrupted by all of those ideas rushing at you.

Personal Experiences I

There's no better place to look for ideas than in your own life. No one else has your experiences, your past, your dreams, your goals, and your interests. You have a true market on ideas that come from your own life, because no one else has them.

You really have two levels of personal experiences from which to draw ideas. The first level is the emotional one, which consists of your present circumstances, your past and your memories, and your hopes and dreams. These experiences, while they can provide you with plenty of ideas for writing projects, are often hard to tap into because they are so personal. Many writers, in fact, feel as if they are revealing too much of themselves if they write about their personal experiences. They feel vulnerable in sharing these facts with others. If you feel that way, try to tap into these experiences by saying you will write about them for your eyes only.

Look at your present life. What about it could be enlightening or useful to other people? With what fact of your present life could others identify? In order to see your present life in a tangible way, consider it in terms of these categories:

My family life:

My profession/career:

My geographical location:

My daily routine:

Once you have filled in each of these categories, ask yourself what parts of your life could interest other people. What about your present life could educate others? You may find that you now have several ideas for magazine articles.

When most people think of personal experience articles, they often think of nostalgic pieces. Both your past experiences and specific memories can provide excellent fodder for article ideas. Think to your past and complete the following exercise to flesh out specific details:

Places I have lived:

Jobs I have held:

Special recognitions I have received:

Turning points in my life (both professionally and personally):

Places I have visited:

Special family members in my past:

Special friends in my past:

This exercise will help you reacquaint yourself with your past. You will have the foundation for how, where, and with whom you have lived your life. Many of these details can be used as starting points for magazine articles. In looking at my own list, for example, I could write articles on living in college towns, being a single mother (and now, making a second marriage succeed), working as a book editor, traveling the Caribbean, and keeping in touch with childhood friends. Look at your own list, and see what article ideas you can develop.

> *"Nothing is thrown out. Nothing. Everything is saved. Usually when I finish, I have more ideas left over than when I started."*
>
> JACK KEROUAC

Memories go a step deeper than a superficial list such as the one above. Memories refer to specific events or people your mind chooses to remember. To tap into your memories, think as specifically as possible. Think of yourself at a specific age; remember a specific person; try to recall the way you felt at a specific holiday; take yourself back to a location in as specific a way as possible (under that special tree in your grandmother's front yard, for example).

Also included in this first category of personal experiences are your hopes and dreams. Imagine what you would like to accomplish and where you want your life to lead. Could you develop any of these wishes and goals into publishable ideas?

Personal Experiences II

This second category, not quite as intimate as the first, consists of your interests, hobbies, and areas of expertise. It is an excellent way to gather ideas, and it may, in fact, be the origin for most article ideas. Because writers want to write about things they themselves enjoy, this is a very useful idea category. What writer wants to write about pets if he hates animals? Who wants to write about children if he or she never plans on having any? It would make writing feel like a chore—like you had just received a term paper assignment from your high school English teacher.

Determining your interests, hobbies, and expertise is quite simple. Put each heading on a separate sheet of paper (or use Exhibit 3.2 on page 48 to do so). On each sheet, write as many thoughts as you can about the category. Write down anything you can think of, even if you can't imagine that one of your hobbies is something anyone else would care to read about. When looking at your expertise, don't just think professionally. Ask yourself, "What do I do well?" If you are a good listener, write that down. An article on listening tips would be very useful and, if you're good at it, quite simple to write.

Family, Friends, and Acquaintances

Your personal experiences aren't the only ones that would make for good magazine articles. Those of your family, friends, and acquaintances are also up for grabs. Look at the circle of people with whom you spend time. Is there a cousin who has had a dramatic experience? Is there a friend who successfully learned how to deal with a life-altering change? Is there a friend who is an expert at something?

Remember our friend David at the beginning of this chapter? An acquaintance (an insurance sales rep he met on a plane) provided him with a great idea for an article. While you are going through your daily routine, always be on the lookout for people who could provide good information for or be a good subject of an article. Use Exhibit 3.3 on page 49 to size up your circle of relationships.

Observation

Observation may sound simple, but it really isn't. It isn't easy to observe with all of your being—using all of your senses.

- Use your sense of sight to truly notice everything around you. As you go through your daily life and when you are specifically working on a writing project, look at everything closely. Notice colors, shapes, and textures; make note of a person's expressions, gestures, and body language. There is always so much more than the surface of a person or a situation. Teach yourself to look below the surface. As you're working on a writing project, ask yourself, what of these details could make my article more lively and accurate?
- Use your sense of sound to add a new dimension to your writing. The sounds of an environment are often integral to that environment's meaning. Listen closely to *all* sounds.
- Use your sense of touch when details are important to your writing (all of the time, in effect). How does something feel? How can the texture or feeling of an object or atmosphere add a new dimension to your descriptions?

EXHIBIT 3.2 PERSONAL EXPERIENCES II

Interests	Hobbies	Expertise

EXHIBIT 3.3 YOUR CIRCLE OF RELATIONSHIPS

Who do you come in contact with everyday? Your circle of relationships is probably a lot wider than you think. To determine your circle, list the names of people you come in contact with in various environments. Are there any article ideas you can develop from these relationships?

At home:

At work:

Across the miles:

Doing errands:

In civic organizations and other groups:

Having fun:

Random meetings:

- Use your sense of taste if it is necessary to your article. It won't always be part of an environment, but it often will be.

Seasonal Topics, Holidays, and Anniversaries

You can come up with hundreds of article ideas each year by simply reading the calendar. Sound impossible? It's not, if you consider the fact that most magazines accept seasonal articles and stories on historical anniversaries and that the calendar is full of holidays and anniversaries.

The first thing you need to realize in coming up with these ideas is that you need to get yourself in a seasonal state of mind. Most magazines accept articles an average of six months before publication time. This means that you need to be writing about Christmas when you're really celebrating the Fourth of July. (Exhibit 3.4 below is a handy reference to help you determine when your seasonal articles will be needed.)

At the beginning of every year, I like to create a brand-new list of ideas categorized by months. I designate separate file folders for each month and keep them to put ideas in as I get them.

To come up with seasonal article ideas, think about what issues are important at specific times of the year. In January, for example, people are concerned about new beginnings; in February, we all think about love; in March and April, spring is starting to arrive; in May, school is letting out for the kids; in June, brides are getting ready to march down the aisle; in July, hot weather concerns and summer vacations are important; in August and September, school's getting started again; in October, football is popular; in November, it's cold and we're learning to be thankful; in December, of

EXHIBIT 3.4 SEASONAL ARTICLE GUIDE

Today	*Three months ahead*	*Six months ahead*	*One year ahead*
January	April	July	January
February	May	August	February
March	June	September	March
April	July	October	April
May	August	November	May
June	September	December	June
July	October	January	July
August	November	February	August
September	December	March	September
October	January	April	October
November	February	May	November
December	March	June	December

course, it's the holiday season. There are thousands of different topics that apply to certain parts of the year, and magazines yearn to get good seasonal material—that's a combination that could mean publication for you. If you can come up with a different slant on a traditional holiday, or provide a unique article about a little-known holiday, you will get an editor's attention.

Anniversary articles are, in effect, historical articles. They tell about a significant anniversary of an important event (Columbus's arrival in the New World, the birth of Beethoven, etc.). To get ideas for anniversary articles, invest in a historical timeline book. For information on historical happenings and on little-known holidays, buy a book of days. I guarantee that these two books will give you enough magazine article ideas to keep you busy for the next year.

FROM THE EDITOR'S DESK

"Do your homework and send material we can use."

WENDY WALLER, *WOMAN'S JOURNAL*

Imagination

Have you ever heard a writer say that an idea "just came" to him or her? In these cases, the writer's idea for an article (or short story or novel) came from the imagination.

How do you define *imagination? Webster's Dictionary* defines it as "the mental faculty which apprehends and forms ideas of external objects." I like that definition. With our imagination, we grasp onto something we see and mold it into something new with our minds.

Many of your best ideas can come from simply using your imagination. Usually, imagination will combine with one of the other idea-gathering techniques already listed to create a slant or concept for an article. You might observe a conversation between two friends and *imagine* what it is about; from this imagined conversation, you could develop an idea for a magazine article.

Another way to use your imagination to develop article ideas is to use it in conjunction with writing exercises. These exercises are often good to just get your mind breathing and your hand writing. (For more exercises to attack writer's block, see Chapter 11.) Here are some of my favorite imagination exercises:

- *Editor for an Hour.* Select a magazine for which you would like to write; read through several copies of the magazine. Close your eyes and imagine that you are the editor of that magazine. Your desk is covered with unusable manuscripts. You wish you could get just *one* good article in the mail. Imagine what types of articles you, as the editor, would like to receive. Open your eyes and write the articles down. Could you write any of these articles?
- "*I Love . . .*" Write the statement "I love . . ." at the top of a clean sheet of paper or page on your computer screen. Quickly write as

many items, peoples, places, activities, and so forth on the page. Try not to think about the words as you are writing them; simply write down any you think of. After five minutes of writing, look through your list. Could you turn any of these concepts into article ideas?

- *I Spy.* Look around your study (or kitchen, or wherever you happen to be) and select ("spy") one object. Write down anything pertinent about this object—its appearance, function, smell, meaning to you, and so forth. Is there some aspect of this object that could provide the focus for an article?
- *Down Memory Lane.* Take several minutes (or, if you get into it, a few hours) looking through old photo albums. What memories do you associate with the pictures? What experiences did you have that you had forgotten about? Could you write about any of these experiences?
- *Music Appreciation.* Turn the radio to your favorite station, put your favorite CD (or tape, or record) in the player, or select some music that you've never listened to before. Close your eyes and let your mind wander. What images does the music create? What words does the music make you think of? What type of person might enjoy this music? With what kind of experience does this music go? Open your eyes and write down any images or ideas that the music gave to you.
- *Idea Chart.* Fill in the idea chart in Exhibit 3.5 on page 53; it is guaranteed to provide you with twenty-five magazine article ideas. On the horizontal row, write down five types of magazines for which you would like to write (women's, children's, history, science, etc.). On the vertical row, write down a general subject of interest to you (food, cats, travel, etc.). After you have filled in the two rows, intersect the boxes and come up with specific article ideas from these intersections. For example, if you would like to write for women's magazines and a subject you're interested in is health, you might come up with "Learning to Detect Breast Cancer" as your idea for that intersecting box.

> *"Any man who will look into his heart and honestly write what he sees there will find plenty of readers."*
> EDGAR W. HOUSE

- *Article Idea Match-Up.* In developing ideas for articles, you must realize that there are three important components: the specific audience for which you are developing the idea, the specific topic of the idea, and the type of article you're going to develop from the idea. This exercise will create article ideas from these basic components. On a sheet of paper, write three headings: Types of Articles, Subjects, and Audiences. Come up with at least ten items for each column—ten common types of articles that you find in magazines (you can use the list from Chapter 2 or come up with some additional ideas

EXHIBIT 3.5 IDEA CHART

Types of Magazines → Topics of Interest ↓					

on your own), ten subject areas of wide interest, and ten audiences that are targeted by magazines. Once you have developed your lists, combine them in random order and try to develop a feasible article idea. For example, you might have to come up with an informational article on food for senior citizens, leading to the idea, "Should 'Fat-Free' Matter to You?" Exhibit 3.6 on page 54 shows a sample chart developed from the article idea match-up.

IS MY IDEA A GOOD ONE?

An idea is just an idea if it's one that can't be developed into an article or if it's one that no editor is interested in reading. To determine if your idea is a feasible and publishable one, go through the following checklist. If you can answer "no" to any of the questions, you need to restructure your idea or give it up for a new one.

EXHIBIT 3.6 ARTICLE IDEA MATCH-UP EXAMPLE

Types of Articles	*Subjects*	*Audiences*
1. How-to	1. Family	1. Executives
2. Personal experience	2. Food	2. Newlyweds
3. Descriptive	3. Business	3. Teenagers
4. Personality profile	4. Sports	4. Working mothers
5. Historical	5. Hobbies	5. College students
6. Humor	6. Money	6. Senior citizens
7. Short piece	7. Love and sex	7. Children
8. Travel	8. Music	8. Parents
9. Investigative	9. Environment	9. Singles
10. Opinion	10. Children	10. Sports fans

1. Does the idea interest you enough to spend considerable time with it in writing your magazine article?
2. If the idea is too broad for a magazine article, can you narrow it down?
3. If the idea is too narrow for a magazine article, can you expand it in some way?
4. Are there several magazines for which it would be appropriate for publication?
5. Imagine that you are a reader of each of these magazines. As that reader, do you identify with the topic? Do you enjoy reading about it?
6. Can you state specifically, in a sentence of fifteen words or less, why other people (readers like the one just mentioned) would want to read about your topic?
7. Can you research the topic without unneeded expense or time involvement?

WHAT DO I DO WITH MY IDEAS?

If you internalize these idea-gathering techniques, you should soon have a mind full of ideas. While you once thought you would never have enough ideas to write about, now you have too many. What do you do with the ideas you want to use right now? And what do you do with those ideas that you aren't quite sure about?

One option you should *never* consider is that of throwing an idea out. Other than that, there are several options you can follow.

- *Write it down.* If you haven't followed any advice I have given you so far, do follow this one: Create an idea notebook. Buy a notebook (preferably, a spiral bound one) and carry it with you at all times. Write down any idea as soon as you think of it. Later, write each idea on a separate sheet of paper and write down sources, anecdotes you will use, an outline, and other information for the magazine article. You might also want to create idea file folders. This is a good way to organize your ideas because you can put clippings and loose sheets of paper into the file folders.

FROM THE EDITOR'S DESK

"Be sure to look at a recent copy of the magazine. A new slant on familiar topics often catches our eyes, but avoid generalizing or summing up an old topic. That won't cut it."

MARTHA CARLSON,
COMPLETE WOMAN

- *Use the idea now.* If your idea is one you feel strongly about right now, go ahead and develop the article while the idea is hot. After you have thought through the idea (and determined that it is a good idea based on the checklist above) come up with a list of magazines that might be interested in the article and write query letters to the magazines (see Chapter 12 for query letter advice). Then, get to work.
- *Put the idea on your calendar.* If your idea is one that needs to be written at a specific time of year (or if you currently have so many other ideas that you don't have time yet to devote to this one), designate a date on which you will begin work on the article. Write the idea down in your calendar, and stick to your plans.
- *Save the idea for a rainy day.* You never know when you will need a good idea, so keep plenty of them in store for those times when you can't think of any new ones. Your idea notebook or idea file folders work well in this respect. You can refer to either of them when you need a new idea. Or create an idea jar. Get your hands on a large, open-mouthed jar (a big pickle jar or apple juice jar work well) and, as you come up with ideas you don't want to use right now, write the ideas on pieces of paper and put the pieces in the jar. On that "rainy day," you can take a piece of paper out and write about that idea.

Jumpstart Exercises

1. Purchase a notebook to be used as your Idea Notebook.
2. Use a newspaper to come up with five magazine article ideas. Take one of the ideas and make a rough outline of the article you would produce from it.

3. If you have not done so already, fill out Exhibits 3.2 and 3.3. Come up with three ideas for magazine articles from your responses.
4. If you have not done so already, fill in the idea chart (Exhibit 3.5) and do the article idea match-up (Exhibit 3.6).
5. Go to a public place (a shopping mall, governmental office, park, classroom) and, using all of your senses to observe the area around you, come up with three article ideas.
6. Take today's date and count six months ahead. Based on that future date, come up with three seasonal or holiday article ideas.
7. Select one of the ideas you developed from the above exercises and put it to the test by completing the checklist that helps you determine whether the idea is a good one or not.
8. Take all of the ideas you developed from these exercises and from reading this chapter and record them in your Idea Notebook.

CHAPTER FOUR

YOU CAN'T HIT ANYTHING IF YOU DON'T AIM AT IT

Do you remember the fable about the tortoise and the hare? By assuming he would win the race against the slow-moving tortoise, the hare failed to plan ahead. He did not keep his eye on the finish line—he simply assumed that he would be the first one across it. Without making plans for how he would win the race, the hare was left relaxing on the sideline while the tortoise broke across the finish line.

As someone once said, "You can't hit anything if you don't aim at it." The hare couldn't hit the finish line because he wasn't aiming for it. Likewise, a writer can't complete his or her first magazine article, write in a journal everyday, or get a first article published (or meet any other writing goals) if he or she hasn't aimed at those goals.

If you want to achieve your writing dreams, you must set specific, regular goals. But what kind of goals should you set if you are a new writer? Should you tell yourself you will send off ten magazine articles in your first committed year of writing? Should you make yourself write everyday? Should you simply tell yourself to spend your first six months learning as much as you can about the writing process?

There are no right answers for these questions. The types of writing goals you set for yourself depend, primarily, upon your own personality. You must decide for yourself how much you want to achieve in a certain amount of time.

Although goal-setting is quite subjective, there are some guidelines that will help you determine what goals to set for yourself.

YOUR REASONS FOR WRITING

Before you set any goals, you should ask yourself the all-important question: *Why do I want to write?* Write this question at the top of a clean sheet of paper. On that sheet, write all the reasons you want to write. Some possible responses might be:

- "I want to sort through my own struggles."
- "I want to help others."
- "I like the process of writing."
- "Writing makes me feel good."

- "People tell me I have talent."
- "I dream of seeing my name in print."
- "I want to earn some extra money."
- "I have got some interesting stories to tell."

Don't feel as if your responses must be of a certain nature. Some people write strictly for the love of it; others love to write but also do it for the practical reason of earning a few extra dollars. Both reasons are valid.

Knowing why you want to write is integral to helping you determine what goals to set. As you go through the guidelines for setting goals in this chapter, realize that you should set goals that match your reasons for writing.

> *"When I am dead, I hope it may be said: 'His sins were scarlet, but his books were read.'"*
>
> HILLAIRE BELLOC

If your main reason for writing is to help yourself or to impart knowledge to others, you shouldn't make promises that stress publication as the number one goal of writing (although you don't want to overlook the possibilities for marketing your work, as you become comfortable with that idea). If your main reasons for writing are to be published and make some money, you shouldn't set goals to only write in your journal or to read about writing as much as possible. You should have goals that will result in publication.

WHAT KINDS OF GOALS SHOULD I SET?

Just as New Year's resolutions come in a variety of flavors, writing goals are many and varied. Generally, however, they appear in three different incarnations:

1. *Write a specific amount each day.* Many writers designate their goals by how much time they spend writing or by how many words they write. These types of goals work great for beginning writers because they are very structured goals. By telling yourself to write 150 words a day or to write for thirty minutes a day, you have a very specific goal to meet. And, you know with these goals that you will be *writing* something. New writers need to have goals that not only make them *think* about writing, but that actually make them write.
2. *Complete a project.* You may decide to have your writing goals revolve around the completion of certain projects. As a new writer, these are good goals for you because they show positive results from your efforts. You will actually see yourself complete what you set out to complete. Just remember to give yourself plenty of time to complete your projects—giving yourself too little time will create unnecessary frustrations and time management woes. Some examples of these

EXHIBIT 4.1 GOALS FOR BEGINNING WRITERS

Listed below are some of the goals that beginning writers made at a recent workshop. Maybe you can get some ideas from them.

"I will write in my journal fifteen minutes a day."
"I'm going to come up with a list of ten ideas for magazine articles every week."
"I will write every morning from 6:00–6:30, before my kids get up."
"I will write one double-spaced typewritten page every day."
"Every month, I will send out one query letter."
"I'm going to join a local writer's group, and actively take my material to be read and critiqued by others."
"No matter how hard it hurts, I'm going to send out my first article to an editor by the end of the year."
"I will write two hundred words every night."
"I'm going to complete an article every month."
"I'm finally going to write about all those things I said I should write about."
"I'm going to send out a query letter every Monday."
"I'm never going to let anyone tell me I can't be a writer again."

types of goals might be to complete an article a month, send out one query each week, read a writing book a month, or write five articles within the next year.

3. *Get published.* For those new writers who are up to the challenge, the goal of getting published is admirable—and attainable. Again, be sure that your specific goals are practical and within your reach.

There are other types of goals, of course. You might, for example, make it a goal to join a writer's group and go to meetings regularly, to finish reading this book and complete most of the exercises, or to enter a writing contest by year's end. Try, however, to set goals in at least one of the three areas mentioned above. Exhibit 4.1 above shows you some popular goals from beginning writers.

BASIC GOAL-SETTING GUIDELINES

As you look ahead to what you want to accomplish in the future as a writer, be aware of the following guidelines in setting your goals. They will make your goals easier to meet and more rewarding when you do meet them.

- *Start simple.* Your goals should not be the same as a writer who has been writing seriously for five years. Start out with simple goals. Make a list of the reasons you want to write and from this list decide what you, reasonably, would like to accomplish by this same time next year. Don't worry if these goals do not seem lofty enough. For a new writer, the ability to reach a goal is more important than achieving a seemingly insurmountable goal. You must be realistic in your goal-setting. As a new writer, you shouldn't be able to get published in *The Atlantic* during your first year of writing. If getting published is your goal, it is just as exciting and motivating to make your first sale to *Needlecraft Monthly*. Remember, new writers must start small and simple. Stay with simple goals as long as you need to, allowing yourself to get comfortable with the fact that you expect your writing to go somewhere. Then, slowly move on to bigger goals.

FROM THE EDITOR'S DESK

"Try to write a piece that leaves the reader with one strong mental image to serve as a reminder of what you've written about. Be a real person talking to other real people about what it means to live in the midst of real-life situations."

MARY LOU REDDING,
THE UPPER ROOM

- *Challenge yourself.* While you want to start out with simple goals, you do want to have goals that will make you work. You want to be stretching—to be improving as a writer. So, make the goals simple enough that you won't give up in frustration, but make them tough enough so that you're working a little bit.
- *Set goals that fit your personality.* Don't pick certain goals just because you think they are the type that writers should pick. Pick the type of goals with which you can feel comfortable. If you're not a morning person, don't make it one of your goals to get up two hours earlier every morning to write. Set goals that are compatible with your personality.
- *Be concrete and specific.* Many new writers, when asked what their goals are for the next year, will say things like: "To write about the death of my mother," or "To tell people what it's like to be a teacher," or "To inform people about crime." These are admirable goals, but they are too nebulous. Better goals would be: "To complete a personal experience article about my mother's death within the next two months," "To write an article on how to relate to your child's teacher," and "To write an informational article on crime in the schools, and market it to five parenting magazines." When determining your goals, ask yourself if they are too broad. If they are, determine how you can make them more specific and concrete.

- *Share your goals with a few writer friends.* Notice two important words in this guideline: *few* and *writer.* You don't want to share your goals with too many people; instead, pick one or two whose judgment and encouragement you trust. You also don't want to share your specific goals with many nonwriter friends. You can let them know, generally, that you plan on succeeding in the future and that you are working on several projects. Your writer friends, however, are the ones with whom you need to share your specific goals. These few writer friends will, ideally, ask you regularly about your progress. In a way, they will serve as watchdogs. And because they experience similar struggles in reaching their own goals, they will be understanding and encouraging when it comes to difficulties you might experience.
- *Check your progress.* Find a specific way that you can mark the progress of your goals. I have found that there are two excellent ways to do this. First, write your goals down somewhere. Put them in a very visible place—above the computer, on the refrigerator, on a bulletin board in the study. Put them anywhere you can see them regularly while you are writing. It also works well to write them down in your calendar. Write the goal on the date when you want to complete it. If, for example, you have the goal to write everyday for fifteen minutes, write this on your calendar ("Write today for fifteen minutes"). If you have told yourself to complete a certain article by a certain date, write something like "Finish the car repair article by today" on that date. Second, mark off your goals as you achieve them. If you have written them on the wall next to your computer, mark them off with a big red magic marker when you accomplish them. Do likewise if you write your goals in a calendar (or wherever you may choose to write them down). Marking off your goals will do two things: if you achieve them, it will motivate you to accomplish your other goals; if you're not achieving them, it will show you that you either need to work harder or alter your goals in some way.

F. Scott Fitzgerald was just twenty-three when This Side of Paradise *was published in 1920. That made him the youngest novelist ever published by Scribner's.*

FROM THE EDITOR'S DESK

"Come up with a unique or timely idea that will appeal to our audience and be able to back it up with facts and interviews."

ALEX GORDON, *INSIDER*

- *Stick to it.* Goals are set for a specific reason: They are designed to allow you to see what things you want to accomplish and to help you set forth a plan to accomplish those things. Goal-setting has an innate sense of completion in it. So, when you are discouraged or think you don't want to be a writer after all, realize that you set your goals for a reason. You set them so you could move forward in your writing dreams.

In my opinion, the best advertising slogan in recent years has been that one by Nike, which is now ingrained in our culture: Just do it. Just do it. And stick to it. Those should be your personal slogans in goal-setting.

WRITING GOALS

Writing goals should encompass different time periods. In that way, you can see how much time and effort it is going to take you to accomplish certain goals. You can see the big picture.

I think the best way to look at your writing goals is in five different classifications. Develop daily goals, weekly goals, monthly goals, year-long goals, and life-long goals. Start with the big picture and narrow it down. If you know what you want to have accomplished by your life's end (although some people might consider it a little bit morbid), you can take a travel back in time through your life. To accomplish that, you ask yourself, what do I need to accomplish this year? this month? this week? today? It really helps put goals in perspective.

> *"What Napoleon could not do with the sword, I shall accomplish with the pen."*
> HONORE DE BALZAC

As you start out in your writing endeavors, develop at least two goals each for the day, week, and month. Come up with at least one year-long goal for each year, and develop at least one statement about what you want to have accomplished by the end of your life. As your writing develops and the years go by, you might want to add more goals for each classification.

To get started, complete the personal goal-setting checklist in Exhibit 4.2 on page 63. Modify this checklist whenever it needs to be altered, but at the very least, review and make changes to it at the beginning of every year. Finally, put the checklist somewhere you can see it, mark off your progress, and stick to it!

Jumpstart Exercises

1. Look at the paragraphs you wrote in answer to the question "Why do I want to write?" in the "Jumpstart" exercises following Chapter 1 (or do so, if you haven't already). Then, make a list of at least five goals you can reach during the next year that are directly tied into your reasons for wanting to write.

2. On a daily basis, how much time could you devote to writing? How many words do you think you could write everyday? Write down a

EXHIBIT 4.2 MY WRITING GOALS

Daily goals:

1.
2.

Weekly goals:

1.
2.

Monthly goals:

1.
2.

In one year, I will:

In two years, I will:

In five years, I will:

In ten years, I will:

I would like my obituary to mention these things in relation to my being a writer:

practical goal for one or the other (writing for a set number of minutes a day, or writing a certain number of words a day).

3. On the top of a clean sheet of paper, write "My Writing Personality." Below it, write different writing habits and styles that match your personality (for example, if you like to write for short periods of time or if you like to talk to people to get ideas). Realize that these types of traits should affect the types of writing goals you set for yourself.
4. Select an article from a magazine. Imagine that you are the writer of that article. What goals did you have to reach in order to get your article published in that magazine?
5. Think of a writing goal you would like to accomplish by the end of your life. Don't worry if you think it's an outlandish goal ("I want to have articles published regularly in *Good Housekeeping* and *Vanity Fair*"). Think of how you can start now to accomplish that goal. Write down three goals you can set for the next year which will start you on your way.
6. Complete the goal-setting checklist if you haven't already.

CHAPTER FIVE

SO MUCH TO WRITE, SO LITTLE TIME

Isaac Asimov, one of the most prolific writers in American history, wrote about everything from religion to Shakespeare to robots (of course). In his early writing years, he supported his family by selling short stories to popular science fiction magazines. At the end of his life, he had written more than five hundred books. How did he do all of this writing? He woke up every morning at 6:00 and began writing by 7:30. He wrote from then until 10:00 each night.

Anthony Trollope, a nineteenth-century British novelist, also followed a very strict routine and, as a result, published more than a hundred novels. He began writing every day at 5:30 a.m. and wrote for just two-and-a-half hours. He, however, made himself produce at least 250 words every fifteen minutes. So, while he wrote for a reasonably short amount of time each morning, he produced a huge amount of work.

If you are like most other new writers in the world today, you have one primary complaint about the writing life. It's something I hear every month at my local writer's group meeting, something I hear at writer's conferences all the time, and something my writer friends and I complain about almost constantly: "I just don't have the time to write."

Even though I'm known to utter those words every once in a while (especially while in a fit of despair about an upcoming deadline), I truly believe that this statement is very rarely true. We *do* have the time to write. We just have to locate that time.

Jane Austen wrote all of her books in a chair in the sitting room at her parents' house. If anyone came into the room, she would hide the papers under blotting papers.

Magazine writers come in all shapes and sizes. Some are singles who work full-time jobs. Others are married men and women who have spouses, children, and jobs to worry about. Still others are the lucky few who work just part-time. Then there are those writers who also go to school.

With so many different lifestyles, writers must depend on different methods to find time to write. Some can only write at night after their children are asleep. Some have the luxury of dedicating their weekends to writing projects. Others find time within their work day to write for short periods.

Despite these different habits and lifestyles, there are several rules-of-thumb all writers can follow to make their time-management woes a little less troubling.

TIME MANAGEMENT GUIDELINES

There *are* ways to locate time for writing, whatever your schedule might be. Follow these guidelines to help locate time—and, as a result, become productive in your writing.

Have a Set Schedule

You have a regular schedule for your work day. Why shouldn't you also have a regular schedule for the time you spend writing? Setting a specific, regular schedule for your writing will give the time the feeling of importance that it deserves. When you set aside specific time for any project, you are telling yourself that the project deserves your attention—it makes it a priority in your life.

If possible, have a regular schedule every single day. Daily writing will keep you motivated; it will also make the writing process become a more natural part of your life. If you find that you cannot sit down and write for a specific amount of time every day, make sure that you are at least in the writing state of mind everyday (carrying a notebook with you and recording observations; always looking out for ideas; etc.). Do this, however, only if there is no way to avoid it. Try to make daily writing a priority!

Your daily schedule should consist of a specific amount of *time* you will write and a specific *place* you will write. Getting into a routine of normality—knowing that you will always write at your desk, knowing that 9–10 p.m. is always set aside for writing projects—will make your time become productive.

Some ideas for times to write: early in the morning, late at night, during one half of your lunch break, during your child's regularly-set naptime (if you work at home), immediately after dinner time (if you have older children who can clean up the dinner table). There are numerous ways to fit in time to write.

Some ideas for places to write: at a desk in your study, at a desk in your bedroom, at the dinner table (if you know you won't be disturbed), in a makeshift study (for example, a converted laundry room or walk-in closet), at the library, or on your bed (if you can get comfortable). Although you will learn to write in all locations (on the freeway during rush hour), you should have a specific place set aside for your daily writing time. It will make you feel professional and keep you motivated.

FROM THE EDITOR'S DESK

"Read back issues to see which topics have already been explored. Try to find a unique approach to traditional topics."

EILEEN NESTER, *CAREER WOMAN*

Many people use their daily writing time as an opportunity to write in their journal. Make it a habit, however, to do more than this. Journal writing is extremely important; still, you want to reach a point where you are working on specific projects (with the goal, hopefully, of writing something that will be publishable). So, use your writing time not only to write in your journal but also to brainstorm ideas, do writing exercises, write query letters, work on articles, and package your works for submission.

Pick a Comfortable Routine

Writing should not be uncomfortable. Your daily time for writing should not be something you dread. Designate a writing schedule that you can live with. Be aware of your personal likes and dislikes when deciding what your schedule will be.

Ask for Help from Others

A close rival for the most-heard complaint of writers (behind "I just don't have the time to write") is probably "No one understands my desire to write." "No one," in most cases, refers to all of those unfeeling spouses, parents, and children out there.

Chances are that they really aren't so unfeeling. They just don't know how to react to your desire to write. They aren't writers themselves, so they don't know whether they should ever be critical (they're probably afraid you will run away in tears or will yell something like, "You don't know anything about writing anyway" at them) or if they should be ever-praising. They aren't writers, so they also don't understand the process you go through to get words down on paper.

They aren't writers, but chances are they'd like to know your side of the story. They want to know why you want to write. So try to explain it to them. When your significant others understand (or partially understand) your reasons for writing, they will be more willing to sacrifice some of their time with you to your writing projects. Don't be shy in asking for solitude or for assistance. Ask your spouse or partner to respect your thirty minutes each night with no interruptions. Ask that same person to listen to your latest article lead and give his or her unbiased opinion. Ask your children to carry articles to the mailbox—tell them that they can be your personal assistants.

> *"We all have our own rituals. I pace. I say lines out loud a lot. I live alone and my neighbors think I have a very active and busy apartment."*
>
> ALLAN GURGANUS

Be Productive

In many cases, fifteen minutes of writing time can be better than an hour. Fifteen productive minutes are always better than sixty unproductive ones. The primary key to being productive is to plan ahead. You should always know, to some degree, what you will be working on at specific times. At the end of each writing session, write a brief note to yourself about what you will accomplish the next day.

Eliminating distractions will also encourage productivity. Your writing time should be devoted to just that—writing. Try to forget, for the moment, about your dirty kitchen or the projects you have to finish at work tomorrow. Focus solely on your writing goals for that day.

Don't Even Think about Perfection

Many a new writer's stumbling block may well be the desire to be perfect. Don't even think about such a thing when you are trying to set up your writing schedule. Your thirty minutes a day have not been designed for you to produce perfect prose. They have been set up by you to get started writing.

Know in advance when you will be working on rewriting during your writing schedule. On those days you can worry about getting your words just right. On a daily basis, however, focus primarily on spending your minutes in as productive a way as possible—getting words down on paper.

Be Creative

As you will no doubt learn in the near future (if you haven't already), a writer's life does not always run on schedule. While you want to be as rigorous as possible in following your own schedules, meeting your own deadlines, and so forth, there are always times when you will sway from the path a bit.

There will be times when you veer from your writing schedule, and this is not always bad. If you find yourself in a rut, for example, you might want to change your schedule. Write at night for a change, instead of early in the morning. Write at a cafe one day during your scheduled time. Change your venue, change your time—as long as you're still writing!

> **FROM THE EDITOR'S DESK**
>
> "Draw the reader into your story. Don't bore the reader."
>
> SANDRA ZINN, *JUNIOR TRAILS*

If your life is especially hectic, you might need to use creativity to find any time to write. If that's the case, consider some of these creative time-management ideas (provided by some of my busy writer friends):

- If you commute to work, take a tape recorder and record your ideas and goals. If you're ready to write that article, do so with the tape recorder.
- If you're a parent of preschoolers, get your children involved in the writing process. Set them down on the floor next to you and let them "write" on their own notebooks.
- Have several substantial projects going at the same time. The more projects you have to work on, the less chance there is of you just sitting there and staring blankly at your computer screen. Your writing time will be productive.

- Write whenever you can—waiting in line at the doctor's office, while stuck in a traffic jam, during your shower.
- Put a "Do Not Disturb" sign on your door.
- Pick one day and don't write. As long as you are being productive when you do write, there is nothing wrong with giving yourself a break. So, go ahead and take a day off from your writing projects. Take a walk in the park or buy yourself a banana split during your designated writing time. Then, promise yourself to work just as hard the next day on writing as you did today on not writing. It will, in all likelihood, make your writing time tomorrow more meaningful.

Poet William Carlos Williams was a pediatrician in Rutherford, New Jersey. He wrote poetry between house calls.

Jumpstart Exercises

1. Have you ever said anything like, "I just don't have the time to write"? Write a list of all the reasons you think you don't have the time (job, family, etc.). Be as specific as possible.
2. At the end of a day, sit down and write your daily schedule in as much detail as possible. Where might there be openings to find time for writing? Write down a list of five possible ways you could fit a daily writing time into your schedule.
3. Who are the important people in your life? Write all of their names down. Next to their names, write what you think they think about your writing dreams. After doing so, ask them what they think about them. Did you have any unjust opinions of any individuals' feelings? Were there people who felt just as you thought they would? How can you use these feelings to develop a regular writing schedule? What help will you need from these individuals to make your schedule a reality?
4. Write down your daily writing schedule, listing both the amount of time you will spend writing and the place you will write. Stick to this schedule for two weeks. At the end of the two weeks, evaluate how the schedule worked. Should you readjust at all? Find a schedule that works for you and stick to it for good!
5. Buy a "Do Not Disturb" sign and use it one night this week during your writing time!

CHAPTER SIX

A WRITER'S TOOLS

I get all types of questions from aspiring magazine writers. A long time ago, I stopped wishing for questions like, "How do I deal with questions of ethical integrity?" and "How can I make my writing more stylistic?" I stopped wishing for such erudite, thoughtful questions—questions that dealt with the craft of writing or the struggles that many aspiring writers feel—for one reason. I was never getting them. Aspiring writers weren't talking with me about these issues for some reason.

Instead, I got—and still get—questions like, "Should I print my articles in fancy type?" and "Do I need to buy a file cabinet?" For some reason, aspiring writers are fascinated with all the *things* they need to make it as a writer. This fascination, though not necessarily bad, is something on which you don't need to dwell. To be a magazine writer who acts in a professional manner, there are a number of different items that you need. Your shopping list, however, is not extensive. After you have acquired the necessary tools (the must-haves listed below), the purchase of additional tools for your writing area depends, primarily, on your personal taste.

THE MUST-HAVES

I have found that the following items are essential to a productive, professional writing life.

Desk

Whether it's an antique roll-top desk or a cheap metal desk (or, as one of my friends used years ago, an ironing-board-turned-desk), you need some sort of tabletop area on which you can write. A desk is important because it serves as a centralized location at which to store information and supplies, display items of inspiration, and actually write.

Computer

We have all heard of those quaint stories about writers who still write in longhand or on an old Smith Corona typewriter. However, I recommend that you work on a computer if at all possible. Computers are worth the investment, if not solely for their ability to store information. They save writers immeasurable amounts of time (you don't have to retype anything) and headaches (you can't lose much of anything, if you follow directions).

Computers, however, can do much more than this. They can provide you with storehouses of information (with Internet systems and CD-ROMs), allow you to make your own letterhead (with graphic art programs), let you communicate with other writers across the nation (through e-mail), and let you send articles to magazines without using your mailbox (with a fax hookup). The possibilities afforded to writers through computers keep growing and growing.

> *"When I quit writing for the day, I do mean I quit. I don't mope around the rest of the day thinking what I'm going to write tomorrow. I put it out of my mind."*
>
> T. R. Pearson

"But I'm not a techno-whiz," you may say. That's okay. Computers are getting more and more user-friendly all the time. Knowing that you need a user-friendly model will make the buying process easier. Take some time to get the right computer for you, then take some time to learn how to use it. Read the manuals; get help from other writer friends who understand computers better than you; don't be afraid to ask questions; and always try to learn more.

Also, realize right now that you simply need a computer terminal, keyboard, and printer. You don't have to have the CD-ROM capabilities, the modem and fax hook-ups, and other frills right now. In looking for your basic equipment, you can go the route of an IBM (or IBM-compatible) computer or a Macintosh computer. Both types have advantages. Talk to other writers about what they use; then talk to a number of computer dealers so you get the best deal.

"But I don't have the money to buy a computer," you may also say. Computers, especially if loaded with all the available frills, can get expensive. Start out by purchasing the bare necessities; you can buy the extras later. You might also want to look into the possibility of buying a used computer. And if you can't afford a computer at all right now, make yourself a goal to save money and buy one by a certain time (even if it takes you a year to do so). I guarantee that your investment will be worth it—in both time and productivity!

A Current *Writer's Market*

This book is often referred to as the writer's Bible. If you have the ultimate goal of getting published, you must buy an updated copy of this book every year. It provides the nuts-and-bolts of how to market your work for all the major magazines in the United States. It tells you what types of articles magazines want, to whom to submit manuscripts, payment rates, special tips from the magazines' editors, and much more. It can be found in the writing or reference section in bookstores everywhere.

Notebooks

If you have gotten this far in the book, you no doubt know that I love notebooks. I like them for recording observations, for storing ideas, for working on actual stories, and for taking notes. Keep a notebook with you at all times.

Camera

I like to think of a camera as a visual notebook—it's invaluable for recording impressions and details of a place, person, or event.

I recently accompanied a writer friend on a research trip she was taking for a project about William Faulkner. To understand the intricacies of the writer's lifestyle and to remember the details of his Oxford, Mississippi, home, a camera was a necessity. She took pictures of his study and his gardens, and months later, as she put the finishing touch on her piece, she was able to recall details by looking at her pictures.

> *"There are hours and hours of a writer's time that aren't worth the paper he is not writing anything on."*
>
> E. B. White

A camera is also important if you want to submit photographs along with your articles. Photograph submission will earn you additional money from the magazine. If you're using a camera primarily for research and personal purposes, a simple automatic will do fine. If you want to take photographs for publication, you will probably want to consider purchasing a 35-mm camera.

Submission Log

When you get to the point where you're sending articles out to magazines, this is an essential tool. With a submission log you can keep track of where your articles are. In a notebook, or in a computer file, list what articles you have sent out, when you sent them out, and to what magazines you have sent them. Then, record the type of response you get for each article. You can also keep track of payments on the submission log. Exhibit 6.1 on page 73 shows how to set up a page in your submission log.

Calendars

Get a good calendar with which to keep up-to-date with your projects. Better yet, get a few calendars. I like to keep my personal deadlines and goals written down on both a wall calendar and a pocket calendar.

Dictionary, Thesaurus, and Book of Quotations

All writers should have some sort of personal reference library in their own home. The more reference materials you have, the more information you have at your fingertips. The essential reference materials, in my opinion, are these three books. The dictionary and thesaurus are the most important

EXHIBIT 6.1 A SAMPLE SUBMISSION LOG

Query letter	*Date sent*	*Magazine sent to*	*Response*

because they illustrate the essence of writing—the individual word. Each will help you to learn more about the language (something writers need to constantly do) and, more specifically, will help you find the perfect words for your articles. The book of quotations is wonderful for all writers of nonfiction. I often like to see what other people have said about my article topic. Many times, these quotations actually make their way into my articles.

Paper

Sounds simple, doesn't it? Paper, along with the pen or other writing utensil, is the most basic of writing tools. Yes, it is simple, but keep it that way. Buy quality typing paper and nothing more. Many new writers think they must send their articles out on fancy, bond paper, because they think it will impress some editor somewhere. What will impress an editor is a quality query letter or manuscript, not your ivory-colored, woven paper. So, buy plain white, quality typing paper (you don't want the thin, cheap stuff), and buy it in bulk—you never want to run out of paper.

The only "fancy" touch you might want to add is some sort of letterhead at the top of your paper. This can be prepared by a local printer or, if you have a computer, you can do it yourself. Simply center your name, address, and phone number at the top of the page in a large-sized print. You may also want to use a nice, decorative font.

When you prepare anything for mailing to a magazine, remember that the editor will respect a professional presentation. So make sure the paper is clean (you won't believe how many times editors complain about coffee stains on query letters) and unwrinkled.

Envelopes

If you want to get published in magazines, you will eventually have to mail out your material. You will need plain, business-size (#10) envelopes to send query letters and other correspondence. You will need 9 1/2" x 12 1/2" clasped manila envelopes to send manuscripts (you don't ever want to fold manuscripts into a #10 envelope).

Stamps

You never want to run out of stamps, so keep plenty of them handy. As you start to send out articles on a regular basis, buy the rolls of hundred from the post office.

THE EXTRAS

The following tools aren't necessary to your survival as a writer, but some of them might make your life a bit easier. Others might just make you *feel* a little bit more like a writer.

Business Cards

Yes, these will make you feel like a writer. But will they do any good? Yes and no. Showing an editor a business card that says you're a freelance writer won't convince him or her to buy your article. Business cards are good, though, for making contacts in your own community. Through them, you might meet other writers, editors of local publications, researchers, typists, and the like.

> **FROM THE EDITOR'S DESK**
>
> "Write clear, crisp query letters. Give an idea of number of words and what will be included in your article."
>
> PEGGY MIDDENDORF, *ATLANTA PARENT*

File Cabinet

File cabinets are a luxury to most aspiring writers. If you put an especially high priority on organization, however, or if you already have a large amount of information to store, you might want to consider investing in one. (For ideas on setting up a file system, look to Chapter 14, "The Business and Legal Side of Writing.")

Postal Scale

Depending on the size of your manuscripts, you might need to affix more than one stamp on your package. A postal scale is quite inexpensive and will keep you from taking extra time at the post office.

Tape Recorder

Even an inexpensive tape recorder is good for several things. You can use it to record interviews you might have for an article, or you can use it to record yourself reading your material. This is an excellent exercise for new writers—hearing your words will give you a new perspective on them. It's much easier to spot inconsistencies, flaws in organization, and poor word choice when a story is read aloud than when it is read in the mind.

Video Camera

Today, many people have video cameras to record special events. Why not use that same camera to record the places, events, and people about which you are writing? A video camera is especially good when writing about a certain place. Take a video with the camera, and then come home to watch the footage and take notes. It will save you a lot of time.

Typewriter

If you don't own a computer, you must at least use a typewriter. There are many sophisticated models on the market today, some of which have memory, correction capabilities, and even a spell-check process.

An Inspirational Item

To make your writing station a pleasant place to work, add some personal touches to it. The best way to personalize it—and to make your area a motivational place to work—is to display an inspirational item of your choice. This should be an item that, when you see it hanging above your desk or sitting atop your computer, will make you *want* to write. Do you have a favorite writer? Put your favorite book by him or her on top of your desk to inspire you. Do you still have a copy of something you wrote as a child? Frame it and display it in your work area. Is there a favorite quotation that inspires you? If so, frame and display it. Are your children (or your best friend, or your spouse, or your mother) what inspire you to write? Put a picture where you can see it while you write.

O. Henry began writing while imprisoned in Texas for embezzlement.

At my desk, I have a picture of Emily Dickinson's home (she's my favorite poet; the fact that anyone can write so beautifully is a great inspiration for me) and pictures of me and my husband on our honeymoon (the happiness he and my daughter give me provides me with endless inspiration).

A friend of mine framed a copy of the first check she received for an article she wrote; it sits next to her desk. Another friend has a seashell on her desk from her favorite beach; whenever she comes back from that beach she is full of writing ideas!

Other Reference Books

In addition to the dictionary, thesaurus, and book of quotations mentioned earlier, you might want to invest in some other reference books. These could include a set of encyclopedias, historical timeline books, atlases, and books of facts on different topics. While *Writer's Market* is the best guidebook for marketing your writing, there are others that can help you. *Literary Marketplace,* as well as references for specific markets (*Market Guide for Young Writers, Christian Writers' Market Guide,* etc.), can also help you locate information about where to sell your articles.

Books on Writing

I don't know about you, but I love to read about writing. One of my favorite sections of the bookstore is the writing section, because there you can find helpful books on almost any aspect of writing—from the specifics of grammar to the subtleties of the writing life. You can also find selections of essays by successful writers and books full of creative exercises to get you started writing. (The Appendix, "Resources for Writers," provides additional information about additional reference books and books on the subject of writing.)

Jumpstart Exercises

1. Look at your writing area. What items do you need to make your writing time more productive and your area more conducive to work?
2. Make a list of all the things you would *like* to have in your writing area. Look at your list and narrow it down to those things that are *necessary*.
3. Purchase a copy of this year's *Writer's Market*. Begin to familiarize yourself with its content and purpose. This activity will prepare you for Chapter 12, "What Do I Do with This Article?"
4. Purchase as many of the other must-haves listed in this chapter as you can. Begin to organize your writing area into a functional and practical workplace.
5. What inspires you to work? Write a list of anything (a person, a dream, a favorite writer, etc.) that gives you inspiration. What type of item of inspiration could you put in your writing area?

CHAPTER SEVEN

GETTING STARTED

Okay, you have got a place to write, you have come up with a block of time during which you can write everyday, you have the basic tools to get started writing, and you have an idea for a magazine article that you think might be publishable. You have all of those things, but for some reason you're staring at an empty computer screen or piece of paper.

The path from an idea to a completed magazine article is not always a straight line. There are several things, in fact, that you need to do before you can even start to fill that empty page. You must take your idea and develop it by gathering information. Then, you must organize your information through the use of an outline or some other approach.

Chapter 8 will take you to the next steps—constructing your article; writing the first, second, and other drafts; and editing, revising, and rewriting. Obviously, getting from an empty page to a full one is not an easy or quick process. Once you learn the steps in getting started writing, however, the empty page will not look quite as foreboding.

GATHERING INFORMATION

Before you can even think about writing, you must acquire all the information you need to make your article an effective one. To decide what type of information you need, first think through your article in as much detail as possible. Imagine that you are a reader and ask yourself what primary questions you would want answered. What secondary questions would intrigue you? Make a list of all these questions, then decide what types of information could answer them. Do you need statistics? quotes from experts? quotes from "real-life" sources? interesting anecdotes?

Make another list, this one detailing the different sources of information you plan on tracking down. Designate parts of your upcoming writing schedule to do this research.

Depending on the type of article you are writing, you will need to acquire different types of information. If you're writing an article from personal experience, most or all of your information will be acquired from your own mind. With almost any other type of article, however, you will have to get information from other avenues.

Traditional Research

To get the basic background information on a topic, to obtain statistics, and to get information that may lead you to other resources, consider the following reference tools (available in most libraries).

Encyclopedias • A wide variety of general encyclopedias (*World Book, Encyclopedia Britannica*, etc.), as well as encyclopedias geared to specific topics, provide basic information. Don't rely on encyclopedias as your sole resources; rather, use them as starting points for your knowledge and research.

Books • Better than encyclopedias, books will provide more in-depth information on your topic. Most libraries have excellent card catalog systems (many now have them completely computerized) in which you can look up information according to subject, author, and title. If your library does not have a book you need, you may be able to order it from another library through the Interlibrary Loan Service. Get to know the librarians at your local libraries so they can help you with searches like this.

Reader's Guide to Periodical Literature • This is the best place to locate other pertinent consumer magazine articles on your topic. The guide is bound according to years, and articles are listed by topic. Other indexes can refer you to articles in trade and specialized periodicals (*Education Index, Business Periodicals Index, Religion Index, Index to Legal Periodicals,* and others). Many libraries now have these guides available on computer, so they're even more easy to use.

Government Sources • The government is known for its efficient and cumulative collections of information in all types of areas; you might be able to find quality information among its publications. Most libraries have the *Cumulative Subject Index to the Monthly Catalog of U.S. Government Publications.* The *United States Government Manual* can provide you with names of departments and bureaus that may be able to provide you with information on your topic.

Other Reference Materials • There are hundreds of other encyclopedias, indexes, bibliographies, and reference guides available. Take a Saturday to check out your local library's reference room. Don't forget to also check out any academic libraries in your area; college libraries are especially known for their excellent reference materials.

Computerized Research

Research has moved into the twenty-first century. Writers now have the capability to acquire all the necessary information for an article without leaving their work area. Database services (more popularly called on-line services) can provide you with information as varied as the text of newspaper and magazine articles, legal briefs, and stock quotes.

Some libraries have computers on which you can do information searches, or you can use your personal computer. You must, however, have a computer, modem, an available phone line, and software to handle the dialing and receiving of information. Some of the most popular on-line services today are:

America Online. For more information, contact America Online, 8619 Westwood Center Drive, Vienna, VA 22182. (703) 448-8700.

CompuServe. For more information, contact CompuServe, 5000 Arlington Center Boulevard, Columbus, OH 43220. (614) 457-8600.

Prodigy. For more information, contact Prodigy, 445 Hamilton Avenue, White Plains, NY 10601. (914) 448-8000.

Computer technology is changing and improving almost daily, so keep your ears open for news of other services and changes to these.

Source Location

Articles are always enhanced with quotations from sources, whether they be experts on your topic or ordinary people who have lived through the experience you are writing about. There are several different places to locate sources for your article.

A Local College or University • This is an excellent place to find experts on almost any topic. Professors are often considered to be experts in their field of knowledge. Simply call the department of psychology, nutrition, education, or other appropriate department; secretaries and instructors are usually happy to lead you to the appropriate source.

The Yellow Pages • Businesses, associations, churches, and hospitals are all possible locations to find sources on your topic.

Books and Magazine Articles • You may want to quote the author of a book on your topic or talk to the author of an article on a similar topic. Most book publishers are happy to forward letters to their authors. *Books in Print* lists publishers' addresses for all books. Likewise, most magazines are willing to forward letters to their regular writers. If the author is not a regular, try calling the magazine to see if the staff happens to know the writer's address.

The Grapevine • Often the best way to locate those "real-life" sources is to simply let people know that you are writing an article on a particular topic. It's amazing how many people will say to you, "Oh, I know someone that happened to. I'm sure she'd talk to you about it."

Observational Research

All writing is strengthened by facts and descriptions garnered by observation. If you are writing about a person or persons, a place, or an event, be especially attuned to the importance of observation. In observing, remember to use all of your senses as discussed in Chapter 2. Strong descriptions, vivid details, accurate facts—all of these things can be observed, and all of them make your article a more realistic reading for your audience.

"CAN I QUOTE YOU?"

Until now, I have talked about research that is quite solitary. You have visited the library, looked up information on the computer, observed the world around you for details, and perhaps talked to an expert so you could put some good quotes in your story.

At some point in your magazine writing endeavors, however, you're going to need to talk to people in-depth. You might have to sit down and talk to a person about a topic for an extended period of time. You might even find yourself spending a few days with an individual if you're writing a personality profile.

For some reason, many new writers are intimidated by the possibility of conducting interviews. They are frightened by talking to a stranger, of asking perhaps imposing questions, and of making mistakes (i.e., sounding stupid).

All of us are shy at times. All of us feel inadequate at times, too. But an interviewee need not know that you're nervous. Everyone can learn basic interviewing techniques—I guarantee you will look like you know what you're doing if you follow them. Most importantly, you should always remember the two basic tenets of interviewing: *be prepared* and *be professional.*

You should never go to an interview situation unprepared; you must know what you're going to discuss, and you must be ready for any situation. Likewise, you should never come to an interview looking and/or acting in an unprofessional manner. The way you carry yourself will determine much of whether you will have a good or a bad interview experience.

Interviewing involves three important stages: preparing for the interview, the interview itself, and digesting the information from the interview.

Preparing for the Interview

A lot of your work will actually take place before you conduct the interview. To be completely prepared, you should complete the following steps.

Establish Contact with the Individual and Set Up an Interview Time • Let the person know what your purpose is. Let him know if you need information on the specific topic about which you are writing. Let her know if you are interested in doing a personality profile on her. If the person asks what magazine you're writing for, be honest. Let him know that you are a freelance writer and not a professional staff writer. The best approach is to write a query letter on the topic; once you have a positive response to the query, then do interviews and write your article.

If you can, set up the interview in the person's home or place of business. This will lend a personal touch to the interview situation. Also, a person tends to feel more comfortable talking to a stranger in a familiar atmosphere.

Set up the interview several weeks ahead of time. Then, follow up with a call reminding the person of the interview several days before.

Do Research • The best way to be prepared for an interview is to conduct research before the fact.

If you are interviewing someone about a particular topic, make sure you know enough about the topic yourself. In interviewing an environmentalist about toxic waste, you want to know the basic environmental terms and issues. Read up on the issue before doing the interview. In this way, you can bypass basic questions (which you can answer by reading books or magazine articles) and get to the heart of the matter quickly.

If you are interviewing someone for a personality profile, it is imperative that you learn as much as possible about that person before conducting the interview. If the person is well known, look his name up in the *Reader's Guide to Periodical Literature* to see if any articles have written about him, or look her name up in one of the many *Who's Who* directories. Obtain the person's resume or academic vitae (this will eliminate having to ask about prior jobs, educational background, and so forth).

Prepare Questions • This is the most important element of the preparation stage. Coming to an interview with a full list of questions (and ideas for discussion and emergency questions, in case there's a lull in conversation) will make it run smoothly.

"I am going to hold myself from writing it till I have it impending on me: grown heavy in my mind like a ripe plum; pendant, gravid, asking to be cut or it will fall."

VIRGINIA WOOLF

In preparing questions, you first must understand what you want to get out of the interview. If you're using the person as one source in a story, look at the information you already have. What questions still need to be answered? What else will your readers want to know? Design your questions around those ideas.

If you're writing a personality profile, develop a central idea for the article (you can't chronicle a person's entire life and dreams in one article). What information do you need to give a complete picture of this central idea? What would your readers want to know about the person in that regard?

Interviews are most effective when an individual is asked a wide range and type of questions. Mix in serious questions with casual ones. Don't neglect questions about the interviewee's personal life, even if you're writing an article on her professional career. Ask both straight-answer questions and hypothetical ones. Don't ask too many closed-ended questions (ones that can be answered simply with "yes" or "no"); ask plenty of questions that require thoughtful answers.

Gather Your Materials • The nightmare interview for me would be going into an interview and forgetting to bring a notebook and a pen. The day before your interview, set out everything you need. Take a full notebook and extra writing utensils (a pen always decides to leak at the wrong time). If you're going to use a tape recorder, make sure it is running properly. I recommend using both a tape recorder and a notebook, as that eliminates any possible problems with equipment. Exhibit 7.1 on page 84 provides you with an "Interview Preparatory Checklist."

The Interview Itself

The actual interview is the most important part of the process. There are several tips to make it run smoothly.

Start Casual • The best interviews begin with casual conversation. Ask the person how his or her day has gone; talk about the weather; mention something that, in research, you discovered that the two of you have in common. People being interviewed are often as nervous as the novice interviewer. A casual beginning will put you both at ease.

Take Notes • You will never be able to catch every exact word that a person says, so set up some sort of shorthand for yourself. Develop abbreviations or learn how to write key words down (being sure to pay close attention to what's being said, so you can reconstruct the thought later). If you find a quote especially intriguing and want it word-for-word, there is nothing wrong with asking the person to repeat what he or she has just said.

> *"It is only through hard work that I can give an impression of ease and simplicity."*
>
> HENRI MATISSE

Even though the interviewee will expect you to take notes, try to take them as unobtrusively as possible. You want to give the impression that the two of you are simply having a conversation; this allows a person to be more open and conversational. A good method for being unobtrusive is to make sure you are having eye contact. Look in the person's eyes, nod your head, and then take a moment to look down on your paper and write what was just said.

Even if you use a tape recorder, be sure to take notes. Your tape recorder might break down mid-interview or your tape might decide to unravel later. Even if those tragedies don't occur, taking notes is still a good supplement to recording. You can write notes to yourself about what quotes should be

EXHIBIT 7.1 INTERVIEW PREPARATORY CHECKLIST

Before you actually conduct an interview, make sure you have completed the following steps. Put a check in the blank when you have completed the step and make any notes to yourself in the space following the item.

_____ Establish contact with the individual and set up time

Interview set for:

_____ Do any necessary research

_____ Prepare questions

List of tentative questions:

_____ Gather Materials

Materials I will need to take to the interview:

given high priority. You might even develop a structure for your article while doing the interview.

Be Observant • There is so much more to an interview than the actual words being spoken. Keep your eyes open to facial expressions, body language, and hand gestures. If you're in a home or office, take notes about an award on the wall or a cat that has free roam of the room. You can ask the interviewee about these things during conversation lulls. Details such as these can also add a touch of intimacy to your article.

Stay in Control of the Situation • Keep your purposes for doing the interview in the forefront of your mind. Check questions off your list as they're answered. Don't let the conversation go off track; if the interviewee goes off onto tangent thoughts and topics, bring the discussion back around to the topics in which you are most interested.

Digesting the Information

The first thing you should do after completing the interview is read through your notes, rewrite them if necessary, and compile them in a reasonable order for your purposes. If you used a tape recorder, transcribe your notes as soon as possible. If, after rereading your notes, you have any unanswered questions, call the individual back. Most people are happy to answer additional questions.

Begin to decide how you will use the information you have obtained. What information is very interesting? What tidbit sheds new light on your subject? What quote is especially powerful? Mark this *good* information in some way (highlight it with a highlight pen, put an asterisk next to it, etc.). In your mind, you may have already developed an idea for how you might organize the information. If you have an idea for a good lead or a good conclusion, write it down. Now you are ready to develop an outline for your article.

FROM THE EDITOR'S DESK

"Write a good query letter. Don't use the telephone for first contact. Show me you know our audience and the kinds of things we publish."

WALTER COLLINS,
NOTRE DAME MAGAZINE

ORGANIZING YOUR INFORMATION

After you have done all your research, you will (if you have done it right) have stacks and stacks of notes and photocopies. How do you sift through all this information and put it into some sort of organized system?

Your first inclination might be to throw all your pages in the air and play fifty-two-card-pick-up with them, but resist the urge. Organization will pay off in all steps of the writing process. The first step in organizing your information is to take a close look at all of it. Determine what quotes are really essential and which ones aren't so hot. Decide what facts are repetitive and which ones are unique and necessary.

When evaluating the importance of pieces of information, ask these questions about each one:

- Is this piece of information essential to my article? Will I need it as I write my first draft?
- Is this piece of information important, but not necessarily something that will make it in my first draft?
- Is this piece of information so unessential that I may not use it in my article at all?

Separate all of your items into items of primary importance and items of secondary importance. Set aside any items you have determined you will not use in your article.

Once you have determined what stays and what goes, you should organize your items into a manageable system. Most writers think of the various subtopics they will have in their article. They then organize material by those subtopics. Some writers put their information on index cards and create different piles for different subtopics. Other writers number their items according to subtopics, while still others color code their items. Find a system that will work for you. The most important element of this step is that you understand your system and that it is logical in its organization.

MAKING AN OUTLINE

Perhaps the best way to organize your material is to make an outline. This will get you organized *before* you actually sit down to write.

There are several kinds of outlines you can make.

The Formal Outline

Remember Mrs. Edwards, your sixth-grade teacher? She's the first teacher who taught you the ABC-123 method of outlining. You wrote a short term paper on George Washington that year and, along with your completed paper, you had to give Mrs. Edwards your George Washington outline. It started something like this:

I. George Washington's Beginnings
  A. Family Background
    1. Birth
    2. Influence of father and mother
      a. Father's discipline
      b. Mother's love and affection
  B. Early Education
    1. Schools attended
    2. Favorite subjects

If you still hold Mrs. Edwards up as the exemplary teacher in your childhood, you may decide to continue using this traditional outline method. Most magazine writers, however, have forsaken it in exchange for a simpler method. Most use one of two types of outlines.

The Informal Outline

Most writers simply list the points they want to make in their article in the order in which they will appear. You can number the items if you wish. This was my informal outline for a recent article about consignment shopping for a regional parenting magazine:

1. Lead: Anecdote of two mothers' different shopping methods
2. Introduction of main idea: After learning the basics of consignment shopping, you can save lots of money
3. What are the benefits of consignment shopping? (include quotes from shop owners and mothers)
4. Tips to be a good consignment shopper: Have a plan. Get to know the owners. Don't buy something just because it's cheap. Put your own clothes on consignment.
5. List of local consignment shops.
6. Conclusion: anecdote to tie in with introduction

> *"I used to throw things out saying, 'This isn't great.' It didn't occur to me that it didn't have to be great."*
>
> WILLIAM SAROYAN

While this is a lot less formal than the traditional outline you may use now, it accomplishes the same thing. You know what's important, and you know in what order your information will be presented. It is informal enough that you feel comfortable changing it a bit if, during the process of writing, you find that the structure needs to be altered.

The Cluster Outline

While it is more popular with fiction writers, the cluster outline can also work for nonfiction writers. The idea here is to know the central idea or theme of your article. From that central point, you then branch off into corresponding ideas. It shows you, in a very natural way, the structure of your article. Exhibit 7.2 on page 88 shows you how a cluster outline works.

Jumpstart Exercises

1. Take one of the article ideas you developed in Chapter 3. Pretend that you are the reader of the article. What are the main questions you have about the topic? Write this list down. Now think of the information

EXHIBIT 7.2 CLUSTER OUTLINE

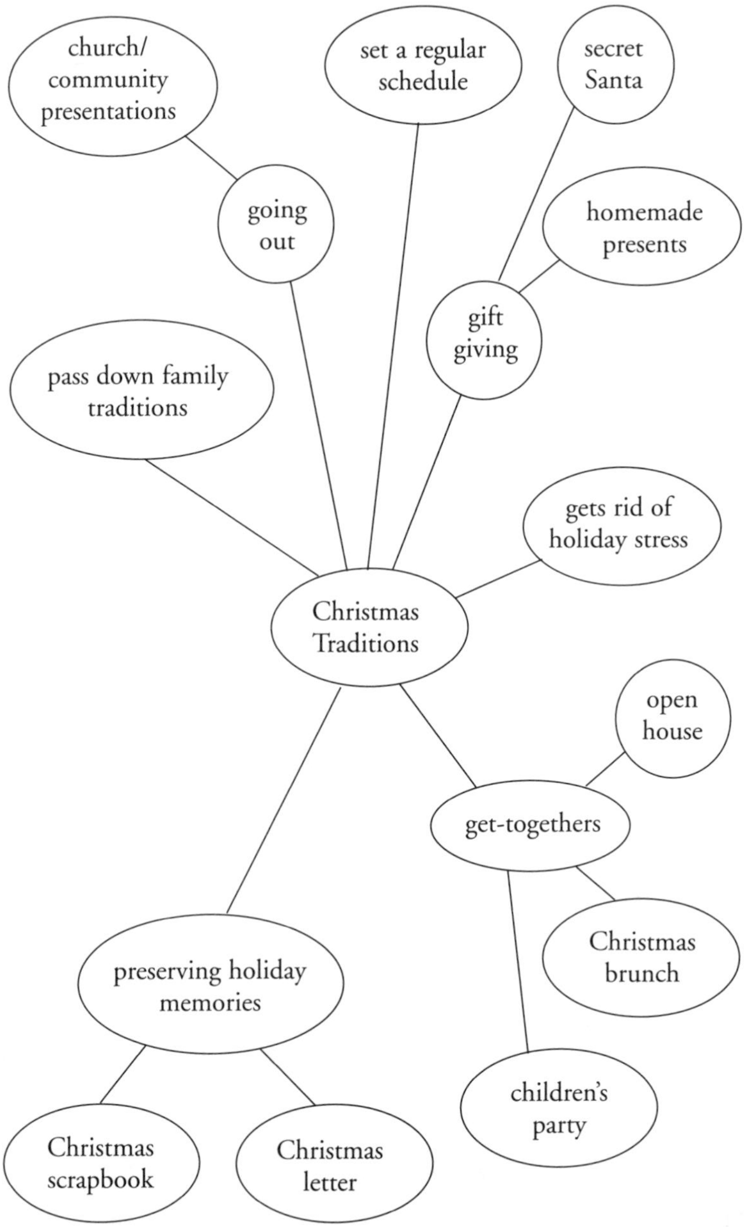
church/ community presentations
set a regular schedule
secret Santa
going out
homemade presents
gift giving
pass down family traditions
gets rid of holiday stress
Christmas Traditions
open house
get-togethers
Christmas brunch
preserving holiday memories
children's party
Christmas scrapbook
Christmas letter

you will need to acquire in order to answer these questions. Write this list of needed information down also.

2. Plan an afternoon to visit your local library (or, if you have several in your area, the one you plan on using for most of your writing research). Introduce yourself to the reference librarian. Get comfortable with the types of reference material the library has.
3. Take the topic "How to Get Rid of Those Extra Holiday Pounds." Write a list of three places from which you could get quotes from expert sources. Write a list of three "real-life" sources you could use.
4. Practice conducting an interview on a family member or friend. Pretend that you are a doing a personality profile on him or her. Follow the steps outlined in the interview section of this chapter.
5. Select another idea you developed from Chapter 3 (select one you would seriously like to complete). Write a formal outline from the idea, then an informal outline, and then a cluster outline.

CHAPTER EIGHT

WRITING THE ARTICLE

In building a house, a carpenter makes plans for the various parts—the foundation, supporting beams, walls, the ceiling. He or she knows how every part works together and plans what he or she will be doing *before* doing it. In writing an article, a magazine writer also makes plans for all the various parts—the introduction (or lead), the body, and the conclusion. The writer knows how all three parts work together and plans how the article will be constructed well before actually sitting down to write it.

Writing your article is, ultimately, a lot more than *writing* your article. It's gathering information, organizing information, and writing an outline (as discussed in Chapter 7). Then it's putting everything together in first, second, and subsequent drafts, and, finally, it's editing, revising, and rewriting.

THE PARTS OF YOUR ARTICLE

All articles contain three basic parts: an introduction, a body, and a conclusion. Each of these parts can be developed in numerous ways. Depending on the tone of your article and the readership to which you are writing, you will develop the parts in a specific way. To write the most effective articles possible, you must learn to determine which approaches to take and when.

The strongest articles are those that have cohesion and unity. Therefore, you cannot look at your article with regards to just the lead or just the body. All parts are equally important, and they must all work together.

The Introduction (or Lead)

The introduction to your article, more commonly called the *lead*, may consist of one paragraph or an entire passage. There are a variety of leads to consider in writing magazine articles. Some of the most effective types of leads include the following ones.

Summary Lead • This straightforward lead summarizes the information to be learned in the article. It will let the reader know almost immediately (usually within the first few words) what the article is about.

The current catch phrase is anything with the words "low-fat" in it. Often, however, this phrase is misleading. An item might be low in fat, but still loaded with calories, sodium, and other unhealthy ingredients. Consumers today need to know that low-fat doesn't necessarily mean healthy.

Anecdotal Lead • This type of lead tells a real-life story that illustrates the point of your article. The anecdote should be brief (a few paragraphs long, at the most), so that readers don't get lost in the story. Most importantly, it should directly bear on your article's topic.

While not always the case, anecdotal leads are many times emotionally-charged. They can be either poignant or humorous. In that way, they can be very strong leads.

It's the night before Sarah's wedding. The images she'd dreamed of for years—the perfect dress, the beautiful vows, the sumptuous reception—now seem to belong only in fairy tales. Her bridesmaids are fighting, her groom still hasn't reported on the state of his self-written vows, and the wrong flowers were ordered. Thinking of the disarray around her, Sarah bursts into tears. This isn't the way her wedding day is supposed to be.

Descriptive Lead • Readers will immediately be transported to the location or be made to feel as if they know the person or thing you are presenting in your article. The descriptive lead puts the person, place, or thing in context by describing it. This approach works particularly well with personality profiles, informational articles, how-to articles, and personal experience articles (especially if they are nostalgic in nature).

A light shroud of early morning fog hangs above the still waters of the pond. Summer insects begin their at-dawn chirping; they rouse themselves from sleep to begin their fly from one bank to the other. A boat, big enough for just two or three people, sits tied to the old wooden pier. It waits expectantly for the man and boy it knows will soon appear.

Suddenly, from out of the fog, comes the yelp of a dog. It's Ranger, the beloved German shepherd belonging to the young boy coming down the slope to the pond. Ranger announces the arrival of the boy and his grandfather to the pond and the insects and the boat.

Unbelievable Lead • This lead grabs your reader's attention by revealing a startling statement. The reader will say, "I almost can't believe that," and then he or she will go on to read the rest of the article. The key to this type of lead is to make sure that your lead is actually believable—it must be true and not misleading.

Twenty-five million American women suffer from osteoporosis.

As startling as that statistic may seem, it's true. Osteoporosis, a condition caused by brittle bones, afflicts a postmenopausal woman every day in this country.

Direct Address Lead • This type of lead puts the reader into the situation by using the word "you." It is effective in making the article seem personal and relevant to the reader.

As a home-based entrepreneur, you know the value of computers. You no doubt use a fax machine to receive and place orders. You probably use e-mail to communicate with other small business owners. You surely use the computer to design promotional materials. You probably don't realize, however, that computers can also cause you problems.

Question Lead • Similar to the direct address lead, the question lead also talks directly to the reader. In this instance, however, it asks a question of the reader ("Have you ever looked helplessly at your rambunctious toddler and wondered if perhaps she belonged to some other parent?").

Who won more games than any college football coach in history? Who sent his team to more bowl games than any other coach? Who had a former president call him "the greatest coach who has ever lived"?

If you're a football fan, the answer to those questions is probably quite obvious to you. You recognize that legendary coach as Paul "Bear" Bryant.

Cliché Lead • This lead should have a warning attached to it: Use this type of lead only when you have a very creative spin on a cliché. The cliché lead takes a familiar saying and puts a spin on it appropriate to your article. Be careful with it, because this type of lead can sound trite if it's not strong enough.

A picture may be worth a thousand words, but it's not worth much of anything if it's out of focus.

There are a number of easy-to-follow tips to make your vacation photos ones to remember.

Quotation Lead • Likewise, this lead should contain a warning: A quote should not open an article unless it is especially powerful. Sources rarely say things outstanding enough to lead your article (but there are always those award-winning exceptions).

"I am a survivor," the 30-year-old blonde says with forcefulness and a smile. "Doctors said that my chance for survival was almost zero, but I still beat this cancer."

Combination Lead • In some cases, you may combine two or more of the preceding types of leads. You might, for example, combine an anecdotal lead with a question lead (presenting your reader with a real-life situation and then asking him if he has ever been through a similar experience).

It can be argued that the lead is the most important part of your article. A reader, after all, has to have some motivation to read your entire article.

The lead will often hook the interest of the reader—or lose it. You should, therefore, spend an adequate amount of time developing your lead. You should be confident that the lead you have constructed is the best possible one for your article. In developing your lead, complete the following steps:

1. Look at all the information you have gathered, study your outline, and write in one sentence the central idea of your article.
2. Look at your information and study your outline again; now look at your central-idea sentence. Ask yourself how you can best introduce the topic to your reader. Does a brief summary, a touching anecdote, or an unbelievable fact fit the bill as the best way to hook the reader?
3. If you know the magazine for which you want to write, study its leads. What type of leads does the editor seem to like? What tone do the leads take? Develop a lead that fits the magazine's style.
4. If you are not writing your article for publication (yet!), you don't know which magazine to study. So, instead, imagine who your reader is. With what type of lead would that reader be comfortable? Develop a lead with a specific reader in mind.
5. Get the reader's attention. Whatever type of lead you choose, your main purpose in writing it is to get the reader's attention and keep it.
6. If you're stuck on the lead, move on to another part of the article. There is no golden rule of writing that says you must write your lead first; that is simply the way it is usually done. If you can't get past your lead, go on to the body of your article. Chances are, your lead will come to you as you're writing another part of your story.

> *"A clean sentence is no accident. Very few sentences come out right the first time or even the third time. Remember this as a consolation in moments of despair."*
>
> WILLIAM ZINSSER

To study some excellent leads, look at the real-life examples in Exhibit 8.1 on page 94.

The Body

The body of your article is where you present all your information, make all your points, give all your suggestions. It is here where you reward your reader for continuing beyond the lead. Here you give him or her the information promised in the lead. Remember that central-idea sentence you wrote a moment ago while developing your lead? This sentence is integral in writing the rest of your article.

Many magazine articles lose steam about halfway through the body. The reader gets lulled away by an interesting commercial on television (at least

EXHIBIT 8.1 TYPES OF LEADS

Read the following leads. They run the gamut of styles. Some are descriptive, some are anecdotal, some use quotes, some spin clichés. They all, however, have one thing in common—they are effective.

> *"Forget oil and cattle; a greater Texas export may be* Tuna*—and that's no fish story. The fare in question is theatrical: a delicious comedy,* Greater Tuna, *and its sequel,* A Tuna Christmas, *which recount the follies of the irresistibly silly denizens of mythical Tuna, the third-smallest town in Texas. Playgoers meet the twenty or so Tunaites—harried housewife, portly sheriff, flirty waitress, local bad boy—all of whom, male and female—are portrayed by a mere two actors, the inimitable duo of Joe Sears and Jaston Williams."*

("Tuna Salad Days," Texas Monthly, *March 1995)*

> *"Dear Ann Landers: I'm a 16-year-old girl who is a nervous wreck from getting yelled at. All I hear from morning till night is, 'Stop smoking, get off the phone, hang up your clothes, do your homework, clean up your room.' How can I get them off my case?—Sick of Parents*
>
> *Dear Sick: Stop smoking, get off the phone, hang up your clothes, do your homework, and clean up your room.*
> *Wouldn't it be great if discipline was that easy?"*

("Discipline: Tools and Assembly Required," ParentLife, *March 1995)*

> *"Would that we could all be Willie Nelson: He motors around in his tour bus, rolls a few joints, sings a few songs, marries some wives, and drinks some whiskey with his buddies."*

("Willie Nelson," Rolling Stone, *March 9, 1995)*

> *"Every old garden rose has its ghosts, each one haunted by a history as fascinating as its halo of fragrance."*

("Roses with a Pedigree," Atlanta, *February 1995)*

> *"'It's like heaven,' says Jessica Lange. It's just four days after her Best Actress win at the Academy Awards, but she's not talking about her Oscar. Heaven, in this case, is the 110-acre horse farm in the rolling hills outside Charlottesville, Virginia that she calls home."*

("A Winner Never Quits," Entertainment Weekly, *April 14, 1995)*

EXHIBIT 8.1 (CONT'D)

"The United States is home to 54.2 million dogs in seemingly endless combinations of shape, size, and personality, and you and your child can introduce yourselves to many of them by taking a quiet stroll around the block."

("Neighborhood Dog Walk," Family Fun, *April 1995)*

"'Mary Catherine Bateson was born on December 8, 1959, and looked very much herself,' wrote her mother, Margaret Mead, in her 1972 memoir, Blackberry Winter. *But today Bateson seems to look more and more like her mother—the same cheekbones, the same broad, open face, the same purposeful eyes, the same self-possession."*

("Mary Catherine Bateson," Publishers Weekly, *May 30, 1994)*

"Miss Barnes had the most beautiful blonde hair I had ever seen. In the back, it flowed silk-like in the groove created by her spine. I was in love with Miss Barnes. I was 6 years old. She was my first grade teacher."

("Reaching for Heaven in the Public Schools," Southern Exposure, *Spring 1995)*

more interesting than your article) or by an enticing spouse (even if the lure is something as unexciting as ironing shirts). Or the reader scratches his head and asks himself, "What does that have to do with anything?" Such responses probably mean one thing: the article lost its train of thought somewhere.

Your central idea should be evident in all parts of the body of your article. Every paragraph and every thought should enhance that central idea. The strongest articles are those that are coherent and unified. To produce a coherent, unified article, keep that central idea in your mind. Write it down where you can see it. As you write the body of your article, stop and ask yourself if your central idea is being communicated.

There are various ways to construct the body of your article so that it is coherent and unified. The two most popular ways are the narrative approach and the topical approach.

The Narrative Approach • A narrative is a story. A narrative approach to the body of your article, therefore, means that you tell it like a story. This usually means that you tell it in a chronological manner. You tell it as events took place; or as a person's life occurred; or as something developed. Obviously, this storytelling approach does not work for all article types, but you might want to consider using it if you're writing a personal experience article, historical article, or a personality profile.

The Topical Approach • This is the method used in most magazine article writing. It takes the central idea and develops it according to secondary topics or themes (thus the other name for this method, the thematic approach). All of the secondary topics relate directly to the central idea. They are often presented with subheads, bullets (•) or other typographic elements, or numerals.

> *"Never correct or rewrite until the whole thing is down. Rewrite in process is usually found to be an excuse for not going on."*
> JOHN STEINBECK

This book is presented in a topical manner. Look, for example, at the section you are reading right now. The main theme of this section is "The Parts of an Article." With that in mind, I set out to present the various topics contained within that main idea (the lead, the body, and the conclusion).

Again, this approach does not work with all article types. It works, though, with the majority of them. It is the perfect approach for informational and how-to articles. And if you choose to analyze a person, an event from your own life, or a historical event by themes (instead of chronologically), it can work for personal experience and historical articles, as well as for personality profiles.

The Conclusion

While the conclusion is not as important as either the lead or the body of your article, you do want to write a strong one. You want to leave a powerful feeling in the reader's mind. You want the reader to be glad that he read your article all the way through. You want the reader to set the magazine down on her coffee table, feeling as if she's better informed or in a better mood than before reading your article.

Consider one of these approaches to your conclusion.

A Final Quote • Select a good quote from one of your sources—not one of the best ones, but a good one—and use it as the concluding thought.

> *Matthew Brady's legacy would make him proud, for he truly wanted to make his mark on history. In his own words, he felt an obligation as a photographer to "preserve the faces of my country's historic men." And he did.*

A Descriptive Scene • Especially if you used a descriptive lead (or if your article was a personality profile or personal experience article), you might want to leave the reader with another look at the place or the person. It will leave a specific image in the reader's mind.

At the end of the day, the beach remains the most indelible image in our minds. The huge moon casts a magical glow on its bright, white expanse and waves crash in the distance. It invites us to sit down once more, to hold hands once more while running our feet through its warm grains. It's what we will miss most about this island after we've left.

A Play on the Title or Lead • You can tie your conclusion in with your article's title or lead paragraph by referring to a similar scene or repeating specific words.

And what happened to the bride mentioned at the beginning of this story? She looked around her and realized that this was her *wedding. She looked at her squabbling bridesmaids, her nervous husband-to-be, and the wrongly ordered flowers and realized that nothing was going to ruin her Big Day. And, of course, it turned out beautifully.*

A Summary Statement • Pull all the information together by providing a summary in your conclusion. This will spell out to the readers what they learned in the article. In this way, the main points will remain in their minds.

It may not be easy, but you can find quality time with your child. By setting priorities, having a regular one-on-one time with your child, communicating openly, and being creative you will find that time spent with your son or daughter can be very meaningful.

Exhibit 8.2 on page 98 shows some effective conclusions from published articles.

A Word about Titles

Yes, the title is part of your article. But it's up to you whether you write a title for your article. To give your article cohesion and to give yourself an idea of your overarching, central theme, creating a title is probably a good writing exercise. Realize, however, that rarely does your chosen title make its way into print. Editors often rewrite titles to fit their magazine's style.

THE FIRST DRAFT

Writer Andre Gide once said, "Too often I wait for the sentence to finish taking shape in my mind before setting it down. It is better to seize it by the end that first offers itself, head and foot, though not knowing the rest, then pull: the rest will follow along."

This is how you should look at your first draft. Your priority in writing the first draft of your article should be to get words on paper. Don't spend time waiting for the sentence to "finish taking shape" or for the perfect word

EXHIBIT 8.2 TYPES OF CONCLUSIONS

Read the following conclusions. Can you recognize what types of conclusions they are? Can you recognize what techniques the writer has used to make them effective?

"What is left of what was once her beauty are her extraordinary eyes, blue as diamonds, and they blaze with light as if, in divine compensation for the dead weight of all that will not cease to haunt her, she has been granted a spark from the hour of an apocalypse others have not seen. Perhaps it's the light offered to victims who have suffered like gods."

(*"Oswald in the U.S.S.R.,"* The New Yorker, *April 10, 1995*)

"By closing the loopholes, voters could 'own' their government and still save on their tax bills."

(*"Bankers' Delights,"* Southern Exposure, *Spring 1995*)

"The experience of communing with people dead for four millennia is one my Chinese colleagues and I would like to share with the whole world."

(*"Mummies of the Tamin Basin,"* Archaeology, *March/April 1995*)

"In retrospect, last summer was one of the easiest, most pleasurable ones I have had with my kids. Thankfully, there are many more yet to come. Now, if I could only get them to sleep fifteen minutes longer in the mornings."

(*"Camp Do-it-Yourself,"* Family Fun, *April 1995*)

"But whatever Macado attempts, critics or no critics, he will survive. He has felt gun-metal in his back before."

(*"Marooned on the Islands of Macado,"* American Theatre, *January 1995*)

"And how do we describe Sundown to anyone who asks? It's terrific."

(*"Atlanta Life: Dining Out,"* Atlanta, *February 1995*)

to appear before you. Be concerned with writing a complete article that contains the main points you want to communicate to your reader. The main points may not be communicated with the exact words yet, but they are there on your page.

In writing your first draft, consider the following points:

- Resist the temptation to edit or revise. You will often find yourself whispering, "This is so awkward . . . so silly . . . so *bad*." It's hard to not want to stop and make everything perfect (or as perfect as you can make it). You must realize that the first draft stage is when you want to get a complete, though likely imperfect, article written. Realize that you will have plenty of time later on to edit, revise, and critique.
- Make broad notes as to what needs work. This may sound like editing, but it's not if you keep it simple. Write brief notes to yourself in the margins, at the bottom of the page, or above words. You might write, for example, "Find a better word" or "Work on description here."
- Realize that you probably can't write a first draft in one sitting. Writers work at different paces, but in your beginning writing days you probably won't be able to complete a draft in one sitting. Most experienced writers (unless they are ultraorganized or very inspired) don't even do so, in fact.

Give yourself plenty of time to complete your first draft. Include it in your writing schedule as long as you need to. And give yourself adequate breaks during the first-draft-writing process. A short rest time will get your brain ready for your next writing session.

THE SECOND DRAFT AND BEYOND

How many drafts should you write? Enough that your article is perfect—or, more realistically, that you're as satisfied as you can be with your work. Many writers write at least three drafts. Some write four or more. As a beginning writer, aim at writing at least three drafts of all your work.

Once you have finished your first draft, your work has just begun. You now need to look at that first draft and determine how it can be improved. At this stage, you will engage yourself in editing and revising, as well as proofreading.

Editing and revising involve looking at your article and working out all the rough spots. It is at this point that you will look at such elements as organization, word choice, transitional phrasing, effectiveness of quotes, and so forth. You will do much rewriting at this stage.

Proofreading involves looking at the technical elements in your article. This involves such things as grammar, spelling, and punctuation. Chapter 9, "The Mechanics of Writing," will introduce you to the major rules you need to follow in making your writing technically correct.

Editing and Revising

As you look at your first draft, ask yourself the following questions and revise as necessary. (Note that editing and revising are learned processes. The more you write, the better you will edit and revise.)

- **Have I left out any pertinent information?** Look at your stacks of information and your outline. Were there any facts you meant to put in, but forgot? Are there any facts you forgot in the entire stage of preparation?
- **Is my information accurate?** If you have inaccurate facts, if you attribute a quote incorrectly, if you spell someone's name wrong you will immediately be considered unprofessional. Double-check all of your facts.
- **Have I selected the best quotes?** Look at the quotes you have used from sources. Do they fit in well with the rest of the article? Quotes should be used, not just as fillers, but as strong complements to your story. Look again at your quotes. Have you used them only when it is the best way to present the information? You should use direct quotes to present unusual or unique information that only the source could provide. You wouldn't use a direct quote for information that could be obtained by observation or common knowledge.
- **Does my article's organization make sense?** This question should take a considerable amount of your time; the editing and revisions that accompany it will probably be the most extensive you do. Your article is well-organized when a reader can read through it without any abrupt stops or surprises and can logically see how all of the points relate to the main topic. Look through your article, piece by piece. Do all of your quotations, anecdotes, facts, suggestions—all elements of your story—relate together to give substance to the main topic? If not, eliminate that element or rewrite it until it does so.

> *"A writer's best friend is the wastepaper basket."*
> Isaac Bashevis Singer

- **Are my transitions effective?** An article's organization directly depends on its transitions. If it has effective transitions, the article will not contain any abrupt stops; it will flow smoothly from paragraph to paragraph and from point to point. If your paragraphs seem to exist separate from one another, you need to work on your transitional words and phrases. To link paragraphs together content-wise and stylistically, consider repeating key words or phrases from one paragraph to the other. You can also use transitional words or phrases. These create a direct tie from one point to another. They are wordings such as "Another way to . . . ," "However," "Then there's . . . ," "You can also . . . ," and "Secondly, (or Thirdly, or Lastly)."

> **FROM THE EDITOR'S DESK**
>
> "Know your subject first-hand and not just from secondary sources. Gather original material. Too many would-be writers only reconfigure information already available."
>
> CHARLES MULLER, *ANTIQUE REVIEW*

- **Are there any words I have used incorrectly?** Or are there other words that would be more appropriate in some places? All words have meaning—both the ones you will find in the dictionary and the ones that people impose on them. You must make sure that each word has the meaning you are trying to convey. Look closely at every word in your article. You also need to be aware of those words that always cause us problems. We have all gotten affect and effect; compose and comprise; capital and capitol confused. Make sure you are using the correct words in all instances.
- **Is my language economical?** Mark Twain once said, "I never write 'metropolis' for seven cents when I can get the same price for 'city.' I never write 'policeman' when I can say 'cop.'" Simple writing is not only easier to use but it is also more powerful in the effect it creates. To achieve a clear, understandable presentation, you must write economically. Get used to using simple words whenever possible. You don't need to send your readers rushing to a dictionary because they don't know what half your words mean. Try also to avoid redundancies; you can often say the exact same thing with two words as you could with five. (Example: in the last sentence, "same thing" is the same as "exact same thing." And it's one word shorter.)
- **Is my language strong?** Just because your writing is simple does not mean it can't be strong. Clear, simple writing can also present a powerful image in the mind of your reader. Strong language consists of vivid details and clear descriptions. Try always to use language that transports your reader to the scene; make your details as real as possible. Strong language also consists of strong action. This means that you should focus on your use of verbs. Verbs are the most powerful words in the English language; take advantage of their power by learning to use active verbs that contain multiple layers of meaning.
- **Can my style be strengthened in any way?** What is style? People use the word in many different ways, but to me it simply means your

personal way of writing. It refers to the personal stamp your writing has. It means that your articles don't read like anyone else's; they are individual, just like you. As you write more, your personal style will develop. Your style will consist of such things as the way you handle descriptions, literary devices you may choose to incorporate, and sentence structures you use. (See Chapter 10, "Writing That Shines" for more information on stylistic practices.)

- **Is there anything left unsaid?** At the end of your editing process, you should repeat the question you asked at the beginning. Is all my information included? Are there any gaps? Have I left any questions in the mind of the reader? Go through your article and look at it in regards to all these questions. (Exhibit 8.3 on page 103 is a checklist for your article.) Mark your article up with a red pen. Then, go back and rewrite it. Then, do it over again.

Jumpstart Exercises

1. Look through several magazines. Find examples of a summary lead, an anecdotal lead, an unbelievable lead, and a combination lead. Which ones were effective? Why?
2. Look through several magazines. Find an example of an article that is organized in a narrative way. Then find an example of one that is organized in a topical way. Did both of the organizations work well? Was one better than the other? Why?
3. Look through Exhibit 8.2. Which conclusions do you like? Take each one and rewrite it using another approach (i.e., if it incorporates a descriptive scene, change it to a summary statement).
4. Take an idea you have developed in a previous "Jumpstart" exercise. Write a first draft, concerning yourself only with getting words on paper. (Leave yourself plenty of time to complete this draft.)
5. After writing a first draft, let it sit for a day or two. Then, write a second draft (and any other drafts, if needed).
6. Again, let the article sit for a day or two. Then, following the steps outlined in this chapter, edit and revise it.

EXHIBIT 8.3 **EDITING AND REVISING CHECKLIST**

As you answer each question, put a check in the blank to the left. Make any comments to yourself in the space below the question.

_______ Have I left out any pertinent information?

_______ Is my information accurate?

_______ Have I selected the best quotes?

_______ Does my article's organization make sense?

_______ Are my transitions effective?

_______ Are there any words I have used incorrectly? Are there any words that would be more appropriate in some places?

_______ Is my language economical?

_______ Is my language strong?

_______ Can my style be strengthened in any way?

_______ Is there anything left unsaid?

CHAPTER NINE

THE MECHANICS OF WRITING

What do magazine editors want in an article? Listen to some of the responses I received when I sent out my survey for the "Twenty-five Great Magazines for Beginning Writers" list (in Chapter 13).

> *"Don't waste words, and be grammatically correct," says George Brand, editor of* Senior Magazine.

> *"All query letters and submissions should be spell checked. A query letter with misspelled words and/or bad grammar is a sure turn off," instructs Bob Shell, editor of* Shutterbug.

> *"Use precise, active, vivid verbs. Avoid overworked adjectives and phrases. Keep a consistent perspective (voice) on both time (past or present) and point of view (first person, second person, etc.)," warns Paul Smith, Adult Editor of* Live.

It's clear that, while it may go hand in hand with an appropriate idea, stylistic writing, and professional presentation, editors expect their writers to know the English language. They want to meet writers who know the rules of grammar, punctuation, and spelling. They want to receive articles that have few or no technical errors.

Although it is so important, few magazine writers are truly masters of the language. Many of us assume we learned all we needed to know because we got through high school English. Many of us don't want to think about the rules of English because they just don't excite us. Many of us even think that we *can't* learn the rules of grammar, punctuation, and spelling because they are just too complicated.

The basic rules of grammar, punctuation, and spelling aren't complicated. Don't let fear of them hamper your writing dreams in any way. The best writers know that good writing is of paramount importance to editors, so they know the basic rules. They aren't afraid when they don't know some of the rules some of the time. And they know where to find answers when they need them. Promise now that you will work on this aspect of your writing if you know it is a weak spot. Even if you feel fairly confident in your understanding of the language, you can always strengthen your skills.

This chapter gives you the basic knowledge needed to write a clean, professional, grammatically correct magazine article. If you feel you need to read more on the subject, I highly recommend William Strunk and E. B. White's *Elements of Style,* William Zinsser's *On Writing Well,* Martin Steinmann and Michael Keller's *NTC's Handbook for Writers*, and Floyd Watkins' *Practical English Handbook.* All of these books should be on the shelves at your local bookstore.

THE BASIC RULES OF GRAMMAR

Whole books have been written on the subject of grammar. The following areas, however, are the most basic and most important ones. Master these ideas and you will look like a pro!

The Eight Parts of Speech

To be a good writer, it is essential that you know the types of words with which you are working. In the English language, you use:

- *Nouns.* The nouns in your writing are the objects or concepts mentioned; they are the names for specific "things" in your sentences (*boy, dog, house, love, liberty,* etc.).
- *Pronouns.* Pronouns are substitutes for nouns; they usually refer to a person in your sentence. There are personal pronouns (*I, you, he, it, we, they, mine, hers, ours, them,* etc.) and relative pronouns (*who, whom,* and *whose*).
- *Verbs.* Verbs express action or a state of being (*run, giggle, sit*) and can be used in one of three tenses: past, present, and future.
- *Adverbs.* Adverbs modify verbs, adjectives, or other adverbs; much of the time they end in *-ly*.
- *Adjectives.* You use adjectives to describe or give more definition to nouns (the adjectives *pretty, blue,* or *wonderful* can describe an object).
- *Conjunctions.* The most commonly used conjunctions are *and, but,* and *or*; they are used to connect words, phrases, and clauses.
- *Prepositions.* Prepositions work with nouns or pronouns to modify other nouns, pronouns, or verbs. They include such words as *in, at, from, to, on,* and *with.*
- *Interjections.* Interjections are words that express strong emotion.

Other Important Terms

In addition to these basic eight parts of speech, there are several other terms integral to your understanding of the language.

- *Verbals.* Verbals are words derived from a verb but used as a noun, adjective, or adverb. The three kinds of verbals are participles, gerunds, and infinitives. A participle is a form of a verb that acts as an adjective (*fascinating* answers, *frightened* boy). A gerund is a form of a verb that acts as a noun (Close the door before *leaving*. A successful chef must enjoy *cooking*.). An infinitive is a form of a verb that usually appears with the word *to* and acts as a noun, adjective, or adverb (I would like *to sleep*. The doctor gave me medicine *to take*.).

- *Antecedents.* Antecedents are the nouns for which pronouns stand. The pronoun should always be in agreement with its antecedent. In the following sentence, *their* is the pronoun and *actors* is the antecedent: "After their performance, the actors went to a party."
- *Clauses.* A clause can be either dependent or independent. In the sentence, "The country surrendered after the fighting stopped," the clause "after the fighting stopped" is a dependent clause because it contains a subject and a verb, but it does not contain a complete thought—it can't stand alone. The clause "The country surrendered" is an independent clause because it could stand alone—it could exist independently, without any other words in the sentence.

The Sentence

As a writer, the sentence is your basic structure for writing. A sentence must meet two requirements: (1) it must contain a subject and a verb, and (2) it must express a complete thought. If you don't meet both of these requirements, you don't have a sentence.

> *Vladimir Nabokov was an internationally known lepidopterist (a butterfly expert) when he published* Lolita *and became an internationally known author.*

You want to avoid the alternatives. One of them is the *sentence fragment*. A sentence fragment is a group of words that does not express a complete thought (there may be instances where you use a fragment for effect, but as you get started writing, attempt to write in complete sentences). The other is the *run-on sentence* (also known as the comma splice). The run-on sentence is created when two independent clauses are connected only by a comma. An example would be, "The couple fell in love, now they are getting married." To correct this mistake, you would separate the two clauses with a conjunction (usually *and*) and a comma, or you could change the comma in the run-on sentence to a semicolon.

Agreement

In writing, your subjects and verbs must always agree in number (that is, whether they are singular or plural). Your pronouns and antecedents must also agree in the same way. Remember, a singular subject takes a singular verb, and a plural subject takes a plural verb. In the sentence, "The girl climbs the stairs," the subject is *girl*. Because it is singular, it takes the singular verb *climbs*. If you were using a plural subject and verb, the sentence would read, "The girls climb the stairs."

In some instances it is hard to determine what your subject is. In the sentence, "The decision of the two girls was to go to a movie," the subject is *decision*, not *girls*. Therefore, your subject must be singular (in this case, *was*).

When you are dealing with pronouns and antecedents, you may get confused when you have more than one subject in your sentence. The sentence, "The committee believed in their decision" is wrong because *committee* is a singular noun (although it probably refers to several people). Therefore, the pronoun should also be singular. The proper handling of the sentence is, "The committee believed in its decision."

Parallelism

In writing a list of actions, the items in your list should be parallel in nature. This mistake can usually be caught in a careful reading. The following sentence, for example, has a mistake in parallelism: "Running around the block, working on the treadmill, and to go to an aerobics class are my forms of weekly exercise." The third item in this list should be reworded "going to an aerobics class." With that change, the items are presented in a parallel (or similar) nature.

Voice

Voice refers to the way in which verbs are used. Verbs can be used actively and passively. If a verb is used in the active voice, the subject is seen as the doer of the action. If a verb is used in the passive voice, the emphasis of action is placed on the object (thus, taking away the fact that the subject is actually doing the action). Passive voice is usually achieved by using a helping verb (like *is* or *was*).

Using active voice, a sentence would read, "Margaret wrote the article." Using passive voice, the same sentence would read, "The article was written by Margaret." In the second instance, the emphasis is taken away from Margaret. To achieve strong, lively writing, you should try to use active voice as much as possible.

Dangling Participles

Sentence meaning can be lost when it is not clear what a phrase at the beginning of a sentence is modifying. The phrase at the beginning of a sentence should always modify the sentence's subject and should be separated from it by a comma. The sentence, "Falling down the stairs, my leg was broken" is confusing because the leg didn't fall down the stairs, a person did. To correct dangling participles, add missing words and make other needed changes (e.g., "Falling down the stairs, I broke my leg.").

Tense

An action can be taking place in the past, the present, or the future. Be consistent in your use of tense. If you start your article in the past, for example, don't switch to the present. Which tense is best to use in magazine articles? As a general rule, write in the past tense; if an action is presently taking place or is an ongoing happening, you may want to use present tense.

THE BASIC RULES OF PUNCTUATION

Punctuation is important because it helps guide your reader through your article. The following punctuation marks are the ones most commonly used; understand their uses and your writing will improve.

End Marks

End marks include the period, the question mark, and the exclamation point. The question mark concludes sentences that ask a question, and the exclamation point is used to conclude sentences that express a strong emotion. The period is used mainly to conclude sentences, but it is also used in several special situations. In addition to using a period at the end of a sentence, you use it to end most abbreviations and after numbers and letters in an outline. When an abbreviation comes at the end of a sentence, you don't add another period; one is sufficient. You would write, for example, "The class ended at 8 a.m." Remember also that, in most instances, periods and other end marks go inside quotation marks.

Commas

Commas are the most-used punctuation mark in the English language, and they are probably the most misused as well. They are primarily used in the following situations:

- Before the conjunction to separate two or more independent clauses

  Example: "The football team has played well so far, and the team hopes to win the state championship."

- To separate three or more words, phrases, or subordinate clauses

  Examples: "Pink, blue, and green are her favorite colors." and "She got to the airport on time by quickly packing her suitcase, driving fast across town, and running through the terminal."

- To separate adjectives of *equal* rank

  Example: "It was a cold, wintry day."

- After an introductory word, phrase, or clause

  Examples: "No, we haven't heard yet." "To complete my article on time, I will have to make deadlines for myself."

- To set off parenthetical expressions (words or phrases that interrupt the flow of a sentence)

  Example: "The encyclopedia gave me, in fact, all of the information I needed."
- To set off nonessential expressions (words or phrases not necessary to the meaning of the sentence)

  Example: "The article, which took three months to write, will appear in this month's issue."
- Various other reasons, including: after each item in an address made up of two or more parts; after the salutation in a personal letter; to set off a direct quotation from the rest of the sentence; and after every third digit from the right in a number of three or more digits.

Colons

Colons are used primarily as introductory devices. They introduce a list of items following an independent clause ("Her research took her to a number of places: the library, historical homes, and courthouses."), a sentence that summarizes or explains the sentence before it ("His reason for forgetting was believable: He stayed up until 2 a.m. the night before."), and a formal appositive that follows an independent clause ("I finally knew what I wanted to do with my life: Write for magazines."). You also use colons in special instances, such as before subtitles of books and magazines, between the hour and minute in times, in biblical references, and after salutations in business letters.

> *"Never stop trying to improve. Never say, 'This is enough.'"*
>
> STEPHEN COONTS

Semicolons

Semicolons are used solely with independent clauses that are closely related in thought and structure. For example, you would use a semicolon to join independent clauses that are not already joined by a conjunction ("I went to the store to buy groceries; the store didn't have everything I needed."). You would also consider using a semicolon to avoid confusion when independent clauses or items already contain commas.

Apostrophes

Apostrophes are used primarily to show possession. To show possession, simply add an apostrophe and the letter *s* (Cheryl's book, Gary's house). To show possession in a word that already ends in *s*, simply add the apostrophe (Carlos' book, Tess' house). To make a plural word possessive, again just add the apostrophe (the teams' helmets, the committees' meetings).

Apostrophes are also used in contractions to add the implied *is*; instead of saying *what is*, for example, you can say *what's*. The problem in this use comes with the word *it*. People, for some reason, have the hardest time with this use. The rule, however, is very simple: *It's* (with the apostrophe) means *it is*, as in *it's a difficult job; its* (without the apostrophe) is the possessive of *it,* as in "its beautiful appearance." *Its'* doesn't exist, so never use it.

Quotation Marks

The primary use for quotation marks is to enclose direct quotes (the exact words that someone says). Remember, commas or periods always go *inside* the final quotation mark. Question marks and exclamation points go inside the final quotation mark if the quotation itself is a question or exclamation; otherwise, they go outside. Colons and semicolons go outside the final quotation mark. If you have a quotation within a quotation, use single quotation marks. Quotation marks are also used around the titles of short works, episodes in a series, songs, and chapters.

For information on other punctuation marks, refer to any of the grammar books listed earlier in this chapter.

THE BASIC RULES OF SPELLING

The best defense against spelling errors is the investment in a good dictionary. Whenever you are unsure of a word, whenever an unfamiliar word is thrust at you, and whenever you have to spell a word with which you have a bad history, refer to your dictionary. Most computer word processing programs also have spelling tools; if you have the capabilities, use these to your advantage also.

> **FROM THE EDITOR'S DESK**
>
> "Learn to write past your own interest. There is no other advice."
>
> JOHN HORAN, *THE SENSIBLE SOUND*

In addition to writing with the dictionary always by your side, also learn to recognize the words that give you problems. There are a number of words that sound alike and are spelled similarly but mean different things. In my experience in teaching beginning writing, the following sets of words create the most problems. Learn the differences between them.

Affect/effect: Affect is the verb; it means to pretend or to produce a change (or *effect*). *Effect* is the noun; it means a change or result.

All right: You never spell it *alright.*

A lot: You never spell it *alot.*

As/like: As is used to introduce clauses. *Like* is a preposition; it requires an object.

Capitol/capital: The seat of government, generally the city, is the *capital.* The actual building where a legislature sits is the *capitol.*

Couple of: You must always use the *of* with *couple.*

Due to/because of: When in doubt, use *because of. Due to* sounds stilted.

Either/each: Either means one or the other, not both.

Elude/allude: Elude means to escape from. *Allude* means to refer to.

Goodbye: Goodby is incorrect.

Hopefully/I hope (or It is hoped): Hopefully should be used to describe a subject being in a hopeful mood. Use *I hope* (or *it is hoped* or some other wording) to refer to something for which you are hoping.

Imply/infer: Imply means to suggest; *infer* means to draw a conclusion from.

Lie/lay: Lie is a state of being; *lay* is the action or work.

Principal/principle: Principal means something or someone first in rank or importance. *Principle* refers to a law, truth, or doctrine.

Reeked/wreaked: Reeked is to have a strong, offensive odor. *Wreaked* means to punish with destructive activity.

Stationary/stationery: Stationary means to stand still; *stationery* means writing paper.

> *"Writing is easy. All you do is stare at a blank sheet of paper until drops of blood form on your forehead."*
>
> GENE FOWLER

Whom/who: Use *whom* when referring to someone who has been the object of an action. Use *who* when somebody has done the action.

Again, refer to a good grammar and spelling book for any more information on these various words. Most basic books provide a list of problem words.

Jumpstart Exercises

1. Select a magazine article you like. Go through it, bit by bit, and analyze its technical qualities. Are there sentences that are unclear? Are there many grammatical problems? Are there misused punctuation marks? Are there are any spelling errors? Chances are, since you like the article, there are few technical errors. If there were, would it change your opinion of the article?

EXHIBIT 9.1 PROOFREADING QUIZ

The greenhouse effect is a theory that stipualates the Earth is going thru global warming. This temperature decrease is caused by the accumulation of certain gasses in the earths atmosphere. The accumulation causes a roof as in a greenhouse that traps heat and sends it back down to the earth.

Ozone deplesion is another problem caused by human's use of harmful chemicals. The ozone layer protects the earth from destructive ultraviolet rays. When certain chemicals encounter the ozone layer, they begin to eat away at it. The ozone layer now has a hole in it that continues to grow. Cholorfluorocarbons, CFC's, are the main cause of ozone depletion. CFC's are found in aerosal cans, refrigerater coolants and isulation.

We have all heard the cry "Save the rainforests" but why is it so important. The destruction of rain forests, as well as hardwood forests throughout the Unieted States is important for several reasons. First, it contributes to the Greenhouse Effect becuase it destroys trees who produce carbon dioxide and oxgyen. It depletes animal species that survive only in those areas. Thirdly, it destroys geograhpical areas where research is still bein gperformed. This research could result in cures for diseases, among other discoveries.

2. Look through the basic rules of grammar, punctuation, and spelling presented in this chapter. Make a list of those rules with which you regularly have problems. Make an effort to perfect your use of those rules.
3. Correct the paragraphs presented in Exhibit 9.1. Look for grammar, punctuation, and spelling problems. The corrected paragraphs are shown on the following page.

EXHIBIT 9.1 (CONT'D.)

Here is the same passage, with corrections marked.

The greenhouse effect is a theory that stipualates the Earth is going thru global warming. This temperature decrease is caused by the accumulation of certain gasses in the earths atmosphere. The accumulation causes a roof as in a greenhouse that traps heat and sends it back down to the earth.

Ozone deplesion is another problem caused by human's use of harmful chemicals. The ozone layer protects the earth from destructive ultraviolet rays. When certain chemicals encounter the ozone layer, they begin to eat away at it. The ozone layer now has a hole in it that continues to grow. Cholorfluorocarbons, CFC's, are the main cause of ozone depletion. CFC's are found in aerosal cans, refrigeratar coolants and isulation.

We have all heard the cry "Save the rainforests" but why is it so important. The destruction of rain forests, as well as hard-wood forests throughout the Unieted States is important for several reasons. First, it contributes to the Greenhouse Effect beacuse it destroys trees ~~who~~ produce carbon dioxide and oxgyen. It depletes animal species that survive only in those areas. Thirdly, it destroys geograhpical areas where research is still beingperformed. This research could result in cures for diseases, among other discoveries.

CHAPTER TEN

WRITING THAT SHINES

Take a moment to read through the following two excerpts:

> *Ernest Hemingway was born in 1899 in a respectable suburb of Chicago. His father, a doctor, often took him and Ernest's five siblings to a lakeside hunting lodge in Michigan. His love of the outdoors, then, he came by honestly.*
>
> *Ernest joined the Kansas City Star as a reporter in 1917, then after a short stint as a volunteer for the Italian army, he returned to America and the Toronto Star Weekly. He became a war correspondent in Europe and took up the romantic life he's so known for—bull-fighting, deep-sea fishing, African safari-hunting, and writing. His books included* A Farewell to Arms, For Whom the Bell Tolls, *and* The Old Man and the Sea. *He won the Nobel Prize in 1954.*

> *Havana was still free that summer—and hot, as it will always be. They still served you frozen daiquiris during the wait for customs at the airport. Castro was a remote shadow in the eastern mountains, and Ernest Hemingway was still alive and working.*
>
> *Papa lived and worked at his Finca Vigia in the suburb of San Francisco de Paulo. It was necessary to stop at the gate just off the main road and get an old man who lived nearby to open it. Then there was a straight road through the woods for perhaps a quarter mile, a curve to the left—and the Finca. It had broad steps, columns, and a feeling of spaciousness, informality, and comfort. It was of not recently painted white stucco, un-airconditioned and a little over-grown. From the back there was a view of the rooftops of Havana with the sea beyond: there was a rectangular pool where each day Mary Hemingway swam her mile, in the nude for freedom of movement, and fired the gardener if he watched. A few yards from the house, but matching it in materials and appearance, was the squarish, three-story tower in the top of which Hemingway did his writing. There were also cats—about fifteen, mostly kittens, which lived in the tower's first floor—the cat house.*

What separates these two excerpts? We may not be able to put an exact handle on it, but we do know that the first piece of writing is sluggish and dull. It gives some good information, but it doesn't excite the reader at all. The second piece of writing, on the other hand, is full of life. It provides information, but it also entertains the reader. It sets the stage for an excellent magazine article. The subject—a profile of Ernest Hemingway—is told in a lively, descriptive, effective manner. We know that the second excerpt is *good*—whatever that means. And we usually say that someone who writes a piece like that has *style.* (The first piece, by the way, was something I wrote, intending it to sound like a dry, encyclopedic entry about Hemingway. The second piece was written by Edward Stafford and published in *Writer's Digest* in 1964.)

THE IMPORTANCE OF STYLE

Style is a term used today in a number of ways. In this instance we are talking about the special marks of a particular writer—the techniques that make his or her writing good and enjoyable to read. If you want to succeed as a magazine writer, you should spend some time on developing your own style. "I don't have a style," you might say. "That's something Faulkner or Hemingway had." It's true that the great writers have a special style, but that doesn't mean you have to be able to write like Faulkner or Hemingway. Some styles are better than others, but we can all aspire to better writing.

Good magazine articles have characteristics that separate them from the ineffective (or mediocre) magazine articles. The good articles lack certain characteristics that pull down an article—characteristics like wordiness, redundancies, and clichés. And they are filled with certain characteristics that set them apart somehow—characteristics such as strong description and literary language. To develop a readable, comfortable writing style, you should work toward eliminating those ineffective techniques and cultivating the effective ones.

WHAT TO AVOID

A piece of writing can fail for a number of reasons. Most of those reasons, however, revolve around the *feeling* the reader gets when trudging through the article (or book, or essay, or whatever). For example, the article might come across as sluggish or indecipherable or unimportant. The following characteristics contribute to those feelings on the part of the reader.

Wordiness

New writers often fall into two wordy traps: Using unnecessary words and using a lot of big or unfamiliar words. If you stop and think about it, it is much easier to write long sentences and be verbose than it is to be concise with your wording. Most of us talk in a rambling way, so we often transfer that style to our writing. Wordiness, however, is a trap that should be avoided in your writing. If you want to achieve a clear style, avoid using unnecessary words. Avoid, for example, phrases like *in the process of doing, at the present time,* and *in a number of instances.* Readers get weighted down by such phrases, which may cause them to completely lose interest.

Also avoid using big or unfamiliar words. You don't need to impress readers with your extensive vocabulary. This doesn't mean you talk down to them—use appropriate words, even if some of them are a bit more complex than others. But don't put in words just because they are long. And definitely avoid using words that will require your readers to rush to a dictionary.

The best way to correct wordiness is to be aware of it when you are editing. Consciously look for ways to make your article more understandable and clear.

Vagueness

If you're writing an article that includes details and facts, make them as precise as possible. "The woman owned two hundred pairs of shoes" is more powerful than "The woman owned a lot of shoes." You can lose readers if they feel your information isn't accurate, and an article has more stylistic force if it comes across as authoritative and strong.

Clichés

These overused words and phrases (*busy as a bee, par for the course, hungry as a bear*) show a lack of originality, and they give the impression that the writer spent little time developing the article. Many of us write in clichés without realizing it, simply because we talk and think in clichés quite regularly. But if you let them seep into your writing, you are being careless. One of your jobs as a writer is to enrich your reader's life, to let their reading experience be enjoyable. Clichés add little newness to their experience.

Triteness

Vagueness and the use of clichés are just two ways that you make your writing sound trite. Empty phrases (phrases that actually contribute nothing to your article, such as the favorite "due to the fact that") also do this. Triteness does little to make an impact on your reader. Ideally, you want the reader to come away from his or her reading experience with some sense of enlightenment. Trite techniques will not leave this type of impression.

Passive Construction

Passive construction does little to move action along in your article. Passive voice (primarily the use of the *to be* verbs) tells you that something happened, but it does little to tell you *why* the event happened. Therefore, passive voice lacks the power of the active voice.

Compare the following sentences: "The expectant wife was driven to the hospital by a frantic husband" and "The frantic husband drove his expectant wife to the hospital." The second sentence is obviously more effective, because it communicates a sense of action. By comparison, the first sentence slows the reader down.

Overuse of Adjectives, Adverbs, and Other Figurative Language

When new writers are trying to develop a style, they often go overboard. In trying to be descriptive, they load up on the adjectives, adverbs, similes, and allusions. The strongest word in the English language is the verb; next in line is the noun. Together, these two words connote action—they present the essential details of whatever it is you are conveying. Adjectives, adverbs, and other figurative words and phrases are add-ons; if not used correctly, they can be superfluous.

Read your article and ask yourself if all the words are necessary. Be especially aware of your use of adjectives and adverbs. Make sure they are necessary and are used precisely. If they aren't, get rid of them.

Exhibit 10.1 on page 118 provides you with a checklist of things to avoid in your own writing; it can also be used to analyze writing other than your own.

FROM THE EDITOR'S DESK

"The more interesting and unique the subject matter the better. A frequent mistake made by writers is failure to provide material with a style and slant appropriate for the magazine, due to poor understanding of the focus of the magazine."

LAUREL LUND,
COLORADO HOMES AND LIFESTYLES

WHAT TO CULTIVATE

Just as there are techniques you should avoid in developing a strong writing style, there are techniques that are important to cultivate. These techniques make your writing stronger, more precise, and more interesting to the reader.

Attention to Word Choice

You should never throw words haphazardly onto the page. You should know why you are using certain words and phrases. Spend time selecting the right ones, so that the message you intend to send is the one being sent.

The word, after all, is the writer's basic tool. Just as electricians know why they use a certain tool in a given situation, writers should know why they are using a particular word or phrase. In particular, pay attention to the way your words flow on the tongue. Make sure your language is not wordy or vague, avoid clichés and empty phrases, make sure that your vocabulary is correct, and watch for uneasy transitions and complicated sentences.

Strong Description

Good, strong description comes from a reliance on precise wording and

EXHIBIT 10.1 PROBLEM AREA CHECKLIST

In looking at any article you write, you want to avoid those characteristics that take away from its effectiveness. Your goal should be to write a clean, readable article. To get used to looking for these problems, use this checklist to analyze your article.

Are any of these elements evident in my article?

Wordiness ____________________

Unnecessary amount of words (five words where one will do) ____________________

Big or long words ____________________

Unfamiliar words ____________________

Vagueness ____________________

Imprecise facts ____________________

Lack of facts ____________________

Clichés ____________________

Triteness ____________________

Empty phrases ____________________

Passive construction ____________________

Overuse of adjectives ____________________

Overuse of adverbs ____________________

Overuse of figurative language ____________________

Overuse of metaphors ____________________

Overuse of similes ____________________

Overuse of descriptive wording ____________________

Any other problem areas that seem evident in my article:

vivid language. The old adage, "Show, don't tell," is never as true as it is when handling description. When showing, make sure that your wording is precise (accurate and true for the reader) and vivid (lively).

Which is better: "The girl felt like she was being watched from all corners of the room" or "The girl could feel the eyes boring holes in her back and could hear quiet, shrill whispers coming from the far corners of the room"? The first sentence simply tells you what the girl feels; the second one relates the information to the readers by showing them what the girl feels. It assumes the readers' intelligence and gives the readers credit for being able to interpret meaning for themselves.

The best way to learn how to write good descriptions is to practice observational skills. Make it a habit to see every situation or environment as a learning experience. Look around you; listen to the sounds; feel the texture of the place; delve into the actions of people. How could you tell someone what was going on? Then—most importantly—how could you *show* someone the same thing? What type of wording, what language, would show her most accurately and interestingly?

Effective Anecdotes

In the simplest sense, anecdotes are stories that serve as examples. They are another tool for showing meaning.

Anecdotes can be utilized in two primary ways. First, they can help the reader identify with the topic of the article. Anecdotes present the reader with situations or people that are familiar. Note, for example, how this works in the following lead: "John Smith, a college sophomore, recently completed research for a history term paper. He collected information from a 1910 *New York Times,* a California database, and a museum in Connecticut—all without moving from his computer screen." The subject, computer use on college campuses, is made more familiar and interesting with the use of a friendly anecdote that shows (instead of tells) what the story is all about.

> *"Most people never listen. Nor do they observe. You should be able to go into a room and when you come out know everything that you saw there and not only that. If that room gave you any feeling, you should know exactly what it was that gave you that feeling."*
>
> ERNEST HEMINGWAY

Secondly, anecdotes can be used to clarify or accentuate a point. You can do this when a topic is hard to understand or when a point requires more illustration. See how the anecdote works in the following excerpt to provide more clarity to the topic of office romance: "While many companies discourage romantic relationships between employees, there are exceptions. Linda Wells and Mark Shaw, English professors at a small college, hid their romance for months, fearing that one might have to resign. They were pleasantly surprised when their department chairman casually commented one day in the lounge, 'Are the two of you planning on getting married sometime soon?'" The point (that there are exceptions to discouraging romance) is made more relevant and readable with an appropriate anecdote.

Literary Devices

When you hear the terms *simile, metaphor,* and *alliteration,* what type of writing do you think of? I bet your answer was novels, short stories, or some other form of fiction. Have you ever thought about using these and other literary devices in your magazine writing? If you haven't, you need to consider the notion. Nonfiction writing can be made more interesting—more sparkling—with these devices.

The *metaphor* is perhaps the strongest of literary devices you can use in your article writing. When you use a metaphor you are referring to something familiar in order to clarify or improve an image. You are comparing one thing to another in a way your reader will understand.

Classic literature gives us many familiar metaphors. Metaphors can describe the sky: "I remember how the world looked from our sitting-room window as I dressed that morning: the low sky was a sheet of metal; the blond cornfields had faded into ghostliness at last" (Willa Cather, *My Antonia*). And metaphors can describe the world: "All the world's a stage, and all the men and women merely players" (William Shakespeare, *Macbeth*).

> *"I try only to write clearly, and I have the very good fortune to think clearly so that the writing comes out, as I think, in satisfactory shape."*
>
> ISAAC ASIMOV

Similes are very similar to metaphors in that they clarify an image by comparing it to another image. Similes, however, use the words *like* or *as* to do so. Again, literature is resplendent with these devices: "At last the summer was like a green sick dream, or like a silent crazy jungle under glass" (Carson McCullers, *The Heart is a Lonely Hunter*); "Above the darkened square, shrouded by the spent dust, the sky was as clear as the inside of a brass bell" (William Faulkner, *Dry September*); and "In the days when the spinning-wheels hummed busily in the farmhouse . . . there might be seen, in districts far away among the lanes, or deep in the bosom of the hills, certain pallid undersized men, who, by the side of the brawny country-fold, looked like the remnants of a disinherited race" (George Eliot, *Silas Marner*).

Allusion is another powerful literary device. Allusion is the practice of referring to a well-known piece of writing (poem, book, movie, etc.) to enrich the meaning of your image. In doing so, you can allude to it directly or indirectly.

Allusion is effective in a way similar to metaphors and similes. It adds familiarity and understanding to your topic, and it makes the reading more lively to your readers. Note the allusions to familiar songs, phrases, novels, even television shows in the following magazine article titles: "Summer in the City," "Are We There Yet?" "Allergies: Gone with the Wind," "Miami Nice," "Vacation in the Lap of Luxury," "Amazing Grace Kelly," and "Much Ado about Shakespeare."

Alliteration and other lyric devices help add rhythm and cadence to your writing. Alliteration is the repetition of a primary sound, such as in the sentence, "The maddening murmur of the voices haunted his memory." Other lyric devices, such as internal rhyme (rhyme within a sentence), onomatopoeia (the use of words meaning a certain sound, such as *thump* or *gurgle*), and repetition (the repetition of words or phrases), add spice to your writing.

Personal Creativity

Style is very personal. It's often created by the personal likes and dislikes of the particular writer. While it's not recommended for those just starting out, writers can develop a personal style that "bucks the system."

For example, think of Faulkner's page-length sentences or James Joyce's blending together of words and phrases. While not as extreme, magazine writers have also been known to use creative license in putting their articles together. They might write sentence fragments to express urgency, or they might write in a stream-of-consciousness manner to recreate someone's thoughts. Realize that this type of creativity in nonfiction writing should be used only when it is better than the conventional method—when it's done for an important purpose.

THE BOTTOM LINE ON STYLE

Developing a personal writing style can definitely make your magazine articles shine in a way that will win and keep readers. Beware, however, of the tendency to overdo it. Your writing should be precise and accurate, as well as interesting to read. Interesting, however, does not mean overly dramatic or colorful. As you look through your writing, consider these questions:

- **Is the Article Readable?** Sure, it's important that your article has a sense of style—that it has some flair. It's more important, however, that your reader is able to get something out of it. You don't ever want your message to get lost in the presentation. To determine your article's readability, first try to read it with an objective eye. Read it aloud (or record it and play it back) and listen for any problem spots: long, unnecessary words; vague information; clichés; choppy transitions; and passive wording. Ask a writer friend to read the article and look for the same problems. Also ask him or her if the main point of the article is clear. If the main idea is not detectable, your message has gotten lost somewhere.

> *"Don't worry about your originality. You could not get rid of it even if you wanted to. It will stick to you and show up for better or worse in spite of all you or anyone else can do."*
>
> Robert Henri

- **Did You Try Too Hard?** In developing a personal style, many new writers go overboard. While trying to sound creative, they actually come across as amateurish. They distract the reader by throwing in overly colorful descriptions and overloading on literary devices. For your writing to be both stylistic and effective, you must remember that a little bit goes a long way. Your similes won't work if they're found in every other paragraph. Your anecdotes won't communicate anything if they're not balanced with convincing information. If you're interested in working on a more lively style of writing, start out slow. Consciously count how many times you use allusion, keep your number of adjectives small, and limit yourself to so many anecdotes in an article. By practicing restraint, you will learn where these devices are truly needed.

Remember Your Audience

We're back to the most basic point of writing publishable magazine articles: remember who your audience is. Before you write your article, review the tone and style of your target magazine. Not all magazines accept anecdotal, descriptive articles, for example. Some, in fact, want straightforward stories with little creativity. Also be aware of your actual reader. Learn as much as you can about the magazine's typical reader, and then imagine that you are one of those readers. Never underestimate your readers, but also try not to talk over them. You're writing so that your reader will learn something and perhaps enjoy his or her time spent with your article. Never forget that that is your goal.

Remember Your Topic

Every topic does not warrant the same style. An article on household cleaning is probably not the place to show off your skill in using ten alliterations on one page; it *is* the place to provide your readers with good, useful information and tips. Don't forget: your presentation should never overshadow your message.

Jumpstart Exercises

1. What does *style* mean to you? Write a one-page essay on the term's meaning to you, and then elaborate on the type of style you would like to develop.
2. Select a magazine article that you like. Read through it, then mark up any problems you see. In particular, look for wordiness, vagueness, clichés, triteness, passive construction, and overuse of figurative language. Rework the problem areas, rewriting sentences and phrases. Does it read better now?

3. Consider the following situations. Use all of your observational skills, as well as your imagination, to describe the situation in as much detail as possible.
   - The last time I talked with my best friend
   - The place I am reading this right now
   - The best vacation I have ever had
   - The scene at a local shopping center
4. Consider the following article topics. Write an anecdote for each one (you can use imaginary individuals) that clarifies or enhances the topic.
   - How to change a tire
   - A profile of a homeless person
   - What it means to be "in love"
   - An analysis of the health care crisis
   - Ways to make Christmas special
5. Select the article you wrote for Chapter 8 (or select another article you have written). Read through it, analyzing it for the characteristics you should avoid (wordiness, clichés, etc.) and the characteristics you should cultivate (effective descriptions, literary devices, etc.). Are there many problem areas? Does your article "shine" at all? Rework the article with these points in mind.

CHAPTER ELEVEN

WRITER'S BLOCK

"I haven't been able to write for a week. I'm just stuck."

"I know what I want to say. For some reason, I just can't say it."

"I really want to write this article. I just can't sit down and do it."

"But . . . well, I have writer's block."

When I hear these excuses I just want to scream from the mountaintops, "You don't have writer's block! You can't have it, because there's no such thing as writer's block!" No such thing as writer's block, you say? I do believe you have what you consider writer's block. I often have what you consider writer's block. In my mind, however, that is too harsh of a name for the problem. A block is something insurmountable, something impassable. I like to call what you consider writer's block by another name: Writer's Pause.

There are going to be times when you feel stuck. You have written the lead on your first draft, but now you don't know where to go (even though you have an outline sitting right in front of you). You have written your first draft, it now has red marks all over it, and you can't seem to get the energy up to go back to your computer and rewrite the article (although the hardest work has been done).

Yes, these are legitimate problems. All writers have them. But, they are not insurmountable. In fact, they should be only temporary problems. You should only *pause* for a moment before you are writing again.

REASONS FOR WRITER'S BLOCK

To get past what you consider writer's block, you must understand why you are stuck. There are various reasons that writers get stuck. Most of them, however, are reasons that can be easily overcome. Most of them simply require a change in attitude. You are probably stuck because of one of the following reasons:

1. *You are distracted.* You may be stuck because you aren't in an environment conducive to writing. It's going to be hard for you to write when you feel like you need to clean the bathroom instead, when you really need to be getting ready for a dinner party that begins in thirty minutes, or when your kids are pounding on your door. If

distraction seems to be your problem, rethink your writing plan. You might need to rework your schedule (go back to Chapter 5 for some ideas). You might also need to rework your attitude about writing. You don't have to feel guilty that there are other claims on your time and energy. Writing is part of your life—it is not your *entire* life.

2. *You fear failure.* Many of us, especially as we are just getting started writing, fear that what we will write will not be good enough. That gives us, perhaps unconsciously, a reason to not write. You might have a great idea for an article, you might even have an outline written, but you can't make yourself write the article because that means someone else might eventually see it. You might have to open yourself up to criticism and, possibly, rejection. There's no easy answer to this problem. You must train yourself to think that your writing doesn't have to be perfect. You write because you want to write, not because someone else won't like what you write.

> *"I suppose I do get 'blocked' sometimes, but I don't like to call it that. That seems to give it more power than I want it to have. What I try to do is write. I may write for two weeks 'the cat sat on the mat, that is that, not a rat,' you know. And it might be just the most boring and awful stuff. But I try. When I'm writing, I write. And then it's as if the muse is convinced that I'm serious and says, 'Okay. Okay. I'll come.'"*
>
> MAYA ANGELOU

3. *You still don't understand your article.* It may be that you scrimped on one of the steps of preparation. If you don't adequately know what points you're going to make in your article, you probably will get stuck. If you haven't done all of your research, you will have gaps and will definitely get stuck. Spend plenty of time on preparation. Know your article inside and out before you sit down to write.
4. *You know your article too well.* This article is now your baby. It is going to be your masterpiece. If you are too close to your article, chances are you will get stuck. It may be because you have thought about it too long and your brain is overworked. Or it may that, because you want this article to be perfect, anything you write won't be adequate. So, either way, you get stuck. The way to get past this problem is to put some distance between yourself and your article. Let it sit for a day or two; focus your energy on another project. Go back to it when you feel less concerned about perfection.

Getting Beyond Writer's Block

Once you have discovered the root of your block, you can take steps to get writing again. You need to take that quick pause, then get going again. Sounds too simple, doesn't it? It's not. Depending on the stage you are at, just try one of these exercises to get you going again.

Start at the End (or the Middle) • There's no rule that says you have to write your article from the beginning to the end. If you're stuck on the lead, forget it and work on part of the body. Or go to the end and write the conclusion (that will make you see how it feels to be finished with an article and might give you inspiration to go back and write the rest).

Freewrite • If you know what you want and need to write, but you can't transfer thoughts to words on paper, this exercise should work for you. Don't worry about the proper format of an article. Don't worry if you're putting things in the right order. From your notes, simply write down everything you know about your topic. Get everything you can down on paper, regardless of how it looks. When you finish, you will find that some of it actually makes sense and might even be useable.

Play Twenty Questions • If you are somewhere in the beginning stage of your writing, pretend that you are the typical reader for your article. What twenty questions would he or she ask you about this topic? This will immediately give you ideas for what needs to be included; you can start writing on one of the questions that interests you most.

Play Editor • Another good exercise at the beginning stage of your writing, this is similar to playing twenty questions. This time, imagine that you are the editor of a magazine that might be interested in your topic. What questions would he or she want to know about this topic? What would he or she be concerned about? You can also do this exercise if you have already written the article. Imagine that the editor is reading your final draft. What questions might he or she still want answered? Does it look professional and clean to his or her eyes?

Write It for Yourself • Something that gets us stuck a lot is the fact that we feel pressure to perform. We are stuck because we're afraid that, when we finish, it won't be any good. So we might as well not write it, right? If you ever feel this pressure, stop and realize that you are really writing for yourself. Write everything you want to write about your topic—and don't write it for your spouse, or your mother, or an editor. Write it for the most important person—you. You, after all, are the one who needs to be satisfied with your work. You are the only one who intimately knows your deepest writing dreams. When you write for yourself, chances are you will create a first draft that, at the very least, contains all the important information. At least you got started writing.

> *"Read, read, read. Read everything—trash, classics, good and bad, and see how they do it. Then read! You'll absorb it. Then write."*
>
> WILLIAM FAULKNER

Read Your Target Magazine • If you already have a magazine chosen as a possible market for your article, read several issues of that magazine. Find articles on similar topics as yours. Analyze those articles for the way they are constructed, the tone they take, any special elements they might have. Then go back to your own article, with the intent of writing it in a way that is compatible with your target magazine.

Get Rid of Any Outside Pressure • Make sure that something external is not causing your writer's block. If you haven't had enough sleep, for example, that will hurt your efforts. Make sure that your diet is fine, that you keep yourself healthy, and that you identify any physical or emotional situations that are keeping you from being productive.

Change Your Routine • Perhaps your problem is that you have been working for too long at the same place. You're tired, you're cranky, and you don't care about your article any more. Changing your routine does wonders for your attitude. So, go to the park and work on your lead while sitting at a picnic table. Work on revisions at a local coffee house. Or take a short break and do something completely unrelated to your article—watch the news, pull some weeds. Just don't make this an everyday occurrence. You need to get back to your writing as soon as possible.

FROM THE EDITOR'S DESK

"Know the subject matter. Demonstrate a reader-friendly style that will help make the sometimes complicated subject of investing more accessible to the average person. Fill the manuscript with real-life examples of people who actually have done the kinds of things discussed."

DENNIS FERTIG,
YOUR MONEY

Go Back to the Library • You might have skimped on research, and that is why you're stuck now. If that's it, go back to the library (or talk to your expert source again, or touch base again with whatever the source of your research was) and work some more.

Write a "Dear John" Letter • If you have planned adequately for your article, then you know what you should be writing. You just can't, for some reason, put it into words. Write a letter to John (or some other imaginary person) explaining what you need to be writing. The letter might go something like: "Dear John, I'm working on this article about the ten best beaches for romantic getaways. I have written the lead, and it's pretty good. But now I don't know where to go. I have a list of seven beaches, but my descriptions of them seem bland and dry. I want to let readers know about the romantic, yet adventurous, activities that a couple can do together (like scuba dive and horseback ride). I want to give them a peek at the exotic dinners they can have at the best restaurants for two. And I want to captivate them with the idea of walking together on the beach at nighttime, with only the magic company of the constellations overhead."

From this short letter, you have solved one or two problems. One, you know you only have information about seven beaches (you need to find three more or retitle you article). Second, you know what you want to describe to your readers. You even have a few words that might be useable ("the magic company of the constellations" isn't bad). Writing a letter will help you put into words what you know you need to write, and you might end up writing some good copy as well.

Borrow from the Best • Start now to create a file of articles you especially like, effective leads, well-written sidebars, and catchy conclusions. When you're stuck on a certain element of your article, get out the file and see if you can get some good ideas. If your lead is giving you trouble, look at one of your favorite leads. Can you write your lead in the same style? Does it give you an idea as to how you can treat your lead?

Cut and Piece Together • If you have a draft written and you are stuck at the stage of analyzing your organization, this exercise really works. Take a pair of scissors and cut the article apart, by subtopics. Now, piece the article back together according to how it makes sense. You may find that your planned organization was flawed and that it needs to be done another way.

Start Over with a Different Approach • Look back at your last paragraph (or another section of your article). Rewrite it with a different point of view, new descriptions—any different approach. By looking at your article with a different eye, your writing will become fresh again.

Schedule Yourself a Writing Appointment • Put your project down; get it out of your mind for a while. Make an appointment to get back to the article at a specific time and write the appointment down in your datebook.

Work on Another Project • Do you have another hobby? If so, get out the needlework or carpenter's tools and work on a project totally unrelated to writing. Do you work full-time at something other than writing? Work on a project from work that really needs to get done. Do you need to cook supper? Do that instead. Give yourself a break from writing. You can also work on a totally different writing project. A good idea is to always have more than one article going at a time. When you get stuck on one article, you can let it sit while you work on the other article.

Reward Yourself • Tell yourself something like: "After I write 250 words, I will stop and have a cup of coffee," or "When I finish this article, I will treat myself to a movie." One word of caution, though: be reasonable and don't spoil yourself. You can spend all of your time drinking coffee and watching movies—and very little time working on your articles.

Imagine the Outcome • Sometimes the old adage is true: We don't want to write, but we want to have written. When you're stuck, it seems that the end is totally unreachable. To get motivated again, imagine the outcome of your completing the article. Close your eyes. Imagine the article completely written, edited and revised, and rewritten. Imagine someone reading the article and telling you, "I really loved your article. It meant a lot to me." Imagine seeing the article in print. Imagine receiving a check in the mail for it. Imagine the feeling of satisfaction you have in yourself and your accomplishment.

Jumpstart Exercises

1. Think of the last time you think you had writer's block. Make a list of the reasons you were stuck. How could you deal with each of these reasons?
2. Do you prefer the term *Writer's Pause?* Why or why not?
3. Pick an idea you developed in a previous chapter. Practice freewriting on the topic. Set a timer for ten minutes and don't stop writing until the timer signals you to stop.
4. Pick another idea and play twenty questions with it.
5. Pick another idea and write a "Dear John" letter, describing what you want your article to accomplish.
6. All of the block-busting exercises in this chapter can serve as "Jumpstart" exercises. If you are stuck right now (or when you become stuck), try an appropriate exercise.
7. Use the Exhibit 11.1 worksheet on page 130 to help you in analyzing why you're stuck on any particular project and to help you come up with a plan for dealing with it.

> *"In many ways, writing is the most serious thing in my life. It's also the least serious thing. Sad, pain-filled writing is, fortunately, not for me. I'd rather for my writing to last only a hundred years and be pain-free than last a thousand years and be filled with pain."*
>
> CLYDE EDGERTON

EXHIBIT 11.1 A BLOCK-BUSTING WORKSHEET

Whenever you have writer's block, vow to tackle and overcome it. Determine why you're blocked, and then devise a plan for getting unstuck. Use the following worksheet whenever you're stuck. Be as honest as you can in your answers.

Project I'm Working On:

Stage I'm Stuck At:

Why Do I Think I Am Stuck?

Is There Some External Reason I Am Stuck? (personal problems, health, etc.)

Is There Some Psychological Reason I Am Stuck? (lack of self-confidence, fear of failure, etc.)

What Do I Want to Accomplish with This Project?

What is Keeping Me From Accomplishing That Goal?

How Can I Overcome My Writer's Block on This Project?

What Exercise Am I Going to Use in Overcoming My Block?

What Specific Steps Will I Take to Do This Exercise?

When Will I Finish This Project?

CHAPTER TWELVE

WHAT DO I DO WITH THIS ARTICLE?

Get ready. This chapter will confront the deep-seated fear that many of you have. You may want to fight the knowledge that, soon in your writing adventure, you need to send an article out to a magazine for consideration. Once you get past that hurdle (and once you have gotten over that first rejection), you will begin to feel like a real writer.

Up until now, this book has been relatively comfortable. You have had a chance to sit comfortably at your own desk and come up with ideas, write outlines, put together a first draft, perhaps even complete a magazine article of which you are quite proud. You may have drifted out of your writing hole every once in a while to start to gauge the magazine field and to begin to think of places to submit a magazine article. This chapter will force you to come to grips with the reality of marketing your magazine article, and you may have to deal with your fear of rejection. You will probably have to learn to handle rejection. But you won't have to live with the fear for very long.

Marketing to magazines is a learned process. Once you learn the tricks of the trade, you will be well on your way to seeing your first article in print. Effective marketing involves several skills: understanding the markets, writing a good query letter, submitting a manuscript properly, and being professional.

UNDERSTANDING THE MARKETS

You would never go on a trip without first knowing as much as you can about your destination. You would never go on a job interview without knowing something about the company or position for which you're interviewing. You would never start a romantic relationship without knowing enough about the person with whom you're getting involved. Likewise, you would never send a query letter (more on them in a moment) or magazine article to a magazine about which you know nothing.

You will want to know about a possible market's attitude toward freelance writers, types of articles frequently published, specific articles recently published, writing style, and position in the marketplace. New writers often make the fatal mistake of sending out an article to a magazine without really knowing whether it fits that magazine's editorial plan or style. They don't realize that one of the keys to getting published is knowing the markets. In not realizing this, these novice writers come across to editors as uninformed and sloppy.

As you develop an idea for a magazine article, you need to have a specific magazine for publication in mind. By thinking of a specific magazine to which you are going to target your article, it is much easier to go to the next steps—querying that magazine and writing your article.

How, then, do you find a specific target magazine? How do you determine where your article will best fit? How do you find out which editors and magazines are most receptive to your type of article? There are several key ways to do this.

Read *Writer's Market*

If you only had time to do one thing to market your articles, this would be the step you would not want to omit. *Writer's Market* is integral to every magazine writer's life.

Writer's Market, published annually by Writer's Digest Books, is a guide to all the markets for your writing, whether they be magazine articles, books, short stories, novels, plays, scripts, greeting cards, or fillers. The magazine article field is the primary area of focus.

Each year the book is updated so that all the information about publishers is current; new markets are also introduced each year. A recent edition, for example, included seven hundred new markets and is updated by 85 percent over the previous year's book. This information is invaluable to you because it keeps you up-to-date on the opportunities available in the market. And, more importantly, it gives you current, step-by-step instructions on how to submit your article.

Writer's Market divides magazines into different categories—women's, health and fitness, regional, juvenile, travel, and so forth. Each category lists specific magazines and vital information about them. Information on the magazine's circulation, staff, editorial needs, payment, and other important topics is included.

How then would you use the *Writer's Market*? Let's say you have an idea for a magazine article about your personal experience with aging parents. The first thing you would do (even before you write your article) is find a magazine to query. Turn to the table of contents in the *Writer's Market* and go through the various magazine categories. You might determine that general interest, religious, and women's magazines fit your needs. At that point, look up specific magazines in each category and read their entries.

A typical entry in *Writer's Market* looks like this:

> ***McCalls,*** *110 Fifth Ave., New York, NY 10011-5603. (212) 463-1000. Editor: Kate White. Executive Editor: Lynne Cusack. 90% freelance written. "Study recent issues. Our publication carefully and conscientiously serves the needs of the woman reader—concentrating on matters that*

directly affect her life and offering information and understanding on subjects of personal importance to her." Monthly Circ. 5 million. Pays on acceptance. Publishes ms an average of 6 months after acceptance. Offers 20% kill fee. Byline given. Buys exclusive or First North American rights. Reports in 2 months. Writer's guidelines for #10 SASE.

Nonfiction: The editors are seeking meaningful stories of personal experience, fresh slants for self-help and relationship pieces, and well-researched action-oriented articles and narratives dealing with social problems concerning readers. McCall's buys 200-300 articles/year, many in the 1,500-2,000 word lengths. Pays variable rates for nonfiction. Subjects of interest to women: health, personal narratives, celebrity biographies and autobiographies, etc. Almost all features on food, fashion, beauty and decorating are staff written. Sometimes pays the expenses of writers on assignment.

Tips: Query first. Use the tone and format of our most recent issues as your guide. Preferred length: 1,500-2,000 words. Address submissions to executive editor unless otherwise specified.

> *"Any man who keeps working is not a failure. He may not be a great writer, but if he applies the old-fashioned virtues of hard, constant labor, he'll eventually make some kind of career for himself as a writer."*
>
> RAY BRADBURY

You can see that the entries in *Writer's Market* will provide you with several items of importance: (1) address and phone number of publication; (2) information about editors and to whom articles should be directed; (3) information about how much freelance material is used; (4) circulation information; (5) publication and contract information (how much the magazine pays, what rights it buys to your article, when it pays, whether you get a byline, when it responds to your query, etc.); (6) editorial needs and topics of interest; and (7) specific tips the editor thinks are important.

When writing a query letter to a specific magazine, follow its guidelines as much as possible. If the entry in *Writer's Market* says it takes articles no longer than a thousand words, don't suggest a seventeen-hundred-word article. If it says it only takes how-to articles and yours is a humor article, send the query to someone else.

You should now see why this guide is so important. It gives you all the basic information about thousands of possible outlets for your magazine articles. See Exhibit 12.1 for an exercise on getting the most out of your *Writer's Market.*

Be a Student of Magazines

I have talked about this before, but it's worth repeating. As an aspiring magazine writer, magazines should be one of your main interests. You should enjoy going to newsstands and perusing the shelves. You should know how to pick up a magazine from that newsstand (or from your mailbox) and

EXHIBIT 12.1 GETTING THE MOST FROM YOUR *WRITER'S MARKET*

You need to learn to be very comfortable with the *Writer's Market.* It is an invaluable tool and it will work better for you if you understand how it can help your marketing efforts. Use the following worksheet any time you are trying to find a suitable market for an article idea. It should help you develop several possible markets for the article.

My idea:

Audiences who might be interested in this topic (i.e, women, sports enthusiasts, travelers, etc.):

Categories of magazines (i.e., women's, juvenile, general interest, etc.) these audiences read:

Type of article into which this idea might develop (i.e, how-to, profile, etc.):

A possible target magazine for this article and additional information I need to know about it (i.e., word limits, tips of editors, etc.):

Another possible magazine and additional information:

Another possible magazine and additional information:

Another possible magazine and additional information:

study it from cover to cover. You should be familiar enough with the field that you notice when a new magazine is being published or when one goes out of business.

These skills are integral in marketing your work. If you have an idea for an article, you can go to the newsstand and find several possible markets. If you are an avid reader, you will know if several magazines have recently published an article similar to yours.

Once you decide on a specific magazine for which you want to write, obtain several copies of the magazine and study it. In particular, notice

- the types of topics it publishes.
- specific articles it has published in the last year.
- any particular interests the editor might have (you can find these by reading the editor's page).
- the use of freelance writers, as compared to staff writers (you can do this by comparing bylines with names in the staff box).
- the style of writing the writers practice, especially the structure of articles.

Send Off for Writer's Guidelines

Once you have determined for which magazine you would like to write, send off for its writer's guidelines. These will give in-depth information about opportunities available for writers at that particular publication. You will learn about how to submit your material, what topics are especially important to editors, and often (and most importantly) what its editorial calendar is like. An editorial calendar is the staff's plan for the magazine in the next year or two. It will show you what specific topics will be covered in future issues. Some magazines also have theme issues, and the calendars will identify these for you. By looking at the editorial calendar, you can gear articles very specifically to the magazine's needs.

Writer's guidelines are important to obtain, because *Writer's Market* does not list editorial calendar information. Also, guidelines are more current; changes may occur before the next issue of *Writer's Market*, and the guidelines would reflect these changes.

When you request writer's guidelines, ask also for a few sample copies. Sample copies will usually cost you a little extra, but they are definitely worth it. There is no better way to understand a magazine than to look at recent copies.

Keep Up-to-Date on Market Changes

Somewhere in your writing journey you will want to subscribe to some writing magazines. While they are lots of fun to read and usually have very informative articles on the craft of writing, the best reason to subscribe is that they publish monthly marketing information.

The markets are constantly changing. A magazine may get a new editor, may begin to accept new types of articles, or might even go out of business. You want to stay abreast of these changes, as it will keep you from wasting time and energy and will make you look like the professional you are.

THE ALL-IMPORTANT QUERY LETTER

Query letters, query letters, query letters. You have heard about them several times, both in previous chapters and in this one. If you know any magazine writers at all, you have heard about them before. But what exactly are they?

A query letter is how you sell your article idea to a magazine editor. It asks an editor if he or she is interested in seeing the article you are planning to write. It tries to grab the editor's attention and make her realize that she needs the article for her magazine.

A query letter should not be longer than one page. It should, briefly and succinctly, sell your article idea. Although it can be written in a number of ways, I tell writers that the best query letter is written in a four-step fashion. It contains four integral parts, each of which represent one paragraph. (As you read through this description of a query letter's parts, refer to the examples in Exhibits 12.2, 12.3, and 12.4.)

FROM THE EDITOR'S DESK

"Write a clear and compelling query letter. Know the audience you are proposing to write for and make that clear in topics and focus you propose."

ROBIN ALLEN,
MILITARY LIFESTYLE

Elements of a Query Letter

An effective query letter contains these four integral parts. Each part usually represents one paragraph.

Paragraph 1: An Attention-Getting Introduction • Set your query letter apart by making it interesting to the editor. Start it off with an interesting anecdote that gives insight into your article idea. Make a startling statement or ask a thought-provoking question. Don't give any details about your actual article—simply get the editor's attention.

Paragraph 2: The Details • Once you have captured the editor's attention, explain the topic of your article. Briefly describe the nature of the article: what information will be provided, what will be explained, etc. Give some idea as to the nature of your article (will it be anecdotal? informational? humorous? serious?). If you will be using sources, list them here. Tell how long your article will be. If you have any "extras" (sidebars, photographs, etc.), give that information in this paragraph. The key is to not tell everything about your article but to tell enough to provide the editor with an accurate description.

EXHIBIT 12.2 SAMPLE QUERY LETTER

Cheryl Sloan Wray

000 Anywhere Road • Birmingham, AL 00000 • (205) 000-0000

February 24, 1996

Leigh Anne Perialas
Assistant Editor, *Family Times*
1900 Super Fine Lane
Wilmington, DE 19802

Dear Ms. Perialas,

It's a beautiful spring Saturday and Caroline and Robert have wonderful plans for spending the day with their eight-year-old daughter Morgan. After a picnic in the park, they plan to see the newest exhibit at the local art museum. When Morgan hears the plans, however, she erupts: "I'm not going there. Museums are boring!"

Many parents today would get similar responses from their children. With the disappearance of arts programs from many schools, as well as the continuing popularity of television and movies, children don't appreciate the arts as they should. I have in mind an article for *Family Times* that would deal with this issue. It would include general guidelines for teaching children to appreciate the arts (such as "Be an example," "Encourage learning," and "Take family excursions"), as well as specific activities geared toward making art, music, and literature fun. The article would be anecdotal and warm, with real-life examples from parents and their children. The article would also be informative, backed up by quotes from experts (such as directors of museums and music programs). It would run approximately 1000 words in length, although I can vary it according to your needs.

I am a freelance writer who specializes in parenting topics. My articles have appeared in such magazines as *Growing Parent, Living with Preschoolers, Accent, Alabama West, Christian Single,* and *Dimension*; I am also the coauthor of two books. Most of my article ideas come from life with my energetic, almost two-year-old daughter McKenna.

Thank you for considering my article idea. I have enclosed a self-addressed stamped envelope for your reply. I look forward to hearing from you soon.

Sincerely,

Cheryl Sloan Wray

EXHIBIT 12.3 SAMPLE QUERY LETTER

Cheryl Sloan Wray

000 Anywhere Road • Birmingham, AL 00000 • (205) 000-0000

July 12, 1995

Gary D. Suggs
Editor, *Senior Magazine*
3565 S. Higuera St.
San Luis Obispo, CA 93401

Dear Mr. Suggs,

The same old shirt and tie. A pretty—but not entirely useful—candy dish. Pot holders for the kitchen. A book you're not sure if the recipient has read or not.

Deciding what to give as Christmas gifts is a perpetual problem. Everyone wants to give something nice, but sometimes it's hard to come up with the perfect present. An easy answer is to use your creativity to make a special present with your own two hands. Gifts from the kitchen are perfect examples—they are creative, reasonably inexpensive, and totally appreciated. Who wouldn't want to receive a huge tin full of chocolate-covered delicacies, a basket full of custom-made drink mixes, or a collection of homemade salsas?

I have in mind an article for *Senior Magazine* tentatively titled "Christmas Gifts from the Kitchen." It would let readers know the benefits of giving food gifts at the holidays. Then it would provide specific ideas and recipes for various gifts. Some of the recipes included are Easy Chocolate Truffles, A Potpourri of Snack Mixes, Homemade Chunky Salsa, and Peppermint Cocoa Mix. The article would run approximately 1,000 words, although I can vary it according to your needs.

I am a freelance writer who has had approximately 150 articles published in a variety of magazines, including *Accent, Alabama Alumni, Atlanta Parent, ParentLife, Southern Hospitality*, and *The Student.* I also love to make and give food gifts for Christmas.

Thank you for considering my article idea. I look forward to hearing from you soon and have enclosed a SASE for that purpose.

Sincerely,

Cheryl Sloan Wray

EXHIBIT 12.4 SAMPLE QUERY LETTER

Cheryl Sloan Wray

000 Anywhere Road • Birmingham, AL 00000 • (205) 000-0000

July 23, 1995

Camille Pomaco
Editorial Director, *Quilting International*
All American Crafts, Inc.
243 Newton-Sparta Rd.
Newton, NJ 07860

Dear Ms. Pomaco,

What is the highest compliment paid to a quilter? An award given at a local arts and crafts show? A lucrative commercial business? Sincere thanks from people who prize her creations?

Quilter Yvonne Wells of Tuscaloosa, Alabama, recently received two compliments of a much higher order: the display of her work at the White House and the use of her work on a national line of greeting cards.

Wells, who's an elementary teacher full time, had a quilted Christmas ornament chosen for President and Mrs. Clinton's Christmas tree skirt last Christmas. Soon after, her quilt "Soul Sisters" was chosen to be featured on a Mother's Day card for Hallmark's Mahogany line (a line geared to African American consumers). Hallmark bought the rights to several other quilts, and they will soon be seen on more cards. Wells says she views herself not only as a quilter, but as a storyteller. "I could tell you what it [the "Soul Sisters" quilt] means to me, but my story is my story, and what people see is their interpretation and that's important to me," Wells says.

Would you be interested in a profile of Wells and her acclaimed work for *Quilting International?* It would focus on her two recent successes, as well as discuss her attitude toward quilting and her role as an African American artist. The article would run approximately 1200 words, although I can vary it according to your needs. I could also contribute photographs.

I am a full-time freelance writer who has had articles published in approximately 150 magazines, including *Alabama West, Atlanta Parent, ParentLife, Southern Hospitality*, and *The Student.*

Thank you for considering my article idea. I look forward to hearing from you soon (and have enclosed a SASE for your reply).

Sincerely,

Cheryl Sloan Wray

Paragraph 3: A Little about Yourself • Take the opportunity to tell the editor why you are the person to write the article. Provide information about where you have previously been published. If you don't have any credits (and there's absolutely nothing wrong with that), explain your connection to or expertise with the article topic. If you're proposing an article about dieting and you just lost ninety pounds, for example, that shows your personal experience with the topic.

Paragraph 4: A Last-Minute Sell and Niceties • Thank the editor for taking the time to read your query. Encourage him or her again to consider your idea ("I look forward to hearing from you soon" or "May I send the article to you?"). Don't forget to say you have included a self-addressed-stamped-envelope for his or her reply.

Why a Query Letter?

A query letter—at least a good one—does take time and energy to write. Time and energy, you might think, that could be better spent working on your actual magazine article. Many new writers have this attitude. Many ask me, "Why don't I just send my entire article in to the magazine and let them judge it for itself?" If you stop and think about it, there are two very good, practical reasons for writing query letters. These reasons will actually aid you in selling more of your magazine articles.

D. H. Lawrence grew up near the mines in Nottingham, England, part of a very poor family. He got no encouragement from his father. His mother, however, refused to let her son work in the mines and encouraged him to educate himself and to write.

First of all, editors are busy people. It's much easier for them to find the time to read a query letter than an entire manuscript. A good query letter should give them an idea (in a minute or two) as to whether your article is for them or not. Sending a query is a professional courtesy; most editors prefer them today.

Secondly, writers are busy people. By sending a query letter first, you can save a lot of time. If it turns out that no one is interested in your article idea, you have not wasted time writing an article that will sit on your desk collecting dust. Once you get a go-ahead from an editor (the message that he or she liked your query and now wants to see your entire manuscript), then you can write the article.

One word of caution while we're on the subject: don't write a query letter for an article you can't write. You don't want to get stuck in a situation where an editor wants your article, but you don't know how to write it. Make sure your article idea is doable; if you can do some preliminary research that doesn't take too much time, go ahead and do that. You want to be able to deliver on your promises to an editor.

The Winning Query Letter

Your query letter is a winning one if it

- **Fits in with the market.** Make sure that your article idea matches the magazine's editorial needs.
- **Is quick and to-the-point.** Don't bore the editor with every detail of your article idea. Present the general idea in an interesting way. Remember, your query is just one of many on the editor's desk.
- **Is convincing.** Does it make the editor feel that he needs to read your manuscript? Does it make your article sound interesting, compelling, emotional, or otherwise necessary?
- **Shows that you're the person to write the article.** You need to sell yourself, as well as the article. Let the editor see that you have the inside track on this topic.
- **Is professional.** Double-check your grammar, spelling, and punctuation before you send the query letter out in the mail. Make sure you are sending it to the proper editor at the right address. Check that it looks neat and clean.
- **Promises something you can deliver.** You must be able to write the magazine article in a reasonable amount of time following a go-ahead. Be honest in your proposal to an editor.

For a quick query checklist, see Exhibit 12.5.

Results of Your Query

The day you put your first query letter in the mailbox is an exciting one. You have taken one more step along the path to publication. You have put your work out there to be judged by someone else. But it is not the last step. Your query letter can have a variety of results. It might result in any one of the following scenarios.

Nothing • After all the hard work you have put into writing the query letter, there are times when you will get no response. Perhaps your letter is sitting in the middle of a big pile of query letters at a very busy magazine office, maybe it was sent to a magazine that no longer accepts freelance material, or maybe it is being dealt with by a very slow editor.

Don't let a lack of response get to you. Determine an amount of time you will allow for responses—four to six weeks is usually a long enough time for a response (although some entries in *Writer's Market* will say a certain magazine takes longer)—and then write a short follow-up letter after the time has lapsed. Briefly ask about the state of your query; be polite. If you never get a response, pick out some more possible markets and send off some more query letters.

EXHIBIT 12.5 QUERY LETTER CHECKLIST

The following elements are all very important to consider when writing your query letter. Put a check next to the ones for which you can answer "Yes." If you can't answer in the affirmative, you need to work on that element.

Does my idea fit the magazine? _____

Is the query tailored to fit the magazine? _____

Is it one page long? _____

Is it quick and to-the-point? _____

Does it catch the editor's attention? _____

Is it interesting to read? _____

Does it accurately say what the article will cover? _____

Does it provide specific factual information about the article? _____

Does it show why I should be the one to write the article? _____

Is it accurate and professional? _____

Have I double checked for any mistakes? _____

Does it have a "sell" in the last paragraph? _____

After reading it, does the editor *need* to buy my article? _____

Rejection • It's a fact of a writer's life: rejection will come your way. You simply cannot let it discourage you. I often tell new writers that if they get a 10 percent acceptance rate on their query letters, they are doing great. That means that 90 percent of your query letters will be rejected.

Yes, writing is hard work. The excitement you feel, however, when your query letters begin to be accepted on a more regular basis will make up for any discouragement you may have felt at one time! As time goes by, your success rate will go up. The key is to learn how to write a good query letter and to send out plenty of them.

A Go-Ahead • This is the type of acceptance you will most likely experience. If an editor likes your idea, he or she will tell you to "go ahead" and send it to her. This does not automatically mean your article will be accepted, but the editor is willing to take a look at it.

A go-ahead is a reason to celebrate, but remember that you must take your writing to the next step. You must begin the work on your article and get it back to the editor as soon as you can (make a point to get your completed articles back to the editor within a month of your go-ahead).

A Firm Assignment • Fewer magazine writers get these, although established ones often do. Getting a firm assignment means that the editor knows he will like your article and goes ahead and assigns you the article. You, in essence, have a contract for your article. With firm assignments, you will have a specific deadline and you must make sure you meet it.

MANUSCRIPT SUBMISSION

You sent a query to *Whatever Magazine*, and a glorious four weeks later you received word that the editor wants to see your article. After completing your article (following the guidelines discussed in previous chapters), it's time to send it in. But can you just dash it out of your printer and send it any way you see fit? No. There is a specific way to submit manuscripts to magazines.

Manuscript submission is another step in the writing process that separates the professional from the unprofessional writer. A properly prepared and professional-looking manuscript may take your article one more step toward your goal of publication.

So what does an editor want? Before we discuss the specifics of how your manuscript should be set up, let's talk about some general rules of submission.

Marks of a Quality Submission

The following guidelines are very basic ones. If you adhere to them, an editor will find it easy and pleasant to read your manuscript.

Submit a Readable Manuscript • You should always submit a typewritten or computer-produced manuscript (never send anything handwritten).

- Use quality paper that doesn't smudge.
- Make sure the print can be read without any problem. That means that you want your type to be dark (make sure your typewriter or printer's ribbon is dark or, if you use a dot-matrix printer, that it uses a high number of pins) and relatively large (10 or 12 point).
- Leave at least one-inch margins on all sides of your manuscript; this keeps your page from being drowned in print.
- Double-space the body of your article; this keeps the editor from straining his or her eyes.

Submit a Correct Manuscript • Have it as your goal to make your article technically perfect. Check and recheck your grammar, spelling, and punctuation. Make sure that no sections are missing and no sentences are incomplete. This is your final chance to sell your article to the editor—make it look as good as possible!

Include a Cover Letter • Use business-letter format in writing the cover letter (type everything flush left; single space the letter copy; double space between paragraphs; sign your signature, with the name typed beneath it).

Your cover letter should briefly reintroduce yourself and your article to the editor. Mention your previous query letter and the editor's interest in your article. Show again your enthusiasm for being published in that particular magazine, and close by thanking the editor for considering your work. Enclose a SASE for the editor to return his or her reply. Exhibit 12.6 on page 145 provides you with an example of a cover letter.

Keep a Copy of the Manuscript • Make sure you are not sending your only copy of the article. If it gets lost in the mail or you receive no response, you want to have a backup copy on hand.

The Format of Your Manuscript

Exhibit 12.7 on page 146 shows what the first, second (and subsequent), and last pages of your manuscript should look like. In putting your manuscript together, the key again is readability.

- In the top left-hand corner of your first page, type your name, address, phone number, and social security number in a block. Skip a line and type the article's approximate word count.
- Drop down one-third of the page and type the article's title, centered on the line. Skip a line and center the word "by" and your name.
- Drop approximately four more lines and begin your article.

EXHIBIT 12.6 SAMPLE COVER LETTER

Cheryl Sloan Wray

000 Anywhere Road • Birmingham, AL 00000 • (205) 000-0000

August 31, 1995

Gina Howard
Editor, *The Student*
127 Ninth Ave. N.
Nashville, TN 37234

Dear Ms. Howard,

Thank you for your positive response to my query letter concerning an article on environmental awareness for *The Student*. Enclosed is the article for your consideration. It is tentatively titled "Responsible for the Earth" and runs approximately 1,500 words in length. I have also enclosed several photographs of college students involved in environmental activities.

As I mentioned in my query letter, I am a freelance magazine writer who has had articles published in approximately 150 various publications. While a graduate student, I was involved in a number of campus-oriented environmental groups and activities.

Thanks again for your interest in my article. I look forward to hearing from you soon and have enclosed an SASE for your reply.

Sincerely,

Cheryl Sloan Wray

- Leave space enough at the bottom of the page (approximately three lines above your one-inch margin) to type the word "MORE." This lets the reader know that there is more copy to come. You continue to say "MORE" until the last page.
- At the top of the rest of the pages, put a one or two word "slug" for your article. A slug is an abbreviated version of your title. If, for example, your article title was "The How-tos of A Second Marriage" you might want to make your slug "Second Marriage." The slug on these other pages ensures that, if the pages of your manuscript get separated, the editor will know with which article they belong.
- On the final page, drop four to six lines after the final line and type "END."

EXHIBIT 12.7 SAMPLE FIRST, SECOND, AND FINAL PAGE FOR ARTICLE SUBMISSION

Cheryl Sloan Wray
0000 Anywhere Road
Birmingham, AL 00000
(205) 000-0000
Social Security #: 000-00-0000

Approximate word count: 1,000 words

"Shopping Smart: A Parent's Guide to Consignment Stores"

by Cheryl Sloan Wray

It's a beautiful, crisp Saturday. Jennifer wishes she could stay home and work in her yard, but instead she dreads her planned activity for the day—shopping. Looking longingly at the sun-filled sky, Jennifer realizes, however, that eleven-month-old Emma desperately needs summer clothes. She might as well grit her teeth and get the shopping done.

After a day at the local shopping mall, Jennifer comes home tired and depressed. Besides spending all day indoors, Jennifer spent her regular amount of money shopping—*too much!* Although she knows that quality children's clothes come with a price, Jennifer still cringes at the thought that she got only seven items (two dresses, a romper, a pair of denim shorts, a T-shirt with Emma's favorite cartoon character, a bathing suit, and a pair of pajamas), and they cost her $142.

It's the same gorgeous day, but Carla is actually looking forward to shopping for summer clothes for her eleven-month-old daughter, Lacy.

(MORE)

EXHIBIT 12.7 (CONT'D)

Wray/ Consignment Shopping/ Page 2

Instead of spending hours at the local department stores, Carla anticipates shopping at some of her favorite consignment shops. The main reason, however, that she does not dread her day is that she knows she'll get some good deals. She will probably even come home with money to spare!

When Carla gets home, she has a smile on her face. She bought seven items similar to Jennifer's but spent only $27. She even got a dress and a new necklace for herself (and they only added $16 to her bill)!

Chances are that your shopping attitudes and habits more closely resemble Jennifer's than Carla's. Still, many mothers have discovered Carla's shopping secrets. They know that consignment stores are the best places to shop thriftily for a child's wardrobe and other items, and they know the techniques necessary to get the best buys.

Consignment shops are the newest and hottest trend in thrift shopping today. Most large cities have countless consignment shops; they are even arriving in the smallest of communities. The Potomoc area itself has approximately 50 consignment shops.

Consignment shops are unique in that the items for sale come from previous items. The items, however, are not what you would typically call "used." Most store owners take only quality items; usually items have been worn only a few times, and sometimes customers may find items with price tags still on them.

"Consignment shops are great because you can get name brands at

(MORE)

EXHIBIT 12.7 (CONT'D)

Wray/ Consignment Shopping/ Page 5

wear a dress! When trying to decide whether to buy an item, analyze what your child has to wear with it, whether buying it would require extra alterations or other work, and whether or not you're just fascinated by the deep discount.

(4) *Make your items easy to sell.* If you are considering putting your items in a consignment shop, keep in mind what you, as a shopper, like to buy. You like items that are in style and that are in good condition. When taking your items to a store, clean and iron them. Make them as presentable as possible (store owners, after all, don't have to take your items).

(5) *Get to know the store's owners.* It's very important, as both a shopper and consigner, to get to know the owners of the establishment. This will allow you to get early announcements on specials, and you can ask the owners to look out for specific items for you. One consignment store owner says that her relationships with both customers and consigners is the most important part of her job. "When you are truthful and friendly with them," she says, "you build a better and more constant clientele."

By discovering the benefits of consignment stores and being a well-organized shopper, you should be able to find excellent deals on your next shopping trip. When you come home with a Guess outfit for $7 and a French Toast dress for $12, you may be converted to shopping the thrifty way. (And your daughter will look like a million bucks!)

(END)

MULTIPLE MARKETING

One of the most common questions among new writers concerning manuscript submission is, "Can I submit the same article to more than one magazine?" My answer is an emphatic YES—with a few guidelines.

You want to be an ethical writer. Therefore, you should never submit the exact same article to competing magazines (magazines that have the same audience, such as *Family Circle* and *Woman's Day*). You can, however, have the same article published in noncompeting magazines, and you can certainly give the same topic different slants for similar magazines.

Slanting a topic is a wonderful skill to learn if you want to be an expert marketer of your work. By taking a different angle on a topic or just by rewording an article to fit in with a different audience, you can make much more money from your writing. You want to learn to sell a piece as many times as possible. To do so, you must learn several secrets about multiple marketing.

Learn about All the Possible Magazines for Publication

This goes back to one of the foundational tools we have talked about throughout this book: be a student of the markets. Always be aware of the various outlets you have before you. If you automatically think first of the national magazine, take the opportunity to dig a little deeper. Which local or regional publications might be interested? Which specialty magazines might be appropriate?

Let's take a real-life example. A few years ago, a young woman from my state (Alabama) named Heather Whitestone won the Miss America title. In the days and the year that followed, articles about her appeared in a variety of magazines. If a freelance writer had taken advantage of the situation, he or she could have sold articles in a huge number of different types of publications.

Articles could have been written for local, statewide, and regional newspapers and magazines (because of her southern status), and they could have been written for national publications (because Miss America is a contest of national interest). Articles could have been written for teenage magazines (because she is a good role model), for college magazines (because she was a college student at the time), and for women's magazines (because she had a lot to say about women's issues). Finally, articles could have been written for religious magazines (because she was a professing Christian), for arts magazines (because she was a gifted ballet dancer), and for disability magazines (because she was deaf).

Learn as Many Angles as Possible about Your Topic

To know which magazines are good markets, you must know different angles on your topic or different aspects of your subject's personality. With the Miss America subject, for example, you would have to know that she was a dancer, a Christian, a college student, and deaf to get all the possible angles.

To learn these different angles, you must perfect your skills as a researcher and an interviewer. Never see a topic or person from only one side. Research intensely to know your topic inside and out; ask your subject good questions on a variety of topics (not just the main one at hand).

Learn the Various Writing Styles of Your Target Magazines

You would never submit the exact same article to more than one magazine, because every magazine's style is different. If you learn the different styles, you can simply alter your article to fit that style. When you look at a magazine, ask yourself what tone its articles take. Is it informational and formal? Is it casual? Does it use a lot of anecdotes? Does it always use snappy leads? Use this information to slant your article in the appropriate style.

As you can see, multiple marketing is a valuable tool for the beginning writer. By learning to slant, you greatly increase your chances of being published!

THE TEN MAGIC RULES OF MARKETING

There are many aspiring writers who get past their lack of ideas and learn not to be afraid of the empty page. Many are able to complete a magazine article of which they are proud. They actually begin to think of themselves as magazine writers.

Those same aspiring writers, however, aren't able to market their articles effectively. By learning the basics of marketing—how to know the markets, how to write a query letter, how to submit a manuscript, and so forth—the process seems less foreboding. If you want to be a master marketer, remember the following "Ten Magic Rules of Marketing":

1. *Make sure your idea is marketable.* To sell your article it needs to be something that people will want to read. You must come up with ideas that will appeal to someone out there, whether that audience is women, woodworkers, or world travelers. And you must develop ideas that are marketable to specific magazines. If you want to be published, it's not worth your time to write an article that can't fit in any magazine. How do you know if your idea is marketable? Stop and ask yourself if there is a specific group of people who would be entertained by your idea, learn something from it, and so forth. Pretend that you are a reader. Does the topic interest you? If you have a trusted writing friend, use him or her as your idea sounding board. Ask him if it is a good idea. Finally, ask yourself if your idea is too narrow or too broad. Your idea might be okay if it is more thoroughly developed.

2. *Know to whom you're marketing your article.* This goes hand-in-hand with rule number 1. As you're writing your query letter or your article, always remember your audience. Keep a picture of a real-life reader in your mind and develop your article in a way that will appeal to that person. Yes, you are selling your article to an editor. But on another level—one which the editor understands inside and out—you are actually selling your article to readers. If the editor doesn't think his readers will be interested in your article, he won't buy it. Always keep your reader in the forefront of your mind.

3. *Get the editor's attention.* The first step in getting your article in print is planting a thought in the editor's mind. That thought might be: "This is quite a unique idea," "My readers would really get into this," or "This query has panache. Maybe the whole article will be this effective." Spend some time on your query letter. Don't just dash it out. Develop an attention-getting lead and think of specific ways you can make the editor think he or she *needs* your article. Then, spend plenty of time on your article. Again, develop an effective lead. Structure the article in a way similar to other articles in your target magazine. Keep your reader in mind and develop your article in a way that will teach that reader something, entertain him, or make him think about something in a new way. Spend time on every paragraph of your article so that the editor and reader will never lose interest. Finally, try to write a satisfying conclusion.

> *"There's literary creation and literary business. When I first got something accepted, it gave my life a validation it didn't otherwise have."*
>
> RAYMOND CARVER

4. *Use the proper form.* While an editor probably won't dismiss your article because you don't have the appropriate number of spaces after your byline, you do want to make your submission as professional as possible. Use some sort of consistent form and make your submission easy for the editor to understand.

5. *Send a SASE.* It's amazing how many editors in my survey complained about writers not sending SASEs with their query letters or manuscripts. If you don't send a SASE, the editor may assume that you're not seriously interested in succeeding as a magazine writer. All businesses have their traditions and courtesies. The SASE is a courtesy in magazine writing.

6. *Do what you promise.* If your query letter says you will interview a national expert for your article, interview him or her. If you say you

will write a 1500-word article, you had better not run out of ideas after 850 words. When you tell an editor your article will be of a certain type, that is the article the editor expects. By not delivering what you promise you are making your article less marketable to that specific magazine.

7. *Don't just market once.* Learn the art of multiple marketing. Get into the habit so much, in fact, that you never develop an idea that can only be marketed once. The ratio between time spent on an article and money made in publications will be much more to your advantage if you do so.
8. *Keep track of your marketing efforts.* Your efforts to get published will run a lot more smoothly if you keep track of your marketing. The easiest way to do this is to set up a submission log. Write down where you have sent query letters and manuscripts and what type of responses you receive. When you get something published, keep copies of payment stubs. (For more information on keeping records and tax information, look to Chapter 14.)
9. *Make it to the mailbox.* While it's very obvious, this is the most *magical* key to getting published. If you never send anything out, you will never get published. Set goals and find the time to sit down and accomplish them.
10. *Don't let fear get in your way.* There has never been a truer saying than, "The only thing we have to fear is fear itself." When you let fear hold you back, you are giving it power it should never have. When you have the right attitude, there is actually very little to fear about sending out a query letter or a magazine article. Okay, maybe your attempt could be rejected, maybe an editor will tell you what's wrong with your article, or maybe other people will begin to expect results out of you. But let's face it. If your query is rejected, *you* haven't been rejected, your first attempts at writing have. These editors don't know you. They don't dislike you. You simply don't fit their needs at the present. As you continue to write and your writing improves, you will fit in with their needs. You will be published. And about those people in your life who begin to expect results, the ones who want to see you fail so they can say "I told you so"—people who belittle other people's dreams don't deserve your worry. Find yourself one or two people who can support you, and then believe in yourself. If you want to write and dream of being published, you must, despite fear, learn to market yourself.

Jumpstart Exercises

1. Familiarize yourself with the way the *Writer's Market* is set up. Take one of the entries and analyze all the information it provides.
2. Select an idea you have developed while reading this book (or select the article you completed in Chapter 8). Find five magazines in *Writer's Market* that you could consider target magazines for the article. Pick one of these five magazines and send off for writer's guidelines.
3. Choose one of the queries from Exhibits 12.2–12.4. Analyze each paragraph. On a piece of paper, describe what each paragraph tries to accomplish. Do you think the query is effective?
4. Using the same idea as above, write a query letter to one of the five magazines you selected.
5. Taking an idea you have developed (from this chapter or an earlier one), come up with five different angles you could take on the same topic.
6. Locate an article from any magazine. Write down at least five other slants that could be taken on the topic. Write down five other magazines for which the article could be written.
7. Are you afraid of submitting your material? What is holding you back? Write a list of anything you are afraid of in relation to marketing your writing. Take a look at the list. Are these practical fears? How can you overcome them?

CHAPTER THIRTEEN

TWENTY-FIVE GREAT MAGAZINES FOR BEGINNING WRITERS

We have all heard the old truism that you can't get a job until you have experience, but you can't get experience unless you get a job. It's the old catch-22. It seems that there are catch-22s in all aspects of life (you can't stop the dating routine until you get married, but you can't get married unless you're dating; you want to relax and enjoy the good things in life, but to enjoy the good things you have to work all the time). Well, I have some good news for you. The old catch-22 doesn't necessarily apply to beginning magazine writers.

A big complaint of many beginning magazine writers is that they can't get published because they have never had anything published. They find a magazine they want to write for listed in the *Writer's Market,* but its entry says that the magazine must see clips of previously published work along with a query. They get rejection letters with notes from editors that say something like, "We only work with writers we have worked with before."

There are many magazines that do operate in that manner. It's true that many magazines (especially the ones with high circulations) want to know what articles you have previously published and that many magazines like to work with regular writers. Think back, however, to our survey of the magazine field in Chapter 2. There are more than three thousand magazines in operation today, and almost all of them need freelance writers to write their articles. Logistically, every one of these magazines can't expect to have the few, vastly experienced, professional, full-time magazine writers in America writing for them.

When you look more closely at the magazine field, you find that there are many magazines (much of the small ones, but even a few of the big ones) who rely on new writers. To these magazines, the key is not whether you have been published elsewhere or not. They key is whether you can write competently and professionally for them. The job you are doing for them at the present is the only job that is of interest to them.

If you don't believe that there are magazines out there willing to take a chance on new writers, do a little homework. First, visit your local magazine rack as you did when you began reading this book. Reacquaint yourself with the huge number of magazines on the market today. Look at the highly specialized magazines on the racks. Read the writer biographies at the end of the articles; very few of them boast that the writer of the article has been published in two hundred magazines.

Then, browse through the *Writer's Market*. Yes, you will find those magazines that require clips of published work and that "only rely on professional, tested writers." Look, however, at the number of entries that don't even mention a requirement of publication. Most of them simply tell you how to send your idea or article in. There are even those editors who say something like, "I'm always eager to work with new writers."

> *"No one else in the wide world, since the dawn of time, has even seen the world as you do, or can explain it as you can. This is what you have to offer that no one else can. Nobody can know how good you are unless you risk letting them know how bad you might be."*
>
> EDITH LAYTON

When I'm preparing an article for submission, I often run across entries like that. One day, I got curious. How many of those magazines actually work with beginning writers? Do they regularly take chances on new writers (perhaps writers who have never been published before)? Can I provide some consolation and motivation to those new writer friends of mine afraid of sending out their first article?

After sending a questionnaire out to more than one hundred magazines, I learned that, yes, there are many magazines willing to work with new writers. There are even those *eager* to do so—several editors told me that they enjoy discovering fresh voices and are proud to have their magazine be the first place a new writer is published.

In doing my survey of magazines, I sent out questionnaires to 131 magazines. These magazines were selected on the basis of two things: (1) their entries in the *1995 Writer's Market* did not say that it was a requirement to send published credits, and (2) the editor made some remark about being "eager" or "open" to working with new writers.

My questionnaire asked such questions as:

- How much of your material is written by freelance writers?
- How much and when do you pay freelance writers?
- What is your attitude toward working with new writers?
- What are your major criteria for giving a positive response to a query or article?
- What tips would you give to new writers?

From the responses I received, I have compiled a list of twenty-five great magazines for new writers. Some are well-known and have high circulations, while others are regional magazines known only in their area. Some are specialized and may not meet your needs. Others are very small in circulation.

The key, however, is that the magazines' editors are willing to give new writers a chance. The consensus from talking to the various editors seems to be that all writers are given equal consideration at these publications—

it's the quality of your idea, your presentation, and your writing that count!

Read through the following list and see if any of your ideas fit with any of these magazines.

Highlights for Children

Description:	Monthly magazine for children ages two to twelve. Accepts nonfiction on topics like science, technology, nature, sports, biographies, and general interest; fiction including picture stories and stories for beginning readers.
Circulation:	2.8 million
Editor:	Kent L. Grown, Jr.
Freelance Facts:	About 74 percent freelance written; says they use new freelance writers "very often." Pays $100 and up on acceptance. Gives byline and sometimes writer I.D.
Tips:	"Study the magazine. Research for nonfiction should be impeccable." Says the fact that the query or manuscript fits into magazine's editorial plan, that it is a unique idea, and that the writing is of quality are all of top priority.

Kiwanis

Description:	Published ten times a year for business and professional persons and their families. Publishes nonfiction articles about social and civic betterment, small-business concerns, science, education, religion, family, youth, health, and recreation.
Circulation:	276,000
Editor:	Chuck Jonak
Freelance Facts:	80 percent of feature articles are freelance written; editor says, "always interested in query letters with fresh angles from freelancers who previously have not been published in *Kiwanis*." Pays $400–$1,000 on acceptance. Bylines are given. Often makes assignments.
Tips:	"Study our writer's guidelines and a sample copy and then present a viable feature idea." Says that an article that fits into magazine's editorial plan, a unique idea, and quality writing are the main criteria for a positive response to query or manuscript.

The Upper Room

Description:	Bimonthly magazine providing a daily inspirational message, including a Bible reading, text, prayer,

	"Thought for the Day," and suggestion for further prayer.
Circulation:	2.3 million
Editor:	Mary Lou Redding (Managing Ed.)
Freelance Facts:	94 percent freelance written; editor says, "Our magazine is a particularly good place for beginning writers to attempt publication because we enjoy publishing 'the first thing I have ever sold.' Since we want variety in the meditations published in the magazine, we search continually for new contributors." Adds, "Good writing, not a long resume, is what gets our attention." Pays on publication $15 for each 250-word meditation. Gives bylines.
Tips:	"Know the market. Read and study the Bible and write about how it connects with your daily life. Write from your personal, unique perspective on scripture and living the Christian life. Be familiar with our magazine and send material that requires little editing."

Humpty Dumpty

Description:	Bimonthly magazine for children ages four to six; main topics covered include health, nutrition, hygiene, exercise, and safety. Publishes nonfiction, fiction, and poetry.
Circulation:	250,000
Editor:	Janet Flynn Hoover
Freelance Facts:	85 percent freelance written; Hoover says staff is "very open" to working with new freelance writers. Pays up to 22 cents per word on publication. Gives byline to articles.
Tips:	"Read editorial guidelines (free with SASE). Read and study several issues of the magazine."

INsider Magazine

Description:	Monthly magazine covering topics of general interest for college students. Publishes nonfiction, photos, and fillers.
Circulation:	1.1 million
Editor:	Alex Gordon
Freelance Facts:	40 percent freelance written; editor says, "We welcome all new writers and look forward to developing relationships with writers early in their careers." Pays 1 to 3 cents per word on publication. Gives byline and writer I.D.; often assigns articles.

Tips:	"Come up with a unique or timely idea that will appeal to our audience (eighteen- to twenty-nine-year-olds) and be able to back it up with facts and interviews."

Live

Description:	Weekly magazine for adults in Assemblies of God Sunday schools. Accepts nonfiction, photos, fiction, and poetry. Nonfiction is usually written in narrative mode and emphasizes some phase of Christian living in a down-to-earth manner.
Circulation:	150,000
Editor:	Paul W. Smith
Freelance Facts:	100 percent freelance written; Smith says "We appreciate any well-written freelance articles, whether written by a new writer or not" and publishes first-time writers "frequently." Pays 3 cents per word. Gives byline.
Tips:	"Study our publication as to focus and emphasis and pay attention to whether article fits into our editorial plan, the timeliness of the issue, and the quality of your writing."

Your Home

Description:	Monthly in-house magazine of Meridian International, Inc. that covers home/garden subjects. Nonfiction articles cover fresh ideas in home decor, home construction, the outdoors at home, remodeling projects, home management, and home buying and selling.
Circulation:	150,000
Editor:	Attn. Editorial Staff
Freelance Facts:	75 percent freelance written; writer guidelines claim, "We are dependent on freelance writers; if they can meet our unique slant, then we are excited about it." Pays 15 cents per word (maximum 1,000 words) on acceptance. Gives byline.
Tips:	"Request guidelines, study them closely, request copies of back issues and study them. If you can understand our target marketing magazine slant, you have an in."

WordPerfect Magazine

Description:	Monthly magazine of how-to articles for users of various WordPerfect computer software. Topics include step-by-step applications, humor, interview/company profile, new product, and technical.
Circulation:	210,000

Editor:	Lisa Downs Bearnson
Freelance Facts:	40 percent freelance written; Bearnson says, "If they can get our format down quick and provide accurate keystrokes, we like them!" and estimates they use first-time writers at least eight times a year. Pays $500–$800 on acceptance. Gives bylines.
Tips:	"Know WordPerfect well. Know the DOS environment. Learn how to write technical material in a friendly way."

Vegetarian Gourmet

Description:	Quarterly magazine on seasonal vegetarian cooking and low-fat issues. Accepts nonfiction (cooking how-to, book and restaurant reviews), photos, columns, and departments.
Circulation:	112,000
Editor:	Jessica Dubey
Freelance Facts:	85 percent freelance written; editor reports, "We are open to working with any writers, including new freelance writers, who show an interest in our publication and an ability to write." Pays on publication up to $250 for full-length articles of six hundred to eight hundred words with eight or nine recipes; up to $175 for department-size articles of three hundred to five hundred words. Gives byline and writer I.D.
Tips:	"Submit quality manuscripts, following our suggested guidelines, and be willing to work with our editorial team. Recipes must be vegetarian. We prefer those that are relatively low in fat."

MuscleMag International

Description:	Monthly magazine for sixteen- to sixty-year-old men and women interested in physical fitness and overall body improvement. Takes informational, how-to, personal experience, interview, profile, inspirational, humor, historical, expose, nostalgia, personal opinion, and new product topics.
Circulation:	300,000
Editor:	Robert Fortney (Assistant Ed.)
Freelance Facts:	About 60 percent freelance written; editor says they are "very open to new fresh writers" and that they publish first-time writers "quite frequently; if somebody has something useful to say, we let them say it." Pays

	$200–$350 for articles of fourteen hundred to two thousand words. Pays on acceptance and gives bylines and writer I.D.
Tips:	"Take note of the subject matter and steer the article in the proper direction. Write from the viewpoint of the reader—what does he/she want to see?"

Career Woman

Description:	Triannual magazine covering career guidance for college women. Wants career-related articles describing the how-tos of obtaining a professional position and advancing a career.
Circulation:	10,500
Editor:	Eileen Nester
Freelance Facts:	90–95 percent freelance written; editor says, "I am extremely open to working with new freelance writers, and I encourage all submissions." Publishes first-time writers for her magazine in every issue. Pays 10 cents per word on publication. Gives byline and writer I.D. Sometimes makes assignments.
Tips:	"Read back issues of the magazine to see which topics have already been explored. Try to find a unique approach to a traditional career-guidance topics. Approach the subject as if you're sharing advice with a few close friends. I like a light, upbeat writing style."

The Family Digest

Description:	Bimonthly magazine for the Catholic family. Publishes nonfiction on family life, parish life, how-to, seasonal, inspirational, prayer life, and Catholic traditions.
Circulation:	150,000
Editor:	Corine B. Erlandson
Freelance Facts:	About 80 percent freelance written; editor says, "*The Family Digest* publishes at least ten freelance written articles in each issue. I'm very open to reviewing freelance submissions." Pays 5 cents a word (not to surpass one thousand words or $60) on acceptance. Gives byline and writer I.D.
Tips:	"Send a 6 x 9 SASE with 55 cents postage for a copy of our writer's guidelines and a sample copy of the magazine. Also, I prefer to see the actual manuscript rather than a query."

Wired

Description:	Monthly magazine covering technology and digital culture. Covers the digital revolution and related advances in computers, communications, and lifestyles.
Circulation:	180,000
Editor:	Louis Rossetto
Freelance Facts:	90 percent freelance written; editor says, "always looking for good new writers" and submission guidelines proclaim, "We seek young and new voices." Payment is on publication and rates vary. Byline and writer I.D. given.
Tips:	"We know a lot about digital computers and we are bored with them. Tell us something about them we have never heard before, in a way we have never read before. If it challenges our assumptions, so much the better. Give it to us in electronic form or on paper. Microsoft Word for Macintosh is best."

Senior Magazine

Description:	Monthly magazine to inform and entertain the "over fifty" audience. Nonfiction topics include historical/nostalgic, humor, inspirational, personal experience, and travel.
Circulation:	240,000
Editor:	George Brand
Freelance Facts:	50 percent freelance written; Brand says attitude toward working with new freelance writers is "positive" and that magazine "frequently" publishes first-time writers. Pays $1.50 per inch on publication. Gives byline and writer I.D. Sometimes makes assignments.
Tips:	"Don't waste words. Be grammatically correct."

Jack and Jill

Description:	Magazine published eight times a year for children ages seven to ten. Emphasizes health, safety, exercise, and nutrition topics.
Circulation:	334,000
Editor:	Daniel Lee
Freelance Facts:	70 percent freelance written; editor says they are "open" to working with new freelance writers. Pays 17 cents per word on publication. Gives byline.

Tips:	"Always looking for nonpreaching health and fitness material directed to kids ages seven to ten. Study the magazine to learn our style."

Florida Living Magazine

Description:	Monthly lifestyle magazine covering Florida subjects for Floridians and would-be Floridians. Nonfiction topics include general Florida interest, historical/nostalgic, interview/profile, personal experience, travel, and out-of-the-way Florida places.
Circulation:	41,000
Editor:	Holly M. Hays
Freelance Facts:	60 percent freelance written; editor says, "We welcome new freelancers with clear, concise writing styles." Also notes that first-time writers are often published in the "Our Heritage" section. Payment is 5 cents per word on publication. Byline is given.
Tips:	"Read our magazine, submit only sharp photos, and avoid clichés."

Pockets

Description:	Monthly magazine. Christian, nondenominational publication for children ages six to twelve. Accepts nonfiction (interview/profile, religious, personal experience), photos, columns and departments, fiction, and poetry.
Circulation:	94,000
Editor:	Janet R. Knight
Freelance Facts:	About 66 percent freelance written; editor says, "We are happy to work with new freelance writers. Several writers have indicated that we were the first magazine to publish them." Pays 12 cents per word for most articles on acceptance. Gives byline.
Tips:	"Know the magazine and its purpose. Write about children resolving issues and not about adults doing so for them. Avoid stereotypes of all kinds."

Atlanta Parent

Description:	Monthly regional tabloid covering parenting of children from birth to fourteen years old. Nonfiction topics include general interest, how-to, humor, interview/profile, and travel. Are also special theme issues each year.

Circulation: 61,000

Editor: Liz White

Freelance Facts: 90 percent freelance written; White says, "We're always looking for new freelance writers who can write. We're glad to work with them. However, everything that is submitted to us is on spec, and many new freelance writers don't understand that." Pays $15–$30 per article. Gives byline.

Tips: "Write clear, crisp query letters. Give idea of number of words, what will be included in article, and writing credits if have them. Understand the long turn-around time on articles." Also notes that the fit of the idea into the magazine's editorial plan is the top priority in making a positive response to a query letter or manuscript.

> *"Convince yourself that you are working in clay not marble, on paper not eternal bronze: let that first sentence be as stupid as it wishes. No one will rush out and print it as it stands. Just put it down; then another."*
>
> JACQUES BARZUN

Antique Review

Description: Monthly tabloid for an antique-oriented readership. Nonfiction articles concern history and production of furniture, pottery, china, and other quality Americana. Also on antique shows and auctions.

Circulation: 10,000

Editor: Charles Muller

Freelance Facts: 65 percent freelance written; Muller says working with new writers "can lead to long-term positive relationship. We enjoy it." Pays $100–200 on publication. Gives byline and makes assignments.

Tips: "Know your subject first-hand and not just from secondary sources. Gather original material. Too many would-be writers only reconfigure information already readily available."

The Woman's Journal

Description: Monthly tabloid covering professional women's issues. Nonfiction topics include humor, interview/profile, opinion, photo feature, and travel.

Circulation: 15,000

Editor: Wendy Waller

Freelance Facts: 90 percent freelance written; editor says attitude toward working with new freelance writers is "posi-

	tive." Pays 5 cents a word on publication. Gives byline and writer I.D.
Tips:	"Do your homework. Send material we can use." Also says that top criteria for a positive response includes an article's timeliness, its fitting into the editorial plan, and the writing quality.

Junior Trails

Description:	Weekly tabloid covering religious fiction, and biographical, historical, and scientific articles with a spiritual emphasis for boys and girls ages ten to eleven.
Circulation:	65,000
Editor:	Sinda S. Zinn
Freelance Facts:	98 percent freelance written; editor says, "I don't consider whether the writer is new or not." Pays 2–3 cents per word on acceptance. Gives byline.
Tips:	"Follow the guidelines, consider the audience, draw the reader into it (don't bore the reader)." Also stresses that the magazine doesn't accept query letters; manuscripts should fit into editorial plan, be timely, be a unique idea, have quality writing, and have a spiritual emphasis.

Accent on Living

Description:	Quarterly magazine for physically disabled persons and rehabilitation professionals. Nonfiction articles about new devices for disabled persons, medical breakthroughs; how-to articles on everyday living with specific, helpful information.
Circulation:	19,000
Editor:	Betty Garee
Freelance Facts:	80 percent freelance written; Garee says, "We are happy to work with quality writers, whatever the experience level" and that they publish first-time writers "very often." Pays 10 cents a word on publication. Gives byline.
Tips:	"*Accent* readers prefer an informal rather than an academic approach. Effective organization of ideas is important. The successful writer must be willing to cut, polish, check, rewrite, and condense."

Virtue

Description:	Bimonthly Christian magazine for women. Nonfiction

articles are about and by "women who seek candidly and honestly to inspire, challenge, encourage, and affirm one another. Also accepts poetry, fiction, and material for departments.

Circulation: 135,000

Editor: Nancie Carmichael

Freelance Facts: 60 percent freelance written; editor says attitude toward working with new freelance writers is "good—we depend on fresh voices." Managing editor estimates that they use first-time writers about twenty-five times a year. Pays 15 to 25 cents a word on acceptance (for assigned work) and on publication (for unsolicited material). Gives byline and writer I.D.

FROM THE EDITOR'S DESK

"Know the magazine and its purpose. Don't make conclusions too easy. Avoid stereotypes of all kinds."

JANET KNIGHT, *POCKETS*

Tips: Stresses that the development of a good idea is essential. "Writing is technical. It's the development of ideas that is difficult to get!" "For the best way of knowing what we look for, see what we have done. Write for a sample issue of the magazine."

Mothering

Description: Quarterly magazine looking at parenting from an "alternative," healthful, and enlightening way. Accepts nonfiction articles on six regular topics—the art of mothering (the inspirational and spiritual side of nurturing), health, a child's world, pregnancy, birth and midwifery, ways of learning, and family living.

Circulation: 67,000

Freelance Facts: Almost 100 percent freelance written; editor says, "Our magazine is based on a foundation of reader-submitted articles. We welcome unsolicited articles." Payment and time of payment varies.

Tips: "Familiarize yourself with *Mothering*. We are more likely to publish your article if you are familiar with the issues we discuss."

Bride's

Description: Bimonthly magazine for brides, her family and friends, the groom, and his family and friends. Accepts nonfic-

	tion articles on issues related to marriage. Topics include: wedding planning, marriage communication, in-laws, money issues, career issues, sex, step-parenting, religion, family planning, second marriages, engagement problems, marital problems and solutions, and reaffirmation of vows. Also accepts material for departments.
Circulation:	400,000
Editor:	Andrea Feld (Managing Ed.)
Freelance Facts:	40 percent freelance written; editor says magazine is eager to work with new or unpublished writers. Pays $300–800 on acceptance. Gives byline.
Tips:	Likes articles that are "well-researched, relying on quotes from authorities in the field and anecdotes and dialogue from real couples." Guidelines say, "Send us a query or a well-written article that is both easy to read and offers real help for the bride or groom as she/he adjusts to his/her new role. No first-person narratives on wedding and reception planning, home furnishings, cooking, fashion, beauty, travel." Note to send articles to Features Department.

FINDING OPEN MARKETS

The willingness of these magazines to work with new writers is evidence of the wide-open market available today. New writers need only to keep their eyes and mind open to the possibilities. One of the best ways to stay in tune with publishing possibilities is to know the magazine trends. Some writers seem to instinctively understand the trends—they always seem to know when and where to send their magazine articles. It's not some inborn instinct, however. It's an acquired knack for knowing where to look, and it's something that all new writers can learn.

The first trick is to always be up-to-date on the markets. Always have the latest edition of marketing information available to you (whether it's *Writer's Market, Literary Marketplace,* or some other reference guide). Then, keep in touch with the changes in the markets that happen more frequently than once a year (which is when the reference guides are updated). To do this, read magazines about writing and the magazine industry (*Writer's Digest, The Writer, Editor & Publisher, Magazine Week*, etc.). Most of these magazines have regular departments that give up-to-date information about new magazines, changes in editorships, and other information crucial to your ability to publish your articles.

You also want to be knowledgeable of the magazine field in the way that a regular reader would. This means that you should regularly visit the newsstand. You should be able to recognize when a new magazine appears at the stand, recognize magazines that might be receptive to your type of ideas and articles, and generally have a feel for the types of magazines that are popular with readers today.

Lastly, you should understand the types of magazines that are receptive to new writers. There are several types of magazines that are, in general, very receptive to working with new and beginning writers. You can see that these types are represented in a number of the magazines in the list above.

> *"Keep away from people who try to belittle your ambitions. Small people always do that, but the really great make you feel that you, too, can somehow become great."*
>
> MARK TWAIN

New magazines are always a good place to look. More than three hundred magazines are started every year; they need editorial copy from somewhere. If you can get your name known at these offices before the magazine really gets rolling or can get on board right at the beginning, you might have a good shot at publication. The best way to find out about new magazines is to watch the newsstands and read the market updates in magazines.

Regional magazines are excellent places for new writers to start. Look at your community, your state, and your region. What magazines and other publications (newsletters, tabloid-size papers) are available? As a "hometown" writer, you have a good chance of selling yourself and your article to the editor. If there are magazines in your town, see if you can arrange a visit with the editor—the personal touch may be just what regional writers need to have.

Remember that regional magazines are not just those city magazines with which you're probably familiar. They also include such things as regional business tabloids, regional parenting magazines and newsmags, special-interest magazines with a regional slant, and trade magazines published locally.

Just in my city and the surrounding metropolitan areas, there is *The Alabama Baptist,* a Baptist newspaper; *Alabama Business Monthly,* a business magazine; *Alabama Outdoors*, a regional fishing and hunting newsmag; *Alabama West,* a regional magazine; *Birmingham,* a Chamber of Commerce-produced magazine; *Black and White*, a city entertainment guide; *Child Times,* a regional parent magazine; *Directions*, a guide for college students; and *Flicker*, a regionally produced children's magazine. Across the state of Alabama, there are a host of other magazines that provide freelance opportunities.

Special-interest magazines are great for new writers who have special talents, skills, or lifestyles. All of these magazines stress good writing, but they put an equal emphasis on the writer's special knowledge. This means that your first attempts at writing might have a good chance of getting published in special interest magazines, provided you know your subject well.

The subjects of special-interest magazines run the gamut. They include hobby magazines (if you know all there is to know about stamp collecting, there's a magazine for you), sports (there are magazines on everything from soccer to weight lifting to kick boxing), animals (yes, there are magazines solely dedicated to tropical fish), and some trade magazines (these are a good opportunity for you if you are very knowledgeable about a certain profession or subject).

Religious magazines are a great place to start, simply because of the sheer number of them out there. If you look back at the list of twenty-five magazines, you will find that there are several religious magazines listed.

Children's magazines are very receptive to new writers. This fact is obvious by the fact that there are more children's magazines listed in the above list than any other type of magazine. Get a copy of the *Children's Writer's and Illustrator's Market* (available from Writer's Digest Books), and you will see how many of these magazines are open to working with new writers.

The key to writing for children's magazines is to write using the correct manner, language, and tone. You have to learn how to write for children (or teenagers, in some cases).

Jumpstart Exercises

1. Visit your local bookstore to read through several magazines. Find the writer biography at the end of the articles. What writing experience do most of them indicate? Are there many that give a hint as to whether the writer is a new writer?
2. Browse through the most recent *Writer's Market* (or other market guide). Find at least ten examples of magazines that seem open to new writers (aside from the ones listed in this chapter). Were you surprised that any of them in particular said they were interested in working with new writers? Are you surprised by the openness of many magazines?
3. Have you noticed any new magazines on the market recently? Would your writing fit into their editorial style and plan? If so, write a query letter to one of them.
4. What magazines are published in your city, state, and region? Are you interested in the type of writing these magazines publish? If so, write a query letter to the appropriate ones.
5. Look through the lists of ideas you have developed while reading this book. Then, look through the list of twenty-five magazines in this chapter. Could any of your ideas fit into these magazines? If so (you guessed it), write a query letter to that (or those) magazine(s).

CHAPTER FOURTEEN

THE BUSINESS AND LEGAL SIDE OF WRITING

Magazine writing isn't all fun and games (if you ever actually believed that in the first place). Magazine writing—especially if you're getting articles published—entails some *messy* practices about which you need to learn, including things like keeping records, filing taxes, understanding contracts, and knowing about copyrights. The business and legal aspects of your writing life are very important in that they keep you organized, as well as out of trouble.

KEEPING RECORDS

Organization is an integral skill in succeeding as a magazine writer. It keeps you in line and on track—you know where you are on certain projects, and you can easily chart your writing progress. It's also important at tax time, because you can take a number of deductions if you have the records to prove them.

For Your Own Purposes

Keeping records is a good idea for your own state of mind. They keep you organized, letting you know how your marketing is progressing. There are several basic ways to keep records for this purpose.

Set Up Files for Different Projects • You need to know where all your information for a particular project is located. File folders keep you organized in this way.

At the very least, consider setting up file folders for each individual article you're working on. In the folder, store clippings with information for the article, notes you have written, first drafts, and any other information pertinent to that project.

There are a number of other folders you can set up: idea folders (with random clippings and notes of ideas you may use someday), topic folders (with information on a specific topic you plan on writing about someday), marketing folders (with information on target magazines for which you're interested in writing), writing guidelines folders (with guidelines from magazines), and writing tips folders (with articles you clip from writing magazines and tips you get from other sources).

Write Things Down in Your Calendar • Prioritize projects by devoting specific amounts of time to them. You should have at least one calendar on which you keep track of projects. There are other ways to use a calendar, however. Desk calendars are good because they provide you more space on which to write. You can also use page-a-day calendars; these are good because you only see your projects one day at a time. Regardless of what type of calendar you use, use it in a few ways:

- Write down your plans for each day (if you're going to come up with five article ideas, write that down; if you're going to finish an article, write that down).
- Keep track of deadlines (give yourself deadlines before an article is actually due; then, give yourself the actual deadline as a last-minute reminder).
- Check off when you finish projects.

Keep a Query and Manuscript Submission Log • Obtain a notebook to be used strictly as a query and manuscript log, or set the log up on your computer. Use the log to write down anything you send out to magazines. With queries, write down the article idea, the magazine to which you sent the query, and the date you sent it. When you get a response, write it down. Do the same thing for manuscripts—write the article title, the magazine to which it was sent, and the response you get.

Although there are many ways you can set up this type of log, an example is back in Chapter 6 on page 73.

Keep a Payment Log • If you're like me, the ultimate motivation to continue writing is to get paid for my work. Keeping a payment log is not only important for tax matters (see the next section for more on that), but it is also motivational. When you're going through a dry spell, you can look back and see that you have sold to magazines in the past. (If you're not yet ready to get into full-blown marketing, keep this idea for future reference.)

The best way to keep a payment log is to set up another page in your query and manuscript log notebook strictly for that purpose. Write down the article sold, the magazine to which it was sold, the amount paid, and the date payment was received.

Organization invariably means added productivity. By knowing where information is when you need it, you will save time and energy. So, even if you're not a neatnik (I'm certainly not), you need to make organization a priority in your writing life.

For Tax Purposes

This book is not designed to give you all the information you need to file taxes as a freelance writer. The law changes so much, that a book like this couldn't accurately give you all of the information you will need. Before you file every year, make sure you check the most recent tax information. If you have any questions, call your local tax office or ask a personal accountant for assistance.

With that in mind, however, you must realize that there are some consistent guidelines to follow in keeping records. These guidelines will prepare you for tax time. In keeping records for tax purposes, there are two primary things to keep in mind: (1) You must keep accurate records of expenses, and (2) you must keep accurate records of any writing income you receive.

To keep track of both your expenses and income, find some sort of record-keeping system that you like. The easiest way is to get a ledger and record expenses and income in two separate columns. You can divide your ledger up monthly, or you can get more sophisticated and divide your ledger into separate areas (in keeping track of expenses, for example, you could have separate pages for supplies, transportation, postage, printing, and so forth). As a new writer, you should try to keep things as simple as possible. As long as you're recording everything necessary, your system should work!

Stephen Crane's Maggie: A Girl of the Streets *was rejected by all the publishers he sent it to, so he published it himself. He sold one hundred copies of it, then was forced to use the remaining copies to fire his furnace that cold winter. After* The Red Badge of Courage *was published several years later,* Maggie *was released to commercial and critical success.*

Your Writing Expenses • If you're making a profit with your writing, you must pay income taxes (simply because magazines do not take taxes out of the fee they pay you for an article). If you're a "working" writer, then you can go beyond that and deduct expenses. The government considers you a working writer if you make a profit three out of five consecutive years. If you don't, you're considered a writing "hobbyist."

What kind of expenses, then, can you deduct? If you're a working writer, you should keep track of all expenses related to your writing. Keep receipts, canceled checks, and all other proofs that you spent money on any writing-related objects. You can deduct writing supplies such as paper, envelopes, pens, typewriter ribbons, computer diskettes, and file folders. Postage costs and photocopying are also deductible, as are long-distance phone calls related to your writing. Travel to the post office, library, homes of people you're interviewing—any place directly involved in your writing—can be deducted. If you go to a writing conference or workshop (or you pay dues to a writing organization), you can deduct those costs. The same goes for the expense of writing books and subscriptions to writing magazines. Equipment such as typewriters, computers, printers, and fax machines can be depreciated.

If you use a room in your house for writing only, that room can be deducted. This applies whether you rent or own a house. If you rent or own a six-room house and you use your office solely for writing, you can deduct one-sixth of your rent or mortgage. You could also deduct one-sixth of your utility bills, real estate taxes, home repairs, home insurance costs, and other home expenses.

The key, once again, is to keep good records of your expenses. If for some reason the IRS audited you (and they do like to audit self-employed individuals more than employees), you must be able to prove all of your deductions. Keep all of your receipts and use some sort of system to file them. I think the best approach is to use an expanded file folder with different envelopes set up for different types of expenses.

As an added note, if you were to be audited, the IRS would want some proof that you are serious about your writing life, whether it's full or part time. So keep copies of all your published articles and have plenty of items that make you look like the professional you are (letterhead stationary, business cards, memberships in writing organizations, and so forth).

Your Writing Income • As mentioned already, keeping track of the money you earn from writing is, if nothing else, motivational. It might keep you going when nothing else can. It's also important, however, in a practical way. You need an accurate record of your income in order to report it to the IRS.

Most payment checks from magazines will come with a tear-away stub or a separate receipt of payment; if they don't, photocopy the check to use as a record. Keep this and put it in your appropriate record-keeping place (if you're using expandable files as I recommended above, simply have one section for income receipts).

To keep from getting forgetful (or for those of you who simply have an aversion to organization), record your payment as soon as you get it in the mail—or, in the least, as soon as you get to see your name and article in print.

UNDERSTANDING YOUR RIGHTS

Just as there are business aspects to your life as a writer, there are also legal aspects you need to understand. These aspects are vitally important to the way you are treated as a writer and to the type of payment you will receive.

One of the first things you need to understand is your rights. I'm not talking about your right to exercise poetic freedom—to write what you want. I'm talking about the rights to your article that you sell to a magazine. When a magazine purchases your article, it is also purchasing a particular right. It's claiming, in one way or another, ownership of your article. There are several primary types of rights.

All rights means that the magazine is buying all of your ownership to the article—you're giving up the right to use it again. You want to avoid selling all rights to a magazine; after all, as we have already discussed, you want to try to get as much out of your articles as possible.

First rights means that the magazine has the right to publish your article for the first time in published form. After that, all rights to the article belong to you. Sometimes this type of rights is also called *First North American Rights* (since these rights are usually just for North American publications anyway) or *First Serial Rights.*

Second rights (sometimes called *reprint rights*) are usually bought when your article has already been published in another magazine. The magazine is buying the rights to publish it again. These rights are fine to sell, because you can still sell your article again.

One-time rights allow the magazine to publish your article once. These rights are ideal because there is no limitation on your selling the article again and again; you can even sell your article to other magazines at the same time. One-time rights are the most commonly used rights; you can usually assume, if you don't know for sure, that the magazine is buying one-time rights. Only rarely will you come in contact with a magazine that wants to buy all rights. Most magazines understand that freelance writers are trying to make money, and they will not try to control ownership of one particular article.

If you feel slighted, however, when it comes to the rights a magazine wants to buy, you can certainly try to negotiate with the publication. Even if *Writer's Market* says a magazine only buys a certain type of rights, rights are almost always negotiable. You can certainly ask questions about the rights or ask to have something else agreed upon.

In submitting your article manuscript, you might choose to list what type of rights you're offering. At the top right corner of the manuscript's first page, write "One-time rights offered." If you are offering a reprint of an article you have had published elsewhere, write "Reprint rights offered."

To understand what rights the magazine is purchasing—and to understand other intricacies of the publishing process—you need to know some basic information about contracts.

UNDERSTANDING YOUR CONTRACT OR AGREEMENT

Understand, first of all, that you won't always receive a contract (sometimes just called an agreement) for your work. I have had many articles published simply by having an editor notify me that the magazine would be publishing it and then receiving the check for my work a bit later (either upon acceptance of my article or upon publication of it in the magazine).

There are plenty of magazines, however, that will have you sign a contract. Magazine article contracts are usually quite straightforward, with few areas for the magazine to "cheat" the writer. It helps, though, to know what you're looking at. The standard article contract or agreement contains:

1. **The rights being purchased by the magazine.** Follow the guidelines already mentioned in the previous section. If you feel uncomfortable with the agreement, speak up and try to renegotiate.
2. **Arrangement for payment.** The contract will let you know if the magazine pays on acceptance or publication. Ideally, you want to be paid on acceptance, since publication can often occur months (maybe even a year) after your article is accepted. You can try to negotiate this point if you'd like or reach a middle ground by asking for a percentage of the fee on acceptance. If you're a new writer who simply wants to get something published, you should be willing to accept payment on publication. Once you get a few publications under your belt, you will probably be working with magazines that pay on acceptance. The contract will also let you know if the magazine gives a kill fee. This is a fee paid to you even if the magazine fails to ultimately publish your article. The amount is usually a percentage of the total payment.
3. **Editing arrangements.** Most contracts contain a standard sentence like, "The magazine reserves the right to edit for space and style." This can mean many things: the magazine can edit completely as it sees fit, the magazine will edit within parameters (meaning it won't alter it too terribly much), or the magazine can edit in any way but will let you see the changes first. We have all heard stories of magazines accepting an article and then changing it so much that it doesn't even resemble the writer's original work. While this certainly is in the realm of possibility, personally I have never seen this happen. In fact, I have had very few of my words changed for publication; the most editing my articles have ever experienced has been editing for space. My article was too long, so it was cut in a few places to make it fit the allotted space. If you write an article as professionally as possible and write it in the style of your target magazine, you should not experience too much editing or revising by the magazine's staff.

> *"The worst of writing is that one depends so much upon praise."*
> VIRGINIA WOOLF

4. **Arrangements for other elements of the article.** Have you written a sidebar with the article? Are you submitting photographs or illustrations? If so, the contract will handle arrangements for these. You will be told if you will be paid for them separately, what the payment will be, and any details you need to know about submitting them.
5. **Arrangements for author copies.** You should get copies of the magazine in which your article will be published. The contract will tell you how many you will receive; magazines generally send you three to five copies.

6. **Due date (if you're getting a firm assignment).** If the magazine is assigning you to write the article (as opposed to their accepting your manuscript after a go-ahead letter), the contract will give you a deadline for turning it in.

7. **Signatures.** There will be a space for both the editor's signature (which should already be filled in) and your signature. Many magazines will also have you put your social security number next to your signature (for payment purposes).

Be sure to always keep a copy of the contract or agreement for your own record-keeping purposes. The contract should let you know which copy you keep and which copy you return to the magazine.

COPYRIGHT AND FAIR USE

Another legal matter with which you need to be comfortable is copyright and fair use. Undoubtedly, you will come to a point in your writing when you will want to quote from another piece of writing. You may be working on an article about a songwriter and want to quote verbatim some of his songs' lyrics, or you might be writing a piece on the anniversary of the publication of *Gone with the Wind* and want to quote a passage from the book. Can you do this? Do you have to get permission from the writer or publisher to do so?

For some reason, copyright gives new writers more headaches than almost any issue. It is actually, however, a pretty simple issue. There are several main points you need to understand.

Understand What Copyright Means

Anything in published form, as well as in public performance or display, is copyrighted. Whenever something is created—an excerpt from a magazine article, an excerpt from a book, a speech, a song, and so forth—it is protected to prevent anyone from just coming along and using it for their own purpose. This protection is provided by the federal government and its violation is punishable.

Understand a Doctrine Called "Fair Use"

According to the doctrine, you have permission to quote briefly from material that is copyrighted. The key word here is *briefly*. Generally (although it's never been established by law), *briefly* has usually meant up to around a hundred words from an article or similar short piece (excluding poetry and song lyrics) and up to around two hundred words from a book. If you want to use material longer than that, you must obtain permission from its creator or publisher.

Know Copyright Life

In the United States, there are two main rules to remember in regard to copyright. The first is the 1978 rule. For works copyrighted on or after January 1, 1978, those works are protected for the rest of the author's life and another fifty years after his or her death.

The second rule is more important when thinking about quoting from published works in your articles. This is the seventy-five-year rule. If the copyrighted piece was a "work made for hire" (a piece, in other words, written for a publication), copyright on it expires seventy-five years after first publication or one hundred years after its first creation, whichever is earlier.

FROM THE EDITOR'S DESK

"Take note of the subject matter and steer the article in the proper direction. Write from the viewpoint of the reader—what does he/she want to see?"

ROBERT FORTNEY, *MUSCLEMAG*

The main thing that you need to know, then, is when a work was copyrighted. Then, going by the fifty-year or seventy-five-year rule, you can determine whether you must obtain permission to reprint the material you plan on using. If the piece is still protected by copyright and if you intend to use more than a brief amount of it, you must get permission to do so.

Once the years have expired, copyright material falls into the public domain. This means that the material now belongs to the general public and anyone can use it without permission from the original author or publisher. The only restriction is that you must attribute the material to the author.

Under these guidelines, you could quote freely, for example, from any of Benjamin Franklin's writings. He died more than fifty years ago. You don't have to get permission from his estate or from any of his publishers; simply mention that Franklin wrote whatever you're quoting.

Obtain Permission If Needed

To get permission to quote from copyrighted material, you need to make a request to the material's copyright owner. This means, then, that you're usually going to make requests of publishers.

To request permission, write a brief letter to the magazine, book publisher, or other publishing company. You can always find a magazine's address on its staff page or in *Writer's Market*. A book publisher's address is usually located on the book's copyright page or in *Writer's Market*; there is also a reference guide called *Books in Print, Publishers* that will provide you with addresses.

In the letter, explain what you want to quote, where and when it was originally published, and information about the article and magazine in which it will be published. In most cases, the copyright owner is agreeable to your using the material and will simply request that you use a credit line in your article (something like, "Used by permission of ABC Publishing").

There will be instances in which you will have to pay a small fee to use the material. At that point, you simply must weigh the cost against the importance you place on using the material.

One other note about copyright: you never have to personally obtain copyright for your work. I have many writers ask me whether they should copyright their articles. I always give them an emphatic no—it would be redundant. The Copyright Act of January 1978 established that anything you write automatically becomes copyrighted. And if your article gets published, it is automatically copyrighted by the magazine as well.

SHOULD I WORRY ABOUT LIBEL?

Any time we're talking about legal concerns to writers, the topic of libel comes into play. In writing, you must be sure not to write anything that is libelous or slanderous to an individual.

What is libel? That's a good question, because its definition often gets lost in a lot of legalese. Simply put, libel is anything published that is both false and damaging. To qualify as libel, printed information must be false (and the author must know that it is so) and must damage a person's reputation "in the eyes of a substantial group."

Generally, if you follow some sort of ethical code, you will not have to worry about these things. If you believe that it is wrong to falsely accuse someone of a criminal act, if you believe that a person's reputation is more important than a fast buck, then you should be okay.

> *"Writing is easy. All you have to do is cross out the wrong words."*
>
> MARK TWAIN

Where some writers get into trouble is through routine haphazardness. You must always print the truth. Writers sometimes *don't* print the truth simply because they don't double-check facts, not because they intended to lie. Be careful, then, to always double-check certain elements of your article:

1. **Double-check—actually, triple-check—names.** It's amazing how many people have similar names. You don't want to say John Smith was a murderer if your article is for a regional magazine in which a John Smith is a prominent mayor. Clarify any potentially harmful situations. In a less harmful instance, be sure that names are spelled correctly. People hate to have their names misspelled, and it's very embarrassing to you.
2. **Check facts you're sure of.** There are facts you sometimes easily assume are correct. If you have any facts mentioned in your article, check them to make sure they're accurate—even if it seems obvious that they are.

3. **Read material back to sources.** Following an interview, read quotes that you know you will use in your article back to the source. You never want to misquote someone.

The key to protecting your back legally—and to being the professional writer you want to be—is accuracy, accuracy, accuracy.

DO YOU HAVE MORE QUESTIONS?

You may come up against other legal issues as you get started writing. If you have a close lawyer friend, utilize your relationship for casual advice. If you want answers specifically geared to writers, contact the National Writers Union, Suite 203, 873 Broadway, New York, NY 10003. The Volunteer Lawyers for the Arts is another useful resource; it is located at 6th Floor, 1 E. 53rd St., New York, NY 10022.

Jumpstart Exercises

1. Look through the information you have amassed from reading this book. You should have lists of ideas, drafts of several articles, information on marketing, and so forth. Determine what type of file system would work best for you. As a minimum, set up an idea folder, a marketing folder, and topic folders.
2. If you haven't done so already, set up a query and manuscript submission log and a payment log.
3. Set up some sort of ledger system for keeping track of your writing income and expenses. Promise to be as conscientious as possible in keeping these records.
4. Look through *Writer's Market*, noticing what types of rights various magazines purchase. Are there many that buy all rights? What is the most common type of rights purchased?
5. If you have a writer friend who has been published, ask him or her if you could take a look at one of the contracts or agreements. Notice the different elements of the contract; is there anything confusing to you? Talk to your friend about any experiences he or she has had with contracts.
6. Find a magazine article that quotes from published material. How did the writer handle attribution? How did he handle any permissions to quote from the material?
7. Do you believe that writers must live by an ethical code? In regards to your writing, are there any ethical guidelines in which you strongly believe? Write a brief description of your own writer's ethical code.

CHAPTER FIFTEEN

A POTPOURRI OF NEW WRITER CONCERNS

One of the ways I decided what needed to be included in this book was to remember various conversations I have had with new writers. I have tried to recall what aspiring writers have been concerned about. I have tried to reminisce about anguish-filled questions I have been asked.

There are so many topics that are of concern to new writers, but none of them are large enough to constitute an entire chapter. This chapter, then, is what I call a potpourri of topics for new writers. It may not seem to have much semblance of organization. Try to forgive me for my haphazardness, however, for I think you may find some answers to your concerns.

MEETING LIKE-MINDED FRIENDS

I have plenty of close friends who have very little interest in my writing. We laugh together, go to movies together, have each other over for dinner, call each other just to chat, and help each other with problems. They know I love to write and they support that love, but they don't *share* my love. My best friend, in fact, only writes when she has to and does not know that much about the craft of magazine writing.

I have another set of close friends who *do* share my passion. One is a magazine writer similar to me. Another does a lot of academic work. Another publishes her own newsletters. Another dreams of writing mysteries. Still another does technical writing. This set of friends is very special to me. All of these writers know what I'm talking about when I complain about not having enough time to write. They commiserate with me about getting published in that certain magazine. They *understand.*

You may have friends who support your writing dreams, but if they don't understand a little about the business, if they don't have some writing dreams of their own, they will never truly understand your desire to be a writer. Never give up the friends you have—I cherish my nonwriting friends and would be the worse without them—but do try to cultivate some writing friendships.

There are several ways to meet like-minded friends. One is pure chance. As you get into a writing frame of mind and begin to move about like you are a writer, you will be amazed at how many other writers you will meet. You may be standing in the writing section of your bookstore when you meet a fellow writer, or you may be in the park writing observational descriptions and find a like-minded soul. Always be open to others around you.

An excellent and practical way to meet fellow writers is to attend writing conferences. Find a writing conference that suits your individual needs (there are conferences solely for beginning writers, for female writers, for magazine writers, and so on). When you go, take part in as many activities as possible. Don't just go to the open lectures; attend special interest groups and go to critiquing sessions. I guarantee that you will make some new friends.

> *"I think the only person a writer has an obligation to is himself. If what I write doesn't fulfill something in me, if I don't honestly feel it's the best I can do, then I'm miserable."*
>
> TRUMAN CAPOTE

Perhaps the best way, however, to meet fellow writers is to be actively involved in an ongoing writers group. Many communities have writing groups that cater to different types of writers. Try to find one that focuses on magazine writing, although a general writing group can also be helpful. Though these groups are sometimes sponsored by a group or a local college, they are usually started by an individual or group of individuals.

To find out if your community has such a group, first contact your local Chamber of Commerce, as it keeps track of various community organizations. If people there don't know of any, consult the list of group meetings in your local paper. Most Sunday editions include such a listing. You might also touch base with any large meeting places in your area. Conference centers, public libraries, community centers, and so forth are likely meeting places for writing groups. Finally, if you find that your community does not have a writers group, you might want to start one.

HOW TO START A WRITING GROUP

To start a writing group in your area, take the following steps:

1. **Find out if there's an interest and/or need.** If you live in a fairly good-sized community, chances are there are plenty of residents who are aspiring writers. Ask around to see if there would be an interest in a writing group.
2. **Get another hand to help.** Try to locate at least one more person to help you organize the group. You may not want to do all of the initial work by yourself.
3. **Decide on a time and place for your first meeting.** There are several options for this. You can plan your meeting for a weekday or weekend. You may get more people on a Saturday or, like the group to which I belong, you may find that Saturdays are full for most

people and a weekday is better (we meet on Tuesday nights). Nights are probably better than days, since many aspiring writers already have full-time jobs. As for a place to meet, find a site that is central to the area. Also find a site that has several good-sized, comfortable meeting rooms. Some possible places include libraries (my group meets in a conference room at the public library), conference centers, churches, colleges, schools, and community centers. If you're at a loss on site ideas, check under "Meeting Facilities" in the Yellow Pages or call your Chamber of Commerce for ideas.

4. **Publicize the first meeting.** Hang flyers at grocery stores, shopping malls, colleges—any place you can think of where there is a lot of traffic. List the meeting in your local newspaper's club meeting listing. See if there are any other places in your community that offer free advertising (in my town, the Chamber of Commerce has a free community listing on a local television channel, and a classified ad tabloid offers free listing to nonprofit organizations). Include the meeting time and place; say that the meeting is an organizational one for a new group. You might also want to go ahead and select a name for the group (a name gives it credibility).

At the first meeting of your new group, you will need to do the following:

1. **Get to know one another.** Spend plenty of time letting everyone introduce themselves and tell what writing interest they have. Pass around a piece of paper for everyone to write their name, address, and phone number, as you will need to have a way to get in touch with everyone again.
2. **Talk generally about what the group should accomplish.** Should it have informational sessions (there are usually plenty of "experts" who can share knowledge with your group and who are happy to be asked to speak)? Should it include critique sessions in which members can share their writing? New writers might have to get used to this, but it's a good idea to include some sharing in all groups. Should it primarily be a "bull session" for writers to talk about their concerns? Should it be a blending of these different approaches?
3. **Decide on a regular meeting time and place.** Ask attendees if the meeting time and place were good ones. Should they be changed? Decide how often the group should meet. Try not to make meetings too often; people's lives are busy enough. Once or twice a month is plenty.
4. **Brainstorm names of people who might be interested in the group.** Every person can probably think of at least one other person who is interested in writing. Make sure these people are contacted for the next meeting.

5. **Assign jobs**. Have someone be in charge of coming up with a program for the next meeting. Give someone the job of sending out announcements. Ask several people to help publicize the group. At some point—probably during this meeting or the next—you will want to select officers. At the very least, it is good to have a president, secretary, and program chair. There are plenty of other jobs that can be done, however (vice-president, publicity chair, social chair, etc.).

DEALING WITH UNSUPPORTIVE FAMILY AND FRIENDS

What if you have friends and family members who don't understand your writing dreams? What if they don't want to acknowledge your dreams? What if they don't want to help you accomplish your goals? There are several options for you:

- **Find another outlet.** You might want to get involved in a writing group or go to some writing conferences. In other words, find a way to meet people who can be supportive.
- **Look at the problem practically.** Honestly ask your friends and family members what they don't understand. Try to see their point of view. Perhaps they're threatened by your dreams; maybe they think they won't see you anymore if you get too involved. It may simply be a matter of talking to each other like human beings. If the problem is solvable, see what practical solutions can be found. If your spouse is threatened, find a new interest the two of you can share together. If your partner is afraid he or she will lose precious time with you, ask your partner to help you with some of your projects (ask your partner, for example, to read your article and give his or her opinion).
- **Be a little less vocal and give it time.** It may be that your problem can't be easily solved. Your friends and family members may never truly understand what you want to do. You may have to dream your dreams in near silence. Instead of going on and on about your newfound passion, let it ebb a little bit. You may find that time will do wonders for your cause.

HANDLING REJECTION

Rejection is hard, and as a double whammy, it's inevitable in the writing market. The key to handling rejection is twofold: (1) do not take rejection personally, and (2) try and learn something from your rejection. When you find yourself facing rejection, you may be tempted to travel into the Woe-is-Me Zone. This will only lead to more problems—depression and low self confidence, primarily. To escape the Woe-is-Me Zone, remember these four points:

1. **Rejection is not personal.** How many editors would you recognize on the street? Not very many, I imagine. Remember that you don't know editors on a personal level, so they don't know you on a personal level either. When they reject your article, they are not rejecting you. You—the individual—are a valuable person. You—the writer—are still learning!
2. **You can learn from rejection.** Unless an editor is simply in a bad mood, your article is rejected for a reason. It wasn't appropriate for the magazine, it wasn't written in the right style, crucial facts were missing from it, or it lacked zing. When you get a rejection, take a critical look at the article. How could it be better? Is there a better magazine to which to submit the article? Edit, polish, revise, and then send it out again.
3. **If at first you don't succeed . . .** We all know that famous phrase. It may sound trite, but it's very true when it comes to writing. Persistence pays off. By knowing this simple fact, you can better deal with rejection. Remember that Dr. Seuss received twenty-seven rejections for his first book. Remember that all successful writers had to start somewhere. If you believe in your article, and if you have made it the best it can be, stick with it. Eventually, someone else will believe in it too.
4. **Sometimes you need to reject your own work.** Consistent rejection of a piece may mean that you need to let go of it—forever or just for a little while. You can put that article in the trash can. You can put it in a file for later use (it may be that, as you develop your writing skills, you can go back to it later and make it better). Or you can put it in a file of early writing attempts. It's often nice to look back at what you have done and see how far you have come!

You may have to chalk up some of your early writing attempts as experience. You don't have to publish everything you write.

THE JOYS OF A JOURNAL

Many writers have a passion about journals. It might be something that you will also want to catch on to. Journals are nice because they are private. You can write material for your eyes only—you don't have the pressure of producing something for publication. Journals are also a good way to get yourself writing. Structured journal writing provides you a way to write regularly—usually daily.

There are two popular types of journaling for writers. One is the type of journaling we usually think of: freewrite journaling. This type of journaling allows you to write anything and everything you want. You use your journal to write impressions of the world around you, to write your thoughts and opinions, to chronicle your life. It is similar to a diary. (Note that, aside from the writing it allows you to accomplish, this type of journal is wonderful because it is a chronicle of your life to read in years to come and to pass down to your children or other family members.)

FROM THE EDITOR'S DESK

"We want fresh ideas and clean writing, as does every magazine. The stories must be an accurate reflection of our theme. Know your subject."

TRICIA BROWN, *ALASKA*

The other type of journaling incorporates using what would more aptly be called an idea journal. You don't use it as a diary of your life. Instead, you use it as a storehouse for impressions and ideas. You would carry this type of journal around with you, writing down any ideas you have about people, circumstances, events, and subjects. From this journal you would develop ideas for publishable articles. You could also use your idea journal to work on parts of articles as you get inspired to do so outside of your usual work space.

If you decide you like the idea of journaling, you have several things to accomplish:

1. **Purchase a journal.** There are many options here. Depending on your taste and needs, you can purchase a legal pad, ring binder with loose-leaf paper, spiral bound notebook, blank book, or writer's journal. (You could even consider journaling on a computer disk.)
2. **Determine the purpose of your journal.** Will your journal be a diary journal or an idea journal? Would you like to do *both* types of journaling? It's good to know what type of journaling you will be doing. If you don't know that, it will be harder to get started.
3. **Decide how and when to use your journal.** While journaling is generally a creative exercise (it is often, in fact, a way to breathe unstructured time into your writing life), it is still good to have some sort of idea about how you will go about filling it.
4. **Determine the best time for you to write in your journal.** You might want to set up thirty minutes in the morning (which is good for those of you who are alert and creative in the morning), or you may want to write for a set of time in the evening (which I like, because it provides an opportunity to review the day). If you're using your journal as an idea resource for your writing, you should carry it with you wherever you go. You should still set up some time during the day to take a look at what you have written down; you can then see if you have written anything useable.

What If You Have Nothing to Say?

Journals are designed to free your writing spirit—to take off the pressure of writing anything perfect. Still, many people often fail to keep their journaling consistent because they run out of things to say. I will repeat what I said earlier in the book—ideas are everywhere, and that goes for journals also. Here are some easy ways to get your pen moving in your journal:

- **Be observant.** Keep your eyes and ears open. When you hear a fascinating snippet of conversation, write it down. When you see something out of the ordinary, record it in your journal.
- **Keep up with current events.** A great source for journal writing—especially if you're writing one similar to a diary—is your local newspaper or television station. What story makes an impression on you? What is going on in the world that is notable?
- **Look at your life critically.** Don't just record what happens in your day ("I went to the grocery store and the post office"). Write what those happenings mean. Don't just mention the people in your life, write what those people mean to you. All lives are important, and all of our lives have moments of epiphany, moments when you are enlightened with meaning. Be open to seeing your life in this way.
- **Carry your journal with you at all times.** If you have your journal (and a pen) with you all the time, you will be able to record any impression or experience you have—at *that* moment. Time and human memory often change impressions, so it's important to record your thoughts at the time.

BRANCHING OUT WITH OTHER WRITING OPPORTUNITIES

Magazine article writing might be just the beginning for you. Once you feel like you have the basic knowledge for getting started as a magazine writer and once you have a few publications under your belt, you may decide to add something new to your writing repertoire. There are plenty of other writing outlets for you, including children's writing, poetry, mystery novels, biographies, textbooks, newspaper articles, short stories, and technical writing. The list goes on and on.

> Hamlet *earned Shakespeare just five pounds, which was typical payment for all of his plays.*

I would recommend that you first—if you know now that you enjoy magazine writing—stick with this genre for a while. Get comfortable with writing articles. Be confident in your abilities. I would also recommend that you analyze your talents and abilities before moving on. Ask yourself what you like about writing. You may have really enjoyed the instruction on research and interviewing presented in Chapter 7. You might, therefore, enjoy writing more in-depth material that takes even more diligence (technical writing or textbooks, for example). You may have enjoyed learning about editing and rewriting. Perhaps you could edit other people's work. You may have liked the information on imagery, description, and literary devices discussed in Chapter 10. You might, then, want to try your hand at fiction.

James Joyce's The Dubliners *was rejected by at least twenty-two publishers.*

I would finally recommend that you stick with writing that is similar to magazine writing in the beginning. By slowly expanding your field of expertise and interest, your skills will be used in the best way. Other good writing outlets for magazine writers would be, for example, newspaper writing, short pieces (things like reviews, anecdotes, puzzles), and short stories.

CAN I WRITE FULL-TIME?

Let me first tell you that there are very few freelance magazine writers supporting themselves in the United States. Knowing this, if you still ask yourself that question, you might need to ask yourself a few other questions:

1. **Do you have some other means of support?** There are just a few writers who support themselves. Note that this does not count the writers who are working full time but have partners who work. Do you have a partner who can pay the bills until you are bringing in enough money from your writing? There are other ways of supporting yourself. Perhaps you have investments or family money. If you have a supportive partner (monetarily and otherwise) or an independent source of income, you might want to consider writing full-time. If not, you need to think it through a little bit more carefully.
2. **Have you succeeded at marketing your work?** To make money at writing, you must be successful at writing publishable articles and convincing editors that they need to buy them. If you have not done so, begin perfecting your query letters and sending them out. To devote yourself to magazine writing full time, you need to have a very good acceptance rate on query letters and, then, on articles. If your query letters and articles are not being accepted regularly, that's no reason to give up. You simply need to keep working at it and, perhaps, to consider other options in your plan to write full-time. At some point, as you improve at your marketing, you might be able to change your work plan.
3. **Could you consider writing part-time?** By picking up this writing book, you have shown that you are interested in spending some time on writing. If you are to the point that you want to write full-time,

this means you are much more serious about it. To be realistic, however, you should probably consider doing it part-time. But that part-time writing should be *serious.* To get to where you can write full-time, you must spend time equal to a part-time job on your magazine writing. You could do this by working seriously at night and on weekends, or you could get a part-time job and write the rest of the work day.

Beginning writers have so many varied concerns. I recommend that you visit your local bookstore and peruse the writing section. There is a multitude of books on writing topics; there are books solely on ideas, books with instruction for journaling, books that tell you just how to write romances, and books to inspire you.

Jumpstart Exercises

1. Make a list of your best friends. How many of them share your love of writing? If you don't have at least one good writing friend, you should probably consider getting involved in some writing-related activities. Through them, you can cultivate some writing friendships.
2. Is there a writing group in your community? Find out by calling your local Chamber of Commerce and looking at the community listing in your newspaper. If there is a group in your community, call its contact person and ask about the group. Does it sound like there would be like-minded writers there? Are there beginning writers involved in the group? What types of meetings does the group have? Mark the next meeting on your calendar and plan on attending.
3. If there is not a writing group in your community, consider the possibility of starting one. Go through the steps listed in this chapter on how to start a group.
4. Are unsupportive family members and friends a problem? Look at the relationships and determine why there might be a problem. Make a list of reasons why your writing is a strain, and then make a list of practical ways to try and resolve them.
5. Do you handle rejection well? Do you take rejection personally? If handling rejection is a struggle for you, write the four points from this chapter in a place where you can see them. Put these words, for example, above your desk:
   - Rejection is not personal.
   - I can learn from rejection.
   - If at once I don't succeed . . . try, try again.
   - Sometimes I need to reject my own work.

6. Have you always wanted to keep a journal but never have? Now is the time to start. Follow the steps outlined in this chapter on how to start the journaling process. Start writing in your journal today.
7. Look objectively at your writing interests. Is there another avenue of writing you'd like to try? Make a list of other types of writing you'd like to try at some point. After you finish reading this book and feel comfortable with the article-writing process, get your list back out. Pick out one or two other writing types and learn as much about them as possible. Read some books on the subject and give it a try. But please, don't abandon magazine writing. Stick with it. After all, you have come so far by now.

CHAPTER SIXTEEN

TWENTY WAYS TO *NOT* GET PUBLISHED

How do you feel at this point, after reading all of the information provided to you in this book? Do you feel overwhelmed at the amount of information needed to be a successful magazine writer? Do you feel inadequate, still afraid that you can't succeed at getting your magazine articles published? Or do you, perhaps, feel motivated to get out there and get started?

I imagine that you feel a little bit of all three. I hope, however, that you feel more motivation than you did before you picked up this book. I also hope—because it is the main thing I intended for readers of my book to feel once they've come to this point—that you feel prepared for the writing task ahead of you. I wanted all readers to understand that there are many processes and many jobs that they need to learn how to do, but that these processes and jobs are both learnable and attainable. I hope that you now feel that way.

I have a word of warning to those of you, however, who feel like you now know everything there is to know about getting started as a magazine writer: Don't let this knowledge allow you to become complacent. Don't let your new-found confidence allow you to lapse into forgetfulness and easy-way-out solutions.

Even the best of writers become passive and forgetful. Many of us have those days when we think, "I don't really need to spend much time on this query letter," or "I don't know how I ever thought I could be a magazine writer." We forget that preparation and professionalism are important and that belief in our own abilities is paramount.

Within the next month, or certainly the next year, you will probably find yourself going through this phenomenon. You will begin to doubt yourself. You will begin to forget the basic steps needed to succeed at magazine writing. You might even decide to give up. When you get into this frame of mind, open this book back up again and refresh yourself. Remember that you love to write and you desire to become published. Dedicate yourself once more to your goals and dreams.

As you get started writing—even if you have read this book with enthusiasm and attention to detail—you may find yourself lapsing into practices that are not conducive to your success as a magazine writer. I submit to you twenty such practices that will guarantee your failure on your writing journey and in getting published.

1. Tell Yourself, "I'm Not a Writer" or "I Will Never Be a Writer"

A guaranteed way to not be a writer is to tell yourself you're not a writer. Some of the most successful magazine writers I know are not necessarily the most talented. The most successful are those who believe in their capabilities; they have an uncanny ability to believe that they are doing what they should be doing with their life and that they are good at it.

Belief in oneself, as I mentioned in this book's opening chapter, is perhaps the top indicator of success as a magazine writer. Some new writers have a difficult time telling themselves that they are writers or that they know they will be successful someday. I have had several beginning writers say to me, "That sounds vain" or "I don't want to jinx myself." Self-confidence is a learned trait. We must learn that it's okay to believe in ourselves—without, of course, being self-absorbed or vain.

2. Listen to What Other People Say

This goes hand-in-hand with number 1. If, in addition to not believing in yourself, you listen to those people who belittle your dreams and ambition, you are guaranteed to fail. As a writer you need a support system of people who, though they might not be writers themselves or may not even totally understand your desire to write, will uplift you in your endeavors.

You do not need friends, partners, lovers, and work acquaintances who question your talent, who complain about the time spent on your writing, or who wonder (aloud) why you want to write. If you are in a situation where you're not supported, get out there and meet a person or two who will support you (through a writer's group, perhaps); also, constantly remind yourself that your ambition is not futile and that your dreams are not out of reach.

3. Procrastinate

Are you a procrastinator? All human beings are to some extent. For some reason, many beginning writers are procrastinators. We have all heard beginning writers say, "I really should write about that some day" or "That would make a really good story, but . . . ."

> *"Blot out, correct, insert, revise. Enlarge, diminish, interline. Be mindful, when invention fails, to scratch your head and bite your nails."*
>
> JONATHAN SWIFT

If you want to fail at getting started writing and at getting published, you should make these types of statements a regular part of your vocabulary. The more you say them, the more you will act upon them. You will never actually sit down and write about that idea. You will never actually act upon your feeling that you could write a good story.

The key here is to not get into a habit of procrastination. If you do get into the I will-write-about-it-someday habit, you will probably never write.

To keep from becoming a habitual procrastinator, take two steps: (1) set definite goals and (2) develop a writing schedule (we have already discussed those ideas in depth, so you should feel comfortable with them).

4. Write Only When You Feel Like It

If you write only when you feel like it, chances are you won't feel like it very much. You might feel like it on that one perfect spring day when inspiration is screaming at you to sit down at your typewriter. You might feel like it on that rare day when there is no other pressing work to get done (if that type of day actually exists) and you can write at your leisure.

To be productive, you must write regularly. You must learn how to set deadlines for yourself and learn how to say "no" to other things when your writing needs to get done. Writing isn't always inspired; it's usually something you simply "must" do.

5. Have No Definite Goals

If you want to be a writing failure, don't ever really put a finger on what it is you want to achieve. Aimlessly wander along the road to writing success. When people ask you on what writing projects you're currently working, answer, "Oh, several random things." Don't set specific, definite goals. Remember, one of the basic steps in getting started writing is to set goals and stick to them.

6. Write about Everything

Part of the reason for setting goals is that it clarifies your writing projects—it makes your projects more specific, more targeted. You know on what topics you want to write.

Many beginning writers fail because they haven't determined what they want to write about. As a result, they decide to write about everything. They write about the environment, current events, and memories of childhood. They write how-to articles, opinion pieces, humorous essays, and serious informational articles. They aren't focused.

If you want to fail, you should take this exact approach. If you want to succeed, however, you should identify your specific interests and writing abilities. Once you are focused in this way, your writing time will become much more productive.

7. Don't Make Your Writing a Priority

Remember when you first fell in love? You were overwhelmed with the feelings you had for this newly-discovered person. You wanted to spend all of your time with him or her. You wanted your mate to know that he or she was a priority in your life. For some reason, however, many madly-in-love people let the days and the months and the years take their toll. They no longer spend the time and energy on the person they love the most.

If you love writing, it should be a big priority in your life. As time goes by, you should increase the time you spend on it, the energy you expend on it, and your dedication to it. Writing should not be put on a back burner. If you want to fail as a new writer, tell yourself that other things are always more important (notice the word *always*—there are, of course, plenty of times when other details, events, and people must come before your writing) and that your writing projects don't need too much attention given to them.

8. Strive for Perfection

The one thing that seems to hold back beginning writers more than anything is the belief that everything they write must be perfect. Often when I ask a new writer what he or she is working on, the response is something like, "I have this great idea for a story, but I don't think I can write it the way it needs to be written," or "I have actually just finished an article, but I really don't think it's good enough."

Good enough? What is good enough? Nowhere does it say that everything you write has to be perfect. If you want to fail, believe that everything you write must be perfect. Believe that everything Shakespeare wrote was perfect the first time. Believe that Hemingway stopped after one try because his work wasn't perfect. Beginning writers simply need to write. Get that great idea down on paper. Then you can worry about making it better (sometimes almost perfect—but always better).

9. Be Ruled by the Empty Page

What is the scariest stage of writing? Is it the idea-gathering stage? Is it the moment that you realize you must go to the library and do research? Is it the times when you must conduct interviews? Is it the editing stage?

For many new writers, the scariest moment is when they sit down at the computer and see an empty screen. This stage—which should actually be the most exciting one, for it is then when a writer is truly creating—scares many writers like no other. To fail to get started as a writer, let yourself be ruled by the empty page. Believe that you cannot create anything good enough. Believe that writer's block is out to get you. Believe that the empty page can never become full.

10. Walk around with Your Eyes Shut

If you would like to guarantee failure as a writer, tape your eyes shut, stick cotton balls in your ears, plug your nose, and tie your hands behind your back. In this way, you can never truly experience any of life's wonders. You can never see, hear, smell, or touch the world around you. In doing so, you can never develop any ideas for articles from observation and never have any experiences upon which to build your writing.

A writer can never truly separate himself from the world around him. He must be in a constant state of awareness—of both the big and little things. As you walk around with your eyes open, take special care to notice things. Then, remember them and write them down.

11. Never Read

Most of the writers I know read a great deal. I'm imagining that this is also true for you. If you never read, you can never learn to appreciate good—and bad—writing. If you never read, you can never learn what type of writing you want to do yourself; you are, in effect, stopping the learning process.

As a writer, you should read all sorts of stuff. Read nonfiction books (including books on the craft of writing), biographies, best-selling fiction, books of essays, poetry, and magazines (*definitely* magazines). Read anything and everything you can get your hands on. As you read, do so in an active way. Notice how the writer spins his story; take notes of tips you want to remember; wonder how you can incorporate what you have learned into your own writing.

> *"All art is a series of recoveries from the first line. The hardest thing is to put down the first line. But you must."*
>
> NATHAN OLIVERA

12. Only Read (Especially Books Like This One)

Just as never reading will inhibit your growth as a writer, the opposite will also inhibit it. If you spend all your time reading about writing—or going to writing conferences, or meeting with writing groups, or other activities—you will be kept from the activity you actually need to be doing: writing.

I have met many writers who can talk big about writing, but when you actually ask them what they've written, they come up with some statement about working on a novel for several years or having lots of ideas and little time to act upon them. Don't be one of those types of writers. Spend adequate time reading about writing, but take action upon what you're learning in your reading. (Lesson learned: Read this book, and then do what it teaches you.)

13. Take Shortcuts

I remember several vacations as a child when my father would claim that he could find a shortcut through an unfamiliar place. Invariably, the "shortcut" would end up getting us lost and cost us extra travel time. Shortcuts rarely actually work. In writing, this is especially true.

Beginning writers often think that they can cut corners—by skimping on research time, not editing enough, not writing enough drafts, or by sending out sloppy manuscripts. These types of shortcuts only make new writers look unpolished and uninformed. Spend adequate time on your writing. Be as pleased as you possibly can with your final work.

14. Don't Let Your Personality Show

If you regularly read magazines, you know that there are a lot of dry articles written and published everyday. The best articles, however—the ones that readers remember—have a touch of personality. They sparkle and shine. They give readers a glimpse into the writer's passions and personality.

If you don't want to be a good, effective writer, don't let your personality through in your projects. If you want, however, to be a writer whose articles make an impact on the reader, be willing to let your personality show. Be willing to try something different (try a bold lead, tell that fascinating anecdote, use literary devices).

15. Be Consumed with the *Idea* of Being a Writer

There are many people who want to be writers. There are fewer people who still want to be writers once they find out how much work it takes to be one. There are fewer still who actually do the work needed to succeed. Those people who shy away from the work become big talkers. They are consumed with the idea of being a writer and by what they see as the glamour and excitement of the lifestyle, but they never get beyond that stage. If you want to succeed, you do need to like the idea of being a writer, but you don't need to dwell on it. When you dwell on it, you begin to realize that you can never live up to all of your expectations.

16. Take Rejection Personally

My mother is also a writer. She often tells of the time she got her first rejection letter. She had eagerly sent out her first article and waited with bated breath to get her glorious acceptance back in the mail. Two weeks later, she got a form rejection letter. She said she cried for hours over it; today, she laughs at her reaction. She now knows that rejection is part of the game. One of her favorite things to say is, "If I'm not getting rejections, then I'm not writing enough."

> *"Read it over, abridge, and correct it until you get it into the shortest space possible."*
>
> WALT WHITMAN

Most new writers take rejection personally. To succeed, you must get past the idea that a rejection is a personal snub against you. Just because an editor can't use your article does not mean that he or she has a personal problem with you. You may have submitted an idea that the magazine recently published, you might have sent your article to an inappropriate magazine (whereas you didn't do enough homework), or you might have simply caught the editor on a bad day.

Rejections are a fact of the writing life. You must learn to get past them. When you get a rejection, take your article and see if it needs to be altered in any way. Then, send it back out again to another magazine.

17. Be Afraid of Editors

Believe it or not, every magazine editor I have ever met was actually a nice person. Most are truly interested in a writer's welfare; their chief concern is producing an effective, well-written magazine. They are not "out to get" freelance writers. If you want to fail at getting started writing, develop a stereotype of editors. Believe that they are critical and unfeeling. Think that their greatest love is to dash new writers' hopes and dreams. If you want to succeed, however, realize that editors are actually human and approach them in that way.

18. Be Unprofessional

Being unprofessional is one sure-fire way to fail as a writer. Professionalism is the mark of a writer who has developed his craft and who knows what the markets require. This means that you must develop professional practices: keep your manuscripts clean, be courteous in your letters, always send SASEs, address letters to the appropriate editors, make sure your spelling is correct, and don't intrude upon an editor's time. As a new writer, dedicate yourself to being a consummate professional.

19. Send All Your Articles to *Good Housekeeping* and *Esquire*

Not long ago, at the community writers group I'm a member of, I asked an aspiring writer friend about her projects. She said that she was a little depressed because all of her articles had been coming back to her. It was difficult, she said, to send more articles out when they were all getting rejected. I tried to encourage her, telling her she was probably just in a slump and that things would soon turn around.

I then decided to ask her where she was sending her articles, thinking I might be able to give her some advice about specific editors and magazines. She told me that her last three articles had been sent to (and rejected by) *Guideposts, Family Circle,* and *Reader's Digest.*

I hope that one thing you have learned in reading this book is that there are literally thousands of outlets for your writing, most of which are not the well-known, large-circulation magazines. My friend's mistake, and the mistake of many new writers, is that she only thought of the obvious markets. She didn't do research to determine better outlets for her articles.

20. Never Send Anything Out

If you never want to get anything published, never send anything out. This makes absolute sense, and you are probably laughing at the idea that you would ever do it. Believe me, though, many new writers never send any of their articles out for consideration.

Why don't they? There are numerous reasons. They may want to wait until their article is absolutely perfect (and it probably never will be to them). They might not know *how* to send an article out. They, probably, are simply afraid to do so.

Now that you are almost finished reading this book, these reasons should not hold you back. You know that you can never expect your article to be absolutely perfect; you should make it the best you can and then take a chance and send it out to a magazine. You know how to send an article out, you know the fine points of a query letter and manuscript submission, and most of all, you know that you cannot let fear keep you from grabbing hold of your dreams. You have the knowledge and the desire to write for magazines. When you are afraid, you must simply reassure yourself of this fact.

Jumpstart Exercises

1. How do you feel about your prospects as a writer? Write several paragraphs explaining how you feel about the writing process and writing life. Do you think you can succeed? Is there any particular fear still holding you back?
2. Are you a procrastinator? Write a list of the things you wanted to do last week but didn't accomplish. Begin to make lists every week of what you want to accomplish in regard to your writing projects. See if you progress as the weeks go by in accomplishing your goals.
3. What is a priority in your life? Make a list of the most important things in your life. Why are they important? How much time do you spend on them? After you write the list, prioritize them in order of importance (using numbers). Where is writing on your list? Is it in the appropriate place? Is it too important to you, or is it not important enough?
4. Complete the following statement: "I expect my writing to be __________." Write several paragraphs explaining your statement. Do you have high enough standards for your writing? Do you expect it, on the other hand, to be perfect every time?
5. Write five adjectives that describe your personality. Write five verbs that describe your personality. Write five nouns that describe your personality. How can these personal traits be shown in your writing?
6. Select a paragraph of writing that you have finished while reading this book. Does your personality shine through, or is it a dry piece of writing? How can it be made more lively?
7. Think about the last week. How have you been rejected (in all areas of your life, not just writing)? How did you handle that rejection? How could you handle it better?

8. In the process of reading this book, have you sent any articles out to magazines? If you haven't, select a query letter you have written and do so.
9. Look back through the twenty reasons for failure as outlined in this chapter. Honestly look at yourself and determine which of these twenty practices you follow. Where could you improve your attitude? In what area could you have stronger goals? What practices need improvement in your own life?

RESOURCES FOR WRITERS

There is a vast number of resources available to you, the new writer. There are monthly magazines and newsletters that can provide you with regular inspiration. Just take a look at your local bookstore and you can find any number of books on all aspects of writing. Writers' organizations can also provide you with instruction and motivation. Writers' conferences and retreats give you the opportunity to meet other writers, as well as provide you with a chance to learn more about the writing craft.

WRITING MAGAZINES

Writing magazines are excellent resources for several reasons. Most magazines provide basic information about magazine writing on a regular basis. They also give you motivation, as you realize that other people are struggling with the same problems or have the same questions. They are also a lot of fun; I look forward to reading my writing magazines every month to see what new things I can learn.

More and more writing magazines appear on the market everyday; they meet the various needs of different types of writers. The following magazines provide valuable information for magazine writers.

Byline. P.O. Box 130596, Edmond, OK 73013.

Freelance Writer's Report. CNW Publishing, Maple Ridge Rd., North Sandwich, NH 03529.

Housewife-Writer's Forum. P.O. Box 780, Lyman, WY 82937-0780.

New Writer's Magazine. Sarasota Bay Publishing, P.O. Box 5976, Sarasota, FL 34277-5976.

The Writer. 120 Boylston St., Boston, MA 02116-4615.

Writer's Digest. 1507 Dana Ave., Cincinnati, OH 45207.

Writer's Journal. Minnesota Ink, Inc., Suite 328, 3585 N. Lexington Ave., Arden Hills, MN 55126.

Writing for Money. P.O. Box 1144, Hendersonville, NC 28793.

BOOKS ON WRITING

This is is just a partial list of books available on the subject of writing. Most of these deal with aspects of magazine writing, but there are numerous other books available on other writing topics. These are my personal choices, so there may be others books on magazine writing that I have overlooked. The key here is to always stretch yourself—always strive to learn more. All writers—even the very best—can improve. Reading is one way to do so.

Bartlett's Familiar Quotations. Boston: Little, Brown and Co., 1980.

The Complete Handbook for Freelance Writers, Kay Cassill. Cincinnati: Writer's Digest Books, 1981.

The Copyright Book: A Practical Guide, William S. Strong. Cambridge: MIT Press, 1981.

The Craft of Interviewing, John Brady. Cincinnati: Writer's Digest Books, 1975.

Editors on Editing, Gerald Gross. New York: Grove Press, 1993.

Feature Writing for Newspapers and Magazines, Edward Friedlander and John Lee. New York: HarperCollins, 1993.

Find It Fast, Robert Berkman. New York: HarperCollins, 1990.

The Handbook of Magazine Publishing. Stamford, CT: Hanson Publishing Group, 1983.

How to Get Happily Published: A Complete and Candid Guide, Judith Applebaum and Nancy Evans. New York: New American Library, 1982.

How to Write and Sell Greeting Cards, Bumper Stickers, T-shirts and Other Fun Stuff, Molly Wigand. Cincinnati: Writer's Digest Books, 1992.

How to Write Irresistible Query Letters, Lisa Collier Cool. Cincinnati: Writer's Digest Books, 1990.

If You Can Talk, You Can Write, Joel Saltzman. New York: Warner Books, 1993.

The Internet Yellow Pages, Hahn Harley. Berkeley: Osborne McGraw-Hill, 1994.

The Law (in Plain English) for Writers, Leonard D. DuBoff. New York: John Wiley and Sons, 1992.

Literary Marketplace. New York: R.R. Bowker, annual.

The Magazine, Leonard Mogel. Chester, CT: Globe Pequot Press, 1988.

Magazine Writing: The Inside Angle, Art Spikol. Cincinnati: Writer's Digest Books, 1979.

1,011 Best Things Anybody Ever Said, Robert Byrne (ed.). New York: Ballantine Books, 1988.

One to One: Self Understanding Through Journal Writing, Christina Baldwin. New York: M. Evans and Company, Inc., 1977.

Punctuate it Right, Harry Shaw. New York: Barnes and Noble, 1963.

Reference Books: A Brief Guide, Marion Bell and Eleanor Swidan (eds.). Baltimore: Enoch Pratt Free Library, 1978.

Roget's International Thesaurus. New York: T.Y. Crowell Company, 1977.

Secrets of a Freelance Writer: How to Make 85,000 Dollars a Year, Robert W. Bly. New York: Henry Holt and Co., 1990.

The 30-Minute Writer: How to Write and Sell Short Pieces, Connie Emerson. Cincinnati: Writer's Digest Books, 1993.

This Business of Writing, Gregg Levoy. Cincinnati: Writer's Digest Books, 1992.

Wild Mind: Living the Writer's Life, Natalie Goldberg. New York: Bantam Books, 1990.

Working Press of the Nation: Magazines and Internal Publications Directory. New Providence, NJ: National Register Publ., annual.

World Almanac and Book of Facts. New York: World Books.

The Writer's Book of Checklists, Scott Edelstein. Cincinnati: Writer's Digets Books, 1991.

The Writer's Digest Guide to Manuscript Formats, Dian Dincin Buchman and Seli Groves. Cincinnati: Writer's Digest Books, 1987.

Writers Dreaming, Naomi Epel. New York: Carol Southern Books, 1993.

Writer's Handbook, Sylvia K. Buracks (ed.). Boston: The Writer, Inc., 1983.

The Writer's Home Companion, James Charlton and Lisbeth Mark. New York: Viking, 1987.

Writer's Market. Cincinnati: Writer's Digest Books, annual.

Writing from the Heart: How to Write and Sell Your Life Experiences. Cincinnati: Writer's Digest Books, 1993.

The Writing Trade: A Year in the Life, John Jerome. New York: Viking, 1992.

WRITING ORGANIZATIONS

Almost every local community has some sort of writing group. States, likewise, have a number of organizations designed to support writers. My hometown (Birmingham, Alabama), for example, has two writing groups of which I am a member. As a new writer, your main concern in joining any organization is the help and motivation it can provide for you. Are there other new writers in the group? Do members actually encourage writing, and do they critique members' works? Are the members supportive? Talk to other members of the group and get their opinions about the group's personality and effectiveness.

The following organizations are primarily national in scope. They are wonderful resources, but don't bypass your local and statewide opportunities.

American Society of Journalists and Authors, Inc.
1501 Broadway, Suite 302
New York, NY 10036
(212) 997-0947

This is a nationwide organization of independent writers of nonfiction. It promotes high stands of nonfiction writing through monthly meetings, annual writers' conferences, and member publications. It is open to professional freelance writers of nonfiction.

Council of Authors & Journalists, Inc.
1214 Laurel Hill Dr.
Decatur, GA 30033

Established to encourage high standards of writing and to promote interest in writers and their work, the CAJ also holds an annual conference at St. Simons Island, Georgia. Annual dues run from $15 to $100.

The International Women's Writing Guild
Box 810, Gracie Station
New York, NY 10028
(212) 737-7536

This group is a network for the personal and professional empowerment of women through writing. Members receive a newsletter, information on agents and publishing services, access to health insurance plans, and attendance at various writing events. Membership is open to anyone, regardless of writing accomplishments. Annual dues are $35.

National Association of Science Writers, Inc.
P.O. Box 294
Greenlawn, NY 11740
(516) 757-5664

This group is open to anyone actively involved in science writing for newspapers, magazines, or other media. It provides a varied program to improve the quality of science writing. Annual dues are $50.

National League of American PEN Women
1300 17th St., NW
Washington, D.C. 20036-1973
(202) 785-1997

This organization offers networking and workshop opportunities through local branches for receiving manuscript critiques, exchange of ideas, and marketing news. Members receive PEN Women Magazine and statewide newsletters. Annual dues are $25.

The National Writers Club
1450 S. Havana, Suite 620
Aurora, CO 80012
(303) 751-7844

New and established writers, poets, and playwrights can be members. Annual dues range from $15 to $60.

National Writers Union
873 Broadway, #203
New York, NY 10003
(212) 254-0279

Members include more than 3,000 book authors, poets, freelance magazine writers, freelance journalists, and technical writers. The group works to bring equitable payment and fair treatment to freelance writers. Membership is open to writers who have published a book, play, three articles, five poems, one short story, or an equivalent amount of newsletter, publicity, technical, government, or institutional material. Annual dues range from $60 to $150.

Outdoor Writers Association of America, Inc.
2017 Cato Ave., Suite 101
State College, PA 16801-2768
(814) 234-1011

Provides information to professional writers of the outdoors. Membership is by nomination only and includes a monthly newsletter, annual conference, annual membership directory, and contests.

Society of American Travel Writers
1155 Connecticut Ave., NW
Suite 500, Washington, D.C. 20036
(202) 429-6639

Membership is limited to travel writers on staff or freelancers who have a steady volume of published or distributed work about travel. Initial fee is $200; annual dues are $120.

Society of Professional Journalists
16 S. Jackson St.
Greencastle, IN 46135-0077

SPJ has more than sixteen thousand active members and three hundred chapters. It serves the interests of print, broadcast, and wire journalists. Members must spend at least 50 percent of their working hours in journalism. Annual dues are $57.

WRITING CONFERENCES

The following conferences are listed by the states in which they take place. There may be other conferences not listed here. Always keep your eyes and ears open for news of other conferences. Talk to other writers who have attended them and consider going to one yourself.

The key to a good writers' conference is the amount of useful information you acquire. You want a writers' conference that doesn't just consist of successful writers telling you about their work and their lifestyle. You want ones that provide workshops on the practical aspects of writing.

Alabama

Alabama Writers Conclave. Montevallo. 117 Hanover Road, Homewood, AL 35209.

Southern Christian Writers Conference. Samford University, Birmingham. Box 1106, Northport, AL 35476.

Writing Today. Birmingham Southern University, Birmingham. Martha Andrews, BSC A-3, Arkadelphia Rd., Birmingham, AL 35254.

Alaska

Alaska Adventure in Travel Writing. Mike Miller, Box 21494, Juneau, AK 99802.

Arizona

Phoenix Desert Rose Annual Conference. Tempe. Beverly Cohoon, 6117 E. Hobart Dr., Mesa, AZ 85205.

Pima Writers' Workshop. Meg Files, Pima College, 2202 W. Anklam Rd., Tuscon, AZ 85709.

Arkansas

Arkansas Writers' Conference. Clovita Rice, 1115 Gillete Dr., Little Rock, AR 72207.

Ozark Creative Writers. Peggy Vining, 6817 Gingerbread Lane, Eureka Springs, AR 72632.

California

California Writers' Club Conference. Pacific Grove. Dorothy Benson, 2214 Derby St., Berkelely, CA 94705.

Christian Communicators Conference. Santa Clarita. SusanTitus Osborn, 3133 Puente St., Fullerton, CA 92635.

Foothills Writers Conference. Richard Maxwell, English Dept., Foothills College, Los Altos Hills, CA 94022.

Mendocino Coast Writers' Conference. Marlis Manley Broadhead, College of the Redwoods, 1211 Del Mar Dr., Fort Bragg, CA 95436.

Mount Hermon ChristianWriters Conference. David R. Talbott, Box 413, Mount Hermon, CA 95044.

Napa Valley Writers Conference. Napa Valley College. Sherri Hallgren, 2277 Napa-Vallejo Hwy., Napa, CA 94558.

San Diego St. Univ. Writers Conference. Diane Dunaway, 8465 Jane St., San Diego, CA 92129

Santa Barbara Writers Conference. Mary or Barnaby Conrad, Box 304, Carpinteria, CA 93014.

Southern California Writers Conference. Barbara Hartner Sack, 2596 Escondido Ave., San Diego, CA 92123.

West Marin Writers Conference. Point Reyes. Peter Robinson, Suite 201, #1 Weatherly Dr., Mill Valley, CA 94941.

Colorado

Colorado Christian Writers Conference. 2801 Jay Rd., Boulder, CO 80301.

Pikes Peak Writers Conference. Box 25417, Colorado Springs, CO 80936-5417.

The Spring Writers' Conference for Adults. Scoti Domeji, Colorado Christian Communicators, 5209 Del Paz Dr., Colorado Spring, CO 80918.

Vail Writers' Retreat. Vail. Julie Gammack, 1200 Midland Bldg., Des Moines, IA 50309.

Connecticut

Wesleyan Writers Conference. Anne Greene, Wesleyan University, Middletown, CT 06549.

District of Columbia

Washington Independent Writers' Conference. Osolde Chapin, National Press Club, 529 14th St. NW, Washington, D.C. 20045.

Florida

Florida First Coast Writers Festival. Florida Communication College at Jacksonville, Kent campus. Howard Denson, 4501 Capper Rd., Jacksonville, FL 32218.

Key West Literary Seminar. Monica Haskell, 419 Petronia St., Key West, FL 33040.

Southwest Florida Writers Conference. Edison Community College, Ft. Myers. Joanne Hartke, Box 06210, Ft. Myers, FL 33906-6210.

Suncoast Writers Conference. St. Petersburg. Gianna Russo, Dept. of English, University of South Florida, 4202 E. Fowler Ave., Tampa, FL 33620.

Georgia

American Christian Writers Conference. Atlanta. Reg A. Forder, Box 5168, Phoenix, AZ 85010.

Curry Hill PlantationWriters' Conference. Bainbridge. Elizabeth Bowne, 404 Crestmont Ave., Hattiesburg, MS 39401-7211.

Moonlight and Magnolias Writers Conference. Atlanta. Carol Springston, 4378 Karl's Gate Dr., Marietta, GA 30068.

Savannah Writers' Retreat. Savannah. Julie Gammack, 1200 Midland Bldg., Des Moines, IA 50309.

Southeastern Writers Conference. St. Simons Island. Pat Laye, Box 102, Rt. 1, Cuthbert, GA 31740.

Hawaii

Maui Writers Conference. John Tullius, #38, 20 Alacloa, Lahaina, Maui, HI 96761.

Illinois

Blooming Grove Writers Conference. Bettie Story, Box 515, Bloomington, IL 61702.

Mississippi Valley Writers Conference. Rock Island. David R. Collins, 3403 45th St., Moline, IL 61265.

Indiana

Midwest Writers' Workshop. Earl L. Conn, Dept. of Journalism, Ball State University, Muncie, IN 47306.

Iowa

Iowa Summer Writing Festival. Karen Burgus Schootman, 116 International Center, University of Iowa, Iowa City, IA 52242.

Midwest Writers' Retreat. 900 Midland Building, Lake Okoboji, IA 50309.

Prairie Summer Writers' Conference. Meg Fitz-Randolph, Prairie Writers' Group, 201 S. Highland, Fairfield, IA 52556.

Kansas

Heart of America Writers' Conference. Judith Choice, 12345 College Blvd., Overland Park, KS 66210.

Kentucky

Appalachian Writers' Workshop. Mike Mullins, Box 844, Hindman, KY 41822.

Green River Writers' Retreat. Louisville. Mary O'Dell, 11906 Locust Rd., Middletown, KY 40243.

Louisiana

Deep South Writers' Conference. John Fiero, USL, Drawer 44691, Lafayette, LA 70504-4691.

Maine

Down East Maine Writer's Workshop. Camden/Belfast. Janet Barron, Box 446, Stockton Springs, ME 04981.

State of Maine Writers' Conference. Richard Burns, Box 296, 16 Coby Ave., Ocean Park, ME 04063.

Stonecoast Writers' Conference. Freeport. Barbara Hope, University of Southern Maine, 96 Falmouth St., Portland, ME 04103.

Massachusetts

Cape Cod Writers' Conference. Craigville. Marion Vuilleumier, Cape Cod Writers' Center, Conservatory, Rt. 132, W. Barnstable, MA 02668.

Mount Holyoke Writers' Conference. Michael Pettit, Box 3213-W, Mt. Holyoke College, S. Hadley, MA 01075.

New England Writers' Workshop. Jean Chaput Welch, 300 The Fenway, Boston, MA 02115.

Michigan

Midland Writers' Conference. Eileen Finzel, 1710 W. St. Andrews, Midland, MI 48640.

Third Coast Writers' Conference. Tamara Skidmore, Dept. of English, Western Michigan University, Kalamazoo, MI 49008-5092.

Missouri

Heartland Writers' Guild Conference. Cape Girardeau. Heartland Writers' Guild, Box 652, Kennett, MO 63857.

Maple Woods Writers' Conference. Pattie Smith, 2601 NE Barry Rd., Kansas City, MO 64156.

Montana

Fall Writers' Conference. Herb Anderson, 4949 2nd Ave. N., Great Falls, MT 59406.

Yellow Bay Writers' Workshop. Judy Jones, Center for Continuing Education, University of Montana, Missoula, MT 59812.

New Mexico

Gila Writers' Conference. Silver City. Meg Files, 11012 E. Crescent Ave., Apache Junction, AZ 85220.

Southwest Christian Writer's Association. Kathy Cordell, SCWA, Box 2635, Farmington, NM 87499-2635.

New York

American Society of Journalists and Authors Writers' Conference. Michele Aucoin, #302, 1501 Broadway, New York City, NY 10036.

Champlain Valley Nature Writers' Workshop. Plattsburgh. Kathleen Thomas, 40 W. Valley Rd., Lake Placid, NY 12946.

Chautauqua Writers' Workshop. Jack Voelker, Box 1098, Chautauqua, NY 14722.

Hofstra University Writers' Conference. Lewis Shena, Dept. B, University College for Continuing Education, 205 Davison Hall, 110 Hofstra University, Hempstead, NY 11550.

Sarah Lawrence College Summer Sessions for Writers. Susan Guma, Sarah Lawrence College, 1 Mead Way, Bronxville, NY 10708-5999.

Southampton Writers' Workshops and Festival. Cala Caglioti, Southampton College, Southampton, NY 11968.

North Carolina

North Carolina Writers' Network Fall Conference. Asheville. Marsha Warren, Box 954, Carrboro, NC 27510.

Ohio

Columbus Writers' Conference. Angeala Palazzolo, Box 20548, Columbus, OH 43220.

Ohio State's Summer Writing Series. Joen Roettger, 152 Mount Hall, 1050 Carmack Rd., Columbus, OH 43210-1002.

Oregon

Finer Points Writers' Retreats. Coos Bay. Wendy Keller, Box 534, Coquille, OR 97423.

Pennsylvania

Ligonier Valley Writers' Conference. Box 8, RR 4, Ligonier, PA 15658.

St. David's Christian Writers' Conference. St. Davids. Shirley Eaby, 1775 Eden Rd., Lancaster, PA 17601-3523.

Rhode Island

Newport Writers' Conference. Box 12, Newport, RI 02840.

South Carolina

Francis Marion Writers' Conference. David Starkey, English Dept., FMU, Florence, SC 29501.

Texas

Austin Writers' League Workshop Series. Suite E-2, 1501 W. 5th St., Austin, TX 78703.

Golden Triangle Writers' Conference. 4245 Calder, Beaumont, TX 77706.

Rice University Writers' Conference. Box 1892, Houston, TX 77251-1892.

Write Move. Mt. Pleasant. Box 260E, Rt. 6, Pittsburgh, TX 75686.

Utah

Writers at Work Conference. Box 1146, Centreville, UT 84014-5146.

Vermont

Writers' Program at the Vermont Studio Center. Box 613P, Johnson, VT 05656.

Virginia

Highland Summer Conference. Box 6935, Radford University, Radford, VA 24142.

Washington

San Juan Islands Writers' Retreat. Whidbey Island. 1200 Midland Building, Des Moines, IA 50309.

Seattle Pacific Christian Writers' Institute. Humanities Department, SPU, Seattle, WA 98819.

Write on the Sound Writer's Conference. 700 Main St., Edmonds, WA 98020.

West Virginia

The Blue Ridge Mountains Writers' Retreat. Berkeley Springs. 1200 Midland Building, Des Moines, IA 50309.

GoldenRod Writers' Conference. 219 Kingwood St., Morgantown, WV 26505.

Wisconsin

Best Writers' Workshop in the World. Redbird Studios, 3195 S. Superior, Milwaukee, WI 53207.

Great Lakes Writers' Workshop. Box 343922, 3401 S. 39th St., Milwaukee, WI 53234-3922.

Wisconsin Regional Writers' Association Conference. Elkhart Lake. 1232 Audobon Rd., Howards Grove, WI 53083.

Wyoming

Jackson Hole Writers' Conference. Jackson. Box 3972, UW Conferences and Institutes, Laramie, WY 82071-3972.

GLOSSARY

All fields and professionals have their own lingo. Cooks talk of consommés and ragout; electricians talk of amperage and wattage; and accountants talk of P and L's, accruals, and fiscal years. Magazine writers talk of go-aheads, simultaneous submissions, and clips. Sometimes all the lingo can be quite confusing. If you're serious about being a magazine writer, however, you need to understand these terms. Following are some of the terms you'll see quite often.

Anecdote: A true-to-life story used to make a point relevant to your article. Anecdotes enliven an article, providing information or a scenario with which a reader can identify.

Assignment: A firm agreement that you will write an article for a magazine. Assignments are rare for new magazine writers (you will probably start out getting go-aheads from your query letters).

Body of article: The part of your article that includes your main points. The other parts of the article are the lead and the conclusion.

Byline: The line that tells the authorship of the magazine article ("By Cheryl Sloan Wray").

Circulation: The number of a magazine's readers. Circulation can be calculated in different ways: by the number of subscriptions, by the number of subscriptions and magazine rack sales, or by both of those plus pass-along readership (the average number of times one copy is read by people other than the subscriber or buyer). Magazines with high circulation pay more, but they are also harder to break into as a writer.

Clichés: Words or phrases that are overused ("Hanging on for dear life," "One in a million," "You can bet your bottom dollar"). You should avoid clichés if you want your writing to be strong.

Clips: Samples of your previously published work, sometimes called tearsheets. Magazines sometimes request to see clips of your work. Don't send in the original page; the best way is to make photocopies of your articles and send them in.

Conclusion: The final section or paragraph of your article. It sums up the story for the reader.

Consumer magazine: A publication targeted to the general public; it can be of general or special interest.

Contributor's copies: Complimentary copies of the issue in which a writer has had an article published; the number of copies given to the writer varies with magazines. Some small magazines do not pay writers for their article; instead they give the writer contributor's copies as payment.

Copyright: The ownership of written material. To quote from copyrighted material, there are two basic rules: (1) You don't have to attribute the source if you are using just a brief amount of the information, and (2) If you quote more than 250 words, you need to get permission from the original source to use the material.

Cover letter: A letter included with an article submission. The cover letter should, if you have already had a go-ahead on a query letter, reintroduce yourself and your article and thank the editor for taking the time to consider your piece.

Critique service: An individual or business that critiques (or analyzes) magazine articles and other writings. These services usually just recommend changes, but they can sometimes also provide editing.

Deadline: The date on which your article must be finished. You will have a deadline only if you have a firm assignment from a magazine (a go-ahead on a query letter, for example, has no specific date by which the magazine must see your article). Deadlines can also be self-imposed (giving yourself a deadline to complete a project).

Draft: A version of a magazine article prior to the final version that is sent out to a magazine. Writers usually write first, second, third, and final drafts, although there can certainly be more drafts than that written. Between drafts, articles are edited, proofread, and rewritten.

Editing: The process of looking for various types of mistakes in your article. This usually involves in-depth changes you plan to make, such as correcting structure problems, adding material, rewording, and rewriting for clarity.

Editors: Magazine staff members who are involved in some level of editing. *Editors-in-chief* (sometimes just called editors) are responsible for editorial planning and policy, and editorial content (both editorial text and art). *Managing Editors* coordinate the work of various departments on a day-to-day basis; they usually oversee editing and proofreading, and they may work with freelance writers. If a magazine has one, the *Senior Editor* plans feature articles in specialty areas and usually works with freelance writers. *Copy Editors* edit, proofread, and prepare the final copy to send to the printer. *Editorial Assistants* assist in all editorial areas; the job usually involves reading through query letters and manuscripts.

First-person: An article written from your own experience, using first-person attributions ("I" and "you").

Galleys: Copies of the page as it will appear in published form. Some magazines let an article's author see the galleys of his article before it is published. Galleys are sometimes called page proofs.

General interest magazines: Magazines of interest to a large percentage of the general population. Examples are *Reader's Digest* and *Life*.

Go-ahead: A response to a query letter asking the writer to "go ahead" and send the article in for consideration. A go-ahead is not necessarily an acceptance.

Hard copy: The printed copy of an article, as opposed to a copy on a computer disk or hard drive. You should always keep a hard copy for your own reference.

How-to article: An article that tells readers how to do something.

Invoice: A bill sent to a magazine for a writer's services. While most magazines don't request that a writer submit an invoice, a few still do.

Kill fee: The money given to a writer when his article is accepted but then is not actually published for some reason or other. The fee is usually a percentage of the amount the writer would have been paid for the published article.

Lead: The introductory paragraph or section of a magazine article. Written effectively, it captures the attention of the reader and makes him or her want to continue reading.

Monthly: A magazine that comes out once a month (the most common publishing schedule). Magazines can also be bimonthly (coming out once every other month), quarterly (every four months), or annually (once a year).

Ms: The abbreviation for "manuscript."

Newsletter: A publication sold by subscription or distributed free that is smaller in size than a magazine (usually four to eight pages long). Many newsletters provide opportunities for freelance writers, and they are listed in *Writer's Market* along with magazines.

On-spec: The situation in which a magazine wants to see your article "on speculation." This means that the magazine wants to see your article and consider whether it could use it. This, therefore, does not mean that the magazine will automatically accept your article for publication.

Outline: The format in which a writer plans out his article. An outline can be written in the traditional Roman numeral style, the cluster style, or in an informal style as appropriate to the individual writer.

Payment on acceptance: A magazine's policy to pay a writer when his article is accepted for publication.

Payment on publication: A magazine's policy to pay a writer when his article is published.

Personal experience article: An article written from your personal experience.

Personality profile: An article that presents a profile of an individual. The most common types are profiles of well-known persons (celebrities) or ordinary individuals who have done something noteworthy.

Proofreading: The step in which a writer checks his article for grammatical problems, punctuation errors, and spelling mistakes. Proofreading does not involve changing the stylistic nature or structure of the article.

Pseudonym: A name other than his or her own that an author chooses to use for his or her writing. A pseudonym is also called a pen name.

Publisher: The staff member who controls all business aspects of the magazine; he or she may or may not have control over editorial decisions.

Query letter: The letter you write to convince an editor to consider your article for publication. It should contain a snappy lead, a brief explanation of your article, reasons why you should be the one to write it, and a closing that "sells" your idea again.

Quote: The words of an expert or someone else you interview for your article. There are direct quotes, which are the exact words of the person, and indirect quotes, which is your correct paraphrasing of what the person said.

Reprint: The publication of a previously-published article in another magazine.

Rewrite: The process, after proofreading and editing, of restructuring and reworking the various drafts of your article.

Rights: Your ownership of your article (or any other piece of writing). When a magazine buys an article, it buys a certain kind of right to your article. *First North American rights* means the magazine is buying the right to be the first publication to print the article. After publication, you retain the rights to the article. *One-time rights,* similar to First North American rights, mean the publication has the rights to publish the article just this one time (then the rights belong to you again). *Second rights* give the magazine the permission to use an excerpt from a book after its publication in the book. *All rights* give the magazine rights to your article in all its forms (such as reprints or syndication).

Sample copy: A copy of a magazine sent to a writer on request. To obtain a sample copy, write the magazine and request one. Sample copies are usually free with a self addressed stamped envelope, but they sometimes involve a minimal cost.

Slanting: Rewording and restructuring the same article idea for different magazines. Slanting is a powerful tool for getting the most out of each article you write.

Slush pile: The jargon for the pile of manuscripts received by magazines from freelance writers. The bigger the magazine, the bigger the slush pile and the harder to get published. Following professional courtesy in submitting your query letter or manuscript will get you closer to the top of the pile.

Simultaneous submission: The practice of submitting the same article idea or article to different magazines at the same time. Check *Writer's Market* to see if your target magazine prohibits the practice. Generally, you can send the same article to different magazine as long as they're not competitive.

Slug: The one or two word identification of your article on the second and subsequent pages of your manuscript. For example, if your article is titled "The Joys of Gardening," your slug could be "gardening." This helps editors keep track of the different pages of your manuscript.

Special interest magazines: Magazines designed for and written to a specific segment of the population. They do not appeal to everyone.

Spin-offs: Article ideas that are developed from another idea. Spin-offs are an effective tool for maximizing your ideas and time.

Source: The source of your information; it can be a written source or a person. (Look under **Copyright** to see the rule about quoting a source.)

Style: Your unique writing personality. Style can represent everything from the way you write descriptive scenes to the type of leads you like to write.

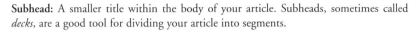

Subhead: A smaller title within the body of your article. Subheads, sometimes called *decks*, are a good tool for dividing your article into segments.

Title: The name for your magazine article. When you submit an article, you should come up with a *working title* (this means that it's a title for the moment, and the magazine may decide to change it).

Trade magazine: A publication written for and distributed specifically to a particular business or industry. A trade magazine is sometimes called a *business magazine.*

Trademark: The name of a product or service that is owned by a specific company (such as Kleenex, Coke, or Xerox). To use a trademarked name, you must get permission from the company or use a generic term (such as tissue, soda pop, or photocopy).

Unsolicited manuscript: An article that is submitted to a magazine without the magazine's prior interest. Magazines usually prefer query letters to unsolicited manuscripts.

Vagueness: An impreciseness in language and word choice.

Word count: The approximate number of words in your article. You should include this count on the first page of your manuscript, because this information is important to editors (magazines have word count limits and average word counts for articles). The easiest way to determine word count is to use a word count command on a computer. If yours doesn't have one, estimate the word count by counting the number of words on one page and multiplying that total by the number of pages.

Wordiness: Using an unnecessary amount of words in your writing. When editing your article, check for wordy phrases such as "at the present time" or "in a number of instances." If one word will do, don't use three or four.

Writer's colonies: Retreats where writers go to write on a daily schedule. Costs of colonies vary, but the cost usually includes all living expenses (including lodging and meals).

Writer's conferences: Meetings at which writers gather to discuss writing topics. These conferences usually run a day or two in length, and they are designed to give writers instruction and inspiration. Some also include manuscript critiques and meetings with editors.

Writer's guidelines: Information regarding a magazine's policy toward freelance writers. The guidelines usually include information on query letter and manuscript submission, editorial calendars, special editorial needs, and other tips.